Praise for _Hello From Heaven!_

"_Hello From Heaven!_ is an ... ...ploration of after-death communication. It will help open a new area of research and experience."

—JAMES REDFIELD, AUTHOR OF _THE CELESTINE PROPHECY_ AND _THE TENTH INSIGHT_

"I am both privileged and honored to be able to recommend _Hello From Heaven!_ I know that it will be a tremendous source of comfort to bereaved parents in many lands. It is a gift of Hope which will encourage and inspire its many readers to look beyond the Valley of the Shadow to the butterflies which dance in the dawning rays!"

—THE REVEREND SIMON E. STEPHENS, FOUNDER OF THE COMPASSIONATE FRIENDS

"_Hello From Heaven!_ is a rare and wonderful book that will give comfort to all, bring peace to the grieving, and open up a whole new dialogue in this fascinating field of after-death communication."

—RAYMOND A. MOODY, JR., M.D., PH.D., PSYCHIATRIST AND AUTHOR OF _LIFE AFTER LIFE_ AND _THE LIGHT BEYOND_

"_Hello From Heaven!_ is a wonderful and uplifting book that will bring tears of happiness to your eyes and goose bumps to your arms. I highly recommend this book to everyone."

—BRIAN L. WEISS, M.D., PSYCHIATRIST AND AUTHOR OF _MANY LIVES, MANY MASTERS_ AND _ONLY LOVE IS REAL_

"_Hello From Heaven!_ is a loving discussion of communications from those who have died. It represents years of scholarly research, yet is warm and very readable. If you are suffering from the death of someone you love, please buy and read this book."

—MELVIN MORSE, M.D., PEDIATRICIAN AND AUTHOR OF _CLOSER TO THE LIGHT_

"We, at Mothers Against Drunk Driving, hear many experiences like those revealed in _Hello From Heaven!_ This collection will, without a doubt, help survivors to know that they are not alone in having experienced an after-death communication."

—JANICE H. LORD, A.C.S.W., NATIONAL DIRECTOR OF VICTIM SERVICES, MADD

"I highly recommend *"Hello From Heaven!* to everyone who is terminally ill or bereaved. Its inspiring messages of love will fill you with comfort, hope, and peace of mind."

—MAGGIE CALLANAN, R.N., HOSPICE NURSE AND CO-AUTHOR OF *FINAL GIFTS*

"Bill and Judy Guggenheim have provided an invaluable service to all those struggling with life-and-death issues. *Hello From Heaven!* is a gold mine of compelling stories that simply cannot be ignored."

—BRUCE GREYSON, M.D., PROFESSOR OF PSYCHIATRIC MEDICINE

"The questions asked by survivors of homicide victims are many. The answers are few. *Hello From Heaven!* offers thoughtful, researched responses to some of the most important questions."

—CHARLOTTE AND ROBERT HULLINGER, FOUNDERS OF PARENTS OF MURDERED CHILDREN

"*Hello From Heaven!* is a very exciting and well researched portrayal of what has happened to so many people. It is well written and one of the few books of the type deserving of belief. I hope it finds a large audience."

—FATHER JOSEPH GIRZONE, ROMAN CATHOLIC PRIEST AND AUTHOR OF *JOSHUA, NEVER ALONE,* AND *JOSHUA IN THE CITY*

"*Hello From Heaven!* is indeed a gift of love to all the bereaved. This book confirms for me, through all the personal accounts of ADC experiences, that there is life after death."

—ADALINE LEIR, PRESIDENT OF THE COMPASSIONATE FRIENDS OF CANADA / LES AMIS COMPATISSANTS DU CANADA

"At last! *Hello From Heaven!* is a message of hope for all of us who wonder if there is life beyond 'good-bye.' "

—DARCIE D. SIMS, PH.D., GRIEF SPECIALIST AND AUTHOR OF *WHY ARE THE CASSEROLES ALWAYS TUNA?*

"*Hello From Heaven!* offers a powerful message of hope. As a grieving parent who has had some ADC experiences, these communications should be accepted for what they are: final gifts that offer the warm and comforting message that love and life continue forever."

—BRUCE J. HORACEK, PH.D., PRESIDENT OF THE INTERNATIONAL ASSOCIATION FOR NEAR-DEATH STUDIES

Hello From Heaven!

A new field of research
~ *After-Death Communication* ~
confirms that life and love
are eternal

Bill Guggenheim & Judy Guggenheim

BANTAM BOOKS

New York   Toronto   London   Sydney   Auckland

To respect everyone's privacy, the names of all the people
interviewed and the names of all the loved ones who appear in
their accounts have been changed. Similarities to other persons
who are physically alive or deceased are unintentional.

This edition contains the complete text
of the original hardcover edition.
NOT ONE WORD HAS BEEN OMITTED.

HELLO FROM HEAVEN!
A Bantam Book

PUBLISHING HISTORY
The ACD Project trade paperback edition published 1995
Bantam hardcover edition published April 1996
Bantam paperback edition / April 1997

ISBN-13: 978-0-553-57634-4
ISBN-10: 0-553-57634-8
Published simultaneously in the United States and Canada

Bantam Books are published by Bantam Books, a division of Random House, Inc.
Its trademark, consisting of the words "Bantam Books" and the portrayal of a rooster,
is Registered in U.S. Patent and Trademark Office and in other countries. Marca
Registrada. Bantam Books, New York, New York.

PRINTED IN THE UNITED STATES OF AMERICA

OPM 30 29 28 27 26 25

This book is dedicated to you
for your willingness to explore the
possibility that life and love are eternal

and to

our special friend and teacher,
Elisabeth Kübler-Ross

Contents

Acknowledgments

Hello From Heaven! is the result of the love, the commitment, and the support of several thousand people. The success of our research and the existence of this book are due to their dedication to The ADC Project.

The greatest credit belongs to the 2,000 men, women, and children who shared their intimate – and often sacred – experiences with us. Their courage, their trust, and their belief in the importance of after-death communications illuminate the pages of this book.

We are very deeply grateful to Reverend Simon Stephens, Iris and Joe Lawley, Paula and Arnold Shamres, Therese Goodrich, Diana Cunningham, and hundreds of American and Canadian members of The Compassionate Friends for all they taught us about unconditional love and its power to heal bereaved families.

We also appreciate the many individuals and organizations who encouraged us during our seven years of research and writing, including Molly Folken, Dick Gilbert, Sally Kopke, Jim Monahan, Kathleen Moore, Shirley Scott, Darcie Sims, Edie Stark, and Ben Wolfe, Association for Death Education and Counseling; Henry Reed, Douglas Richards, and Mark Thurston, ARE; Andrea Gambill, *Bereavement*; Rosalind McKnight, Creative Living Institute; Phyllis Atwater, Nancy Evans Bush, Maggie Callanan, Valerie and Marty Chandler, Diane Corcoran, Mally Cox-Chapman, Ned Dougherty, Elane Durham, Arvin Gibson, Bruce Greyson, Bruce Horacek, Bonnie Lindstrom, Raymond Moody, Melvin Morse, Peggy Adams Raso, Leon Rhodes, Ken Ring, Kimberly Clark Sharp, Jayne Smith, and Harold Widdison, IANDS; Shirley Enebrad, KOMO-TV; Sheryle Baker, The Life Center; Anne and Herb Puryear, The Logos Center; Janet Dunnican and Janice Lord, Mothers Against Drunk Driving; National Hospice Organization; Charlotte and Bob Hullinger and Nancy Ruhe, Parents of Murdered Children; Bill Roll, PSI; Linda and Al Vigil, Sharing and Healing; Beverly Ford, Spiral Circle Bookstore; Elizabeth and Paul Fenske and Ken Hurst, SFFI; and Anne Studner, Widowed Persons Service, a program of The American Association of Retired Persons.

Our heartfelt thanks to the journalists who wrote feature articles about our research for their newspapers: Elaine Jarvik, *Deseret News*; Elizabeth Rhodes, *The Seattle Times*; and Harry Wessel, *The Orlando Sentinel*. And to the dozens of people who told their family members, friends, and support groups about this work, for they were our best source for additional interviews.

Our gratitude is extended to our interviewers: Donna Bishop, Roberta Carson, Gean Peterson, Diane Silkey, and Christina Strickland; and to our first transcriber, Connie Johnson. Also to our special angel, Carole Newman, for her devotion as an interviewer, transcriber, editor, and tireless contributor to The ADC Project. And to our son, Will, for his expert computer assistance.

We warmly acknowledge the first readers of our manuscript for their many insightful ideas: John Audette, Kathy and Jap Becker, Kay and Dick Boza, Kay and Virgil Bryant, Jerry Calder, Debra Davis, David Engle, Paul Fransella, Renate and Jerry Glenn, Lily Kang, Sharon and Gary Kramer, Torie Lane, Wayne Loder, Ralph Losey, Pat Maddox, Mineda McCleave, Kathleen Moore, Robin Moore, Brian Perks, Tom Saunders, Shirley Scott, Michael Smith, Steve Spector, and Merton Stromen. And we appreciate all the improvements made by our fine copy editors, Donna French and Donald Pharr.

Toni Burbank and Irwyn Applebaum, our editor and publisher at Bantam Books, deserve the credit for placing this book in your hands as quickly as possible. Their vision and faith, along with the commitment and creativity of many other people at Bantam, exceeded all our hopes and expectations. And kudos to Gail Ross, our enthusiastic literary agent and attorney, who taught us so much and counseled us so wisely.

We are particularly thankful for the love and emotional support of our family members: Stephanie Guggenheim and Dennis Neal; our two younger sons, Chris and Jon; and Bill's two daughters, Maire and Jaenet. As an anticipated two-year project stretched beyond seven years, they made repeated sacrifices on behalf of this book.

Bill and Judy

Hello
From
Heaven!

PREFACE

Peace:
An Invitation

"How does one become a butterfly?" she asked pensively.
"You must want to fly so much that you are
willing to give up being a caterpillar."
—*Trina Paulus*

Is there life after death? Do we enter another state of existence after we die? Though many people believe death is an ending, you will be introduced to an exciting new field of research that may convince you death is simply a transition from this physical world to life in a spiritual realm.

You are invited to evaluate these uplifting firsthand accounts and determine for yourself if they are authentic communications from deceased family members and friends. If you conclude that they are, you will know with a new certainty that you and all the ones you love continue to live after death. You can then look forward to being reunited with them in a spiritual dimension that will surpass your highest expectations.

If you are willing to read this book with an open mind and an open heart, you may significantly reduce or completely eliminate your fear of death. As a caterpillar once limited to the ground, you might undergo an inner transformation and become like a butterfly free to soar. This new freedom will allow you to live your life more fully and joyously, with a greater sense of peace.

When a caterpillar dies,

a butterfly is born.

CHAPTER 1

The ADC Project:
A Leap of Faith

Death is simply a shedding of the physical body
like the butterfly shedding its cocoon. It is a transition
to a higher state of consciousness where you continue
to perceive, to understand, to laugh, and to be able to grow.
—*Elisabeth Kübler-Ross, M.D.*

Like a caterpillar that was asleep in its cocoon, I was about to be transformed, but I never suspected it at the time. It was summer 1976, and my wife, Judy, and I were living in Sarasota, Florida.

"Bill, come in here! Elisabeth Kübler-Ross is going to be on *Donahue*," she called from the living room.

"I think I've heard her name. Who is she? What does she do?" I asked from my office.

"She's the famous European doctor who works with people who are dying," Judy replied.

This answer didn't thrill me. Why would I want to watch an entire program on a subject that I didn't even want to think about? Formerly a stockbroker and a securities analyst who had worked for two Wall Street firms, I was an avowed materialist. My primary interests were the Dow Jones Industrials Average and earning money on investments. My beliefs about death and life after death could be summed up briefly: "People are like flashlight batteries. When their juice runs out, you simply throw their bodies away. When you're dead, you're dead!"

Judy called again, "Come on, Bill. The show's about to start.

You don't want to miss Elisabeth. She's a really special person!"

"Okay, I'll be there in a minute," I said, though I joined Judy with little enthusiasm. To my amazement, the program turned out to be one of the most engrossing hours of television I had ever seen.

I learned that Dr. Elisabeth Kübler-Ross is a world-renowned Swiss-born psychiatrist. Her pioneering work with the terminally ill was helping millions of Americans overcome their fear of death and dying.

On this show, Elisabeth talked about the near-death experiences her patients had shared with her and of her belief in life after death. She spoke with such compassion, sincerity, and conviction about these issues that I was unexpectedly impressed.

Two weeks later, we watched the same program on another cable channel. This time I felt inspired to send Elisabeth a small donation to help her continue her humanitarian work.

In a few weeks, a package arrived in the mail containing a letter and a set of audio tapes Elisabeth had recorded. Surprisingly, she invited me to attend her five-day "Life, Death, and Transition Workshop," which was to be held in Florida early the next year. At first I felt very flattered to receive her invitation, but I gradually became afraid of participating in such a workshop. Ever since my father had died in 1947 when I was only eight years old, death had been a morbid and distasteful subject for me.

Judy believed I had some unresolved issues concerning the death of my father. Though I denied it at the time, part of me realized this was probably true. I am an only child and had never talked about his death or expressed my feelings about my loss to anyone. Back then the prevailing attitude was "Big boys don't cry!"

In November, on the last day for workshop registration, I called Elisabeth's office in Illinois to decline her offer. I was expecting to speak to someone on her staff, but it was snowing heavily in the Midwest that day, and her secretary had been unable to drive to work. Elisabeth answered the phone, and I recognized her voice immediately. I thanked her for the tapes, then quickly gave a phony excuse for why I couldn't attend her workshop.

Elisabeth remembered me and listened attentively. Then she said in her charming German-Swiss accent, "Bill, I feel you should be there." There was something about the way she said those words that caused me to reply, "If you think so, I will."

Feeling a mixture of curiosity and apprehension, I drove to the retreat center in North Palm Beach in February 1977. All my fears proved to be unfounded, for Elisabeth's workshop was really about life and living, not death and dying.

Seventy strangers rapidly bonded together and soon became a loving family. We supported one another while relating our stories of loss and pain, and we ate together, sang together, played together, and hugged each other freely. Remarkable emotional healings took place as we began to release our accumulated grief of a lifetime. The unconditional love we shared was so tangible that tears of sadness were replaced by tears of joy, and nearly everyone felt safe enough to reveal their innermost self.

Though I didn't realize it at the time, the seeds for this book were being planted within me during Elisabeth's workshop. This process began in a group sharing session when Maggie, a nurse from Illinois, told us she was a bereaved mother. Her 15-year-old daughter, Joy, had been hit and killed by an automobile while she was out walking.

Maggie told us she had had a dream after Joy's death, but added, "It wasn't like an ordinary dream. It was just so real!"

This was right after Christmas, about thirteen months after my daughter was killed. I had been having a bad time, and this particular night, I cried myself to sleep.

While I was sleeping, I dreamed that Joy came to me. We were sitting in a tree on a low, overhanging branch. The landscape was filled with light, and everything was in extremely vivid color. The tree, the green grass, and the blue sky were all very intense.

Joy looked very happy. She was wearing a pastel pink, diaphanous gown. It was very sheer and flowing with long sleeves and a sash around the waist. It wasn't like anything she had owned before.

She sat with me and hugged me and put her head on my left breast. I could feel her weight and her substance.

Then Joy told me she had to go, but that she could come back again. To demonstrate this, she kind of floated away, then came back and sat with me on the branch. She was showing me that my sadness wasn't necessary because we weren't really going to be apart.

Joy was comforting me. She was happy, and she wanted me to be happy too. Then we hugged again and just sat there for a while. But pretty soon, she had to leave.

I woke up feeling very comforted because I felt Joy had really been with me. That's when I began to get better and was able to begin letting go. It was time for my daughter to move on and for me to do other things with my life.

All of us were very happy that Maggie had had such a positive and uplifting experience concerning her deceased daughter, and it was obvious she had undergone much healing since her tragic loss. Because she had called her experience a "dream," that's how I regarded it. I knew people had vivid dreams, but to me dreams were products of our subconscious mind and nothing more.

But Maggie had more to say as she went on to describe an experience her 17-year-old son, Bob, had with his sister:

This happened before my experience, about six to eight months after Joy's death. If anybody was hurting, it was my son, Bob, who was just twenty months older than his sister.

He missed her badly and was really suffering. He went from being one of the most popular kids at school to being a loner, with just one or two friends. He'd come home and say, "It was just terrible today."

So one evening, he was in his room studying, and my husband and I were in the family room watching TV. Suddenly, Bob screamed and came running to us, saying, "Mom! I just saw Joy!" Then he told us his experience.

Bob said that he had been reading, but he really couldn't concentrate. Then he looked up and saw Joy standing in front of his closet.

He told us Joy's hair was like it always was, and she was wearing jeans and a striped T-shirt that he'd never seen on her before. She didn't say anything to him, but he said the expression on her face was like she was fine, like everything was okay.

Bob said he was so startled that he couldn't move or speak for a couple of minutes. Then he jumped up, but Joy wasn't there anymore. That's when he screamed and came running to us.

Could this boy's experience be real? Was it even possible? Could a teenage girl really appear to her brother in Midwest America in the twentieth century after she had been hit and killed by a car? I thought about it briefly, but quickly discounted Bob's experience, attributing it to his grief or wishful thinking or an overactive imagination. I reminded myself, "When you're dead, you're dead."

Elisabeth acknowledged she had heard similar experiences before, and two days later she shared one of her own:

I was at a crossroad. I felt I needed to give up my work with dying patients. That day, I was determined to give notice and leave the hospital and the University of Chicago. It wasn't an easy decision because I really loved my patients.

I walked out of my last seminar on death and dying towards the elevator. At that moment, a woman walked towards me. She had an incredible smile on her face, like she knew every thought I had.

She said, "Dr. Ross, I'm only going to take two minutes of your time. If you don't mind, I'll walk you down to your office." It was the longest walk I have ever taken in my life. One part of me knew this was Mrs. Johnson, a patient of mine who had died and been buried almost a year ago. But I'm a scientist, and I don't believe in ghosts and spooks!

I did the most incredible reality testing I've ever done. I tried to touch her because she looked kind of transparent in a waxy way. Not that you could see furniture behind her, but not quite real either. I know I touched her, and she had feeling to her.

We came to my office, and she opened the door. We went inside, and she said, "I had to come back for two reasons. Number one, I wanted to thank you and Reverend Smith once more for what you have done for me. But the real reason why I had to come back is to tell you not to give up your work on death and dying. Not yet."

I realized consciously that maybe indeed this was Mrs. Johnson. But I thought nobody would ever believe me if I told this to anybody. They really would think I had flipped!

So my scientist in me very shrewdly looked at her and said, "You know, Reverend Smith would be thrilled if he would have a note from you. Would you terribly mind?" You understand that the scientist in me needed proof. I needed a sheet of paper with anything written in her handwriting, and hopefully, her signature.

This woman knew my thoughts and knew I had no intention to ever give her note to Reverend Smith. However, she took a piece of paper and wrote a message and signed it with her full name. Then, with the biggest smile of love and compassion and understanding, she said to me, "Are you satisfied now?"

Once more, she said, "You cannot give up your work on death and dying. Not yet. The time is not right. We will help you. You will know when the time is right. Do you

promise?" The last thing I said to her was "I promise."
And with that, she walked out.

No sooner was the door closed, I had to go and see if
she was real. I opened the door, and there was not a soul
in that long hallway!

When Elisabeth finished speaking, everyone in the workshop was stunned. The room was so quiet that if a pin had
dropped, it would have sounded like a crowbar falling on a concrete floor.

I thought, "Could such things really happen? To a renowned
scientist, no less? Could Elisabeth's experience possibly be
real? Had other people been contacted by someone who was
dead and supposedly gone forever?" If so, the implications
were enormous!

Elisabeth's story defied everything I knew and understood
and assumed was true about death and life after death, and it
forced me to reexamine all my beliefs. My mind raced with
hundreds of unanswered questions as it searched for any logical explanations. Finding none, it finally went "tilt."

Dr. Raymond Moody, Jr., had recently written his best-
selling book about near-death experiences (NDEs), *Life After
Life*, and Elisabeth invited him to speak at our workshop on
Thursday evening. After his talk several people shared their
NDEs, and all of us were deeply moved by their firsthand ac-
counts.

By the time the workshop ended on Friday, my personal beliefs about what was "real" versus "unreal" had been shattered.
The materialistic goals and pursuits I had been taught and had
valued for thirty-eight years suddenly seemed shallow once I
had glimpsed and tasted a much larger, more loving, wonder-
filled universe. I realized I had been touched by the spiritual dimension. Now that my inner eyes and ears and heart and mind
were opening, I felt an insatiable hunger to enter it, to explore
it, and to allow it to become a permanent part of my life.

Upon returning home, I shared as much as I could about the
workshop with Judy. She had previously had a spiritual awak-

ening of her own, so she was very supportive of me and the changes I had undergone.

I immediately decided to find personal answers for some of mankind's oldest and most profound questions: Is there life after death? Do we enter a new dimension or level of existence when our physical life is over? Will we be reunited with our family members and friends who have already died? Is it possible for our deceased loved ones to communicate with us now?

Judy agreed to help me, and we began reading dozens of books about life after death. Some contained experiences similar to the ones Maggie and her son had with Joy, and Elisabeth had with Mrs. Johnson. But no one had ever researched this field thoroughly and written an entire book on the subject. Since there wasn't even a name for these unusual events, we created one ourselves and started calling them "after-death communications" or "ADCs" for short.

We learned that ADCs are probably as old as mankind itself and that accounts of them were recorded over 2,000 years ago. For example, the following is an edited translation of one that appears in the essay "On Divination," by Marcus Tullius Cicero, the prominent Roman statesman and author who lived from 106 to 43 B.C.:

There were two comrades from Arcadia traveling together, and when they reached Megara one of them went to the inn, while the other accepted the hospitality of a friend.

He and his friend finished their evening meal and retired. In his slumber our guest dreamed that his traveling companion appeared to him and said, "The innkeeper has murdered me, flung my body into a cart, and covered it with dung. Please, I beg you, be at the gate early in the morning before the cart can leave the town."

Stirred to the depths of his being by this dream, he confronted at dawn the rustic who was driving the cart out of the gate. The wretch took to his heels in dismay and fright. Our friend then recovered the body and reported the murder to the proper officials. The innkeeper was duly punished.

Because his deceased friend had visited him, the experiencer learned four things in this ADC he could not have known before: that his friend had been murdered, where and when his body could be found, and who had committed the crime.

You may be surprised to learn that the plot of one of the greatest plays in the English language is based upon an ADC experience. In *Hamlet* by William Shakespeare, young Prince Hamlet mourns the death of his father, the King of Denmark, who died when he was reportedly bitten by a poisonous snake. The deceased king makes a full appearance to Hamlet and explains that his brother, Claudius, murdered him so he could marry his widow, Queen Gertrude, and become the new king of Denmark. Hamlet's deceased father also reveals that Claudius poured poison into his ear while he was taking a nap in his orchard to make it appear he had been killed by a snake. He demands that his young son "Revenge his foul and most unnatural murder." Hamlet swears to avenge his father's death, and the fulfillment of his pledge constitutes the rest of the play.

Another ADC is featured in one of the most well-known stories in English literature, *A Christmas Carol* by Charles Dickens. In this tale Ebenezer Scrooge's deceased business partner, Jacob Marley, returns to warn him of his fate if he won't change his materialistic values and replace them with more charitable ones. Scrooge is disbelieving at first but eventually heeds the warning.

Is it merely a coincidence that both of these great works of fiction contain after-death communications? Or is it possible that Shakespeare and Dickens were familiar with contemporary accounts of ADCs and simply adapted them for literary use?

Of course, the best-known after-death communications are the several appearances Jesus made, which are recorded in the Bible, and the multiple appearances of Mary, the Blessed Mother, which are included in the writings of the Roman Catholic Church. Christians believe Jesus and Mary are unique and have vast spiritual powers, and we feel it would be inappropriate to compare their after-death appearances with those made by ordinary human beings.

Six months after the workshop, I wanted to hear Elisabeth again, so I flew to Georgia to attend a lecture she was giving. After her talk, I met John Audette in the audience. John was researching near-death experiences, and we later became close friends.

The next year John founded an association for researchers, experiencers, and others who were interested in studying NDEs. It evolved into the International Association for Near-Death Studies (IANDS) in 1981, and I've been a member since then.

During the next several years my affiliation with IANDS and other organizations allowed Judy and me to meet many researchers in person and to study their work. We also talked with hundreds of people who reported having NDEs, out-of-body journeys, ADCs, and other kinds of spiritual experiences.

Many told us that having an ADC had provided a great deal of comfort and emotional healing. This was especially true for people who were newly bereaved and for those whose experiences included verbal communication. Some also claimed they had been contacted more than once by the same loved one who had died.

Having heard so many firsthand accounts, we wanted to know how frequently after-death communications occur in our culture. To one in a million people? To one in a thousand? To one in a hundred? Regardless of the number, we assumed they must be quite rare.

American Health published the results of a poll conducted by the National Opinion Research Center in its January-February 1987 issue. The poll was directed by Andrew Greeley, the well-known Catholic priest and author. The findings state that 42% of American adults believe they have been in contact with someone who has died. And 67% of all widows believe they have had a similar experience. These figures amazed us because they were much higher than we had suspected.

Assuming this poll is accurate, why do so many people feel they must begin their accounts with disclaimers: "I don't expect you to believe me ..." or "You'll probably think I'm crazy when I tell you my experience ..." or "This is going to sound really weird...."

Why are they so afraid to share such important moments of their lives? Why can't after-death communications be discussed openly and freely? Why aren't they being investigated as potential evidence for life after death? Wouldn't they fulfill the promise of the world's great religions that all of us will survive physical death and have heartwarming reunions with our deceased loved ones?

What would be more comforting for bereaved parents than the knowledge they could be reunited with their deceased children? That widows and widowers who have shared a lifetime of love with their husband or wife might be together again? That all people could once more encounter those they have loved here on earth?

Of course, there is a logical explanation for this. Though most health-care professionals have heard of after-death communications, many of them are convinced ADCs are not genuine. Historically, psychologists, psychiatrists, bereavement counselors, members of the clergy, and others have dismissed these experiences as hallucinations, delusions, or fantasies. The traditional viewpoint has been that ADCs are the result of wish fulfillment, imagination, magical thinking, or memories caused by grief. In fact, they have usually been called "grief-induced hallucinations."

Then one afternoon in the spring of 1988, eleven years after Elisabeth's workshop, I heard a "voice" speak to me in my mind. Powerfully yet lovingly it said, "Do your own research and write your own book. This is your spiritual work to do." This "voice" was familiar because it had spoken to me once before:

It was a damp, gray Sunday afternoon in March 1980, and Judy and I had just finished having a conversation in the living room in the front of our house. As we got up to leave the room, I distinctly heard a voice in my head calmly say, "Go outside and check the swimming pool." Though I didn't feel any sense of urgency, I was definitely puzzled by hearing this voice and receiving such a strange message.

So I walked back to the family room and looked out through the sliding-glass door. Our pool was separated from the house by a 15-foot patio, and I noticed that the gate in the wrought iron safety fence was open. But this wasn't unusual because our two older sons used the pool area as a shortcut to the backyard and sometimes forgot to close the gate.

I walked across the patio to latch the gate, and as I did, I glanced casually at the pool. Suddenly, my heart froze and everything seemed to happen in slow motion. There in the middle of the deep end I saw our youngest son, Jonathan! He was less than two years old and didn't know how to swim.

I ran to the side of the pool and saw our little boy floating face up about an inch or two under the water! He was very still and his eyes were wide open.

I screamed "Judy!" as I jumped into the water feet first. Rebounding off the bottom and kicking my legs furiously, I came up under Jonathan and pushed him toward the side of the pool. Judy had heard my terrified scream and came running. Frantically, I struggled to keep his head above water until she grabbed his arms and pulled him from the pool.

Jonathan immediately began crying and shivering as he coughed up a little water. Miraculously, he was fine. We were probably more frightened than he was as we wrapped him in a big towel and held him in our arms.

Shortly afterward, we learned that Jonathan had gone outside through a bathroom door that opened onto the patio from the far side of the house, for it too had been accidentally left open. When I told Judy about my experience, we realized our little boy must have slipped into the pool only moments before the voice alerted me.

We were immensely grateful we had been given this crucial message because it enabled us to save our youngest son from drowning. And it had spared us the incredible grief that bereaved parents must endure.

When the "voice" spoke to me a second time in 1988 and said, "Do your own research and write your own book," I trusted it but felt I was being called upon to accomplish something much larger than I was capable of achieving. I felt overwhelmed by the sheer size and complexity of such a project. Then slowly it occurred to me that I had been preparing for this assignment for many years and had the time, the means, and a passionate interest in the subject. A new confidence gradually uplifted me, and then and there I made a commitment to follow the guidance of the "voice" as faithfully as possible.

But within a couple of weeks, my resolve began to weaken as a nagging doubt surfaced. My concern was "How can I prove to myself and others that ADCs are not merely bereavement fantasies as so many professionals believe? What evidence, if any, can I find to demonstrate that such experiences might be real?"

By then Judy and I had been divorced nearly four years after being married seventeen years. Later, realizing we still had a lifetime relationship because of our three sons, we chose to work through our personal differences and become friends again. This wasn't easy to accomplish, but the rewards certainly made it worthwhile.

So I called Judy and invited her to my apartment one afternoon to discuss my dilemma. As I was telling her about how the "voice" had spoken to me a second time and of the assignment I had been given, the telephone rang. A friend, Darcie Miller, who knew of my interest in after-death communications, called to tell me about an unusual experience.

Darcie's mother, who was being treated with chemotherapy for cancer, had died unexpectedly in the hospital. Within half an hour, Darcie went in person to inform her mother's lifelong friend, Rose, of her mother's death. When she arrived and before she could say anything, Rose said, "The strangest thing just happened. Your mother came through the wall of my apartment and said, 'I have always loved you and I always will.' Then she left." No one had called or told Rose that Darcie's mother had died. Rose had this ADC before she received any news of her friend's death.

The timing of Darcie's phone call couldn't have been more perfect. My enthusiasm soared, and so did Judy's. We realized that since Rose hadn't known a death had taken place, she wouldn't have been in a state of grief when she had her ADC with Darcie's mother. If this was true for one person, it was very likely other people might have had similar experiences. Here at last was the first piece of evidence that could potentially disprove the theory that ADCs were grief-induced hallucinations. This was the confirmation I had been seeking. Then Judy and I felt ready to begin this work.

Our first step was to determine the boundaries of this field in order to establish which experiences would qualify to be included in our research. This is our definition: An after-death communication or ADC is a spiritual experience that occurs when someone is contacted directly and spontaneously by a deceased family member or friend.

An ADC is a direct experience because no intermediary or third party such as a psychic, a medium, or a hypnotist is involved. The deceased relative or friend contacts the living person directly on a one-to-one basis.

An ADC is a spontaneous event because the deceased loved one always initiates the contact by choosing when, where, and how he or she will communicate with the living person. Since many religions and other sources specifically warn against summoning "spirits," we excluded from our research all experiences that involved any rituals, such as séances, or that utilized ouija boards, crystal balls, or similar devices.

The ADC Project was started in Orlando in May 1988 with 1,000 flyers, 1,000 business cards, a telephone line, a post office box, and a checking account. Diane Silkey, who had previously had her own local television talk show, became our first interviewer.

The flyers asked "Have you been contacted by someone who has died?" and described the types of experiences we were seeking. But how many people would answer "Yes" and be willing to participate in our research? Could we find fifty people to interview the first year? Perhaps a hundred? How long would it take to reach our goal of five hundred interviews? The ADC Project was certainly a leap of faith!

We found people to interview virtually everywhere we went. This included bereavement groups, churches, hospices, personal growth classes, support groups, conferences, social organizations, and spiritual bookstores. We interviewed more than five hundred people the very first year. Our research was proving to be a dramatic success that far exceeded our expectations. It kept growing as if it had a life of its own as many new people came forward to support our efforts.

To our surprise, some of our initial assumptions about this field of study were too limited. They had to be expanded or replaced to keep pace with the quantity and diversity of the accounts we were receiving. So we repeatedly increased the number of interviews to be conducted as we learned of new types of ADCs that hadn't been cataloged before.

Remarkably, doors began to open for us that we had never envisioned. Leaders of local bereavement groups began to ask us to give short talks about our research for the benefit of their members, and these soon evolved into full-length lectures and workshops.

The Compassionate Friends, the largest self-help organization for bereaved parents and siblings in the world, invited us to present two workshops at their 1989 national conference in Tampa. Diane Mason, a feature writer for the *St. Petersburg Times*, attended our workshops and wrote a very informative article about them. As a result, after-death communications gained favorable recognition and credibility in the eyes of the public and the media in our local area.

Subsequent feature articles about our ADC research appeared in *The Seattle Times, The Orlando Sentinel*, and the *Deseret News* in Salt Lake City. These stories were syndicated in twenty-six other newspapers throughout the United States and Canada. Since most of them included our address and telephone number, hundreds of people wrote or called us from all over North America. We even received letters from foreign countries as far away as the Ukraine, Japan, and Australia. Our enthusiasm mounted as we realized we had accepted responsibility not only for exploring an uncharted field of human experience, but also for mapping it thoroughly for readers around the world.

Judy and I appeared on sixteen television and radio programs in the United States and Canada, and each show generated more interviews. Many bereavement groups and other organizations published announcements of our work in more than a hundred of their newsletters and magazines. Several, including Mothers Against Drunk Driving (MADD) and IANDS, also invited us to present workshops at their annual conferences, which we did gladly. And finally, dozens of people enthusiastically promoted our research by word of mouth, and we interviewed scores of their relatives and friends.

Our excitement soared when we heard from people whose lives had been protected or perhaps saved by having an ADC. Some who had been contemplating suicide told us they had refrained from taking their life when a deceased relative or friend intervened. Many reported hearing from a loved one before they were informed of his death, while others declared they had been contacted ten or twenty years later. We also received accounts from people who had shared an ADC experience while together at the same time and place. Increasing evidence for the reality of after-death communications was pouring in by phone and mail daily.

It was obvious to Judy and me that almost all the experiencers, including some who had been devout skeptics, were transformed emotionally and spiritually by their ADCs. By 1993, we too had become convinced that the accounts we were receiving represented authentic contacts with deceased loved ones.

The ADC Project took seven years to fulfill its purpose. During this time we collected more than 3,300 firsthand accounts of after-death communications by interviewing 2,000 people who live in all fifty American states and the ten Canadian provinces. These people are from all walks of life and represent diverse social, educational, occupational, and economic backgrounds. They range in age from an eight-year-old boy to a ninety-two-year-old widower.

Almost all the people we interviewed had a Christian or Jewish religious upbringing, and most still maintain a Protestant, Catholic, or Jewish affiliation. During their interviews some spoke of heaven in its traditional Christian context, while others used it to describe the afterlife in general. In this book we use "heaven" when referring to the higher spiritual realms of life after death.

The average length of a telephone interview was forty-five minutes, although many lasted well over an hour. Everyone was asked a standard set of questions as well as others that pertained specifically to the type of experience being reported. Since an ADC is an extremely vivid and memorable event, the people we interviewed were able to recall the details of their contacts with great clarity even many years later.

Only firsthand accounts of after-death communications are contained in our study. Though we heard a number of impressive secondhand stories, we always passed them by unless we were able to interview the original experiencer. Additionally, for an account to qualify for this book, we needed to have at least two others in our files that were very similar.

Virtually all the people who participated in our research were in good health when they had their experiences. We made exceptions for a few who had their ADC during a health crisis, and this is noted in their narratives. We excluded all people who admitted being under the influence of alcohol or illegal drugs at the time, with the exception of two accounts in Chapter 20, *Saving Grace.*

Many men and women we interviewed expressed the hope that readers would benefit from their ADCs. They wanted to spare others the confusion and pain they had endured when few relatives or friends were willing to believe their stories.

The interviewers, the transcribers, and Judy and I felt honored and were often deeply moved by the highly personal and sacred experiences people entrusted to us. On numerous occasions the interviews became extremely emotional, and some were interrupted by tears from one or both ends of the telephone line.

The transcripts of the interviews total more than 10,000 pages. Our most difficult task was selecting the ADCs that best represent the range and depth of our research and presenting them in a way that would be clear and easy to understand. The format of this book, which is a road map of this complex field, was chosen to showcase the greatest number of firsthand accounts. Each is a complete short story told in the experiencer's own words, and the majority include the emotional and spiritual effects as well. All contain a vitality that can only be derived from reading full-length experiences. Because they speak for themselves, we decided to add a minimum amount of commentary, making it possible for you to enjoy a wide spectrum of accounts. We believe this approach will assist you in evaluating after-death communications and in making your own well-informed judgment regarding their credibility.

Throughout this informal research presentation we've usually written short comments following each of the ADC accounts. Most highlight, examine, or expand upon the significance of a specific experience, while others contain observations about grief and the bereavement process. In some cases you will notice our commentary extends well beyond a particular account. In those instances we generally drew upon the many other interviews in our files. We also incorporated information from numerous additional sources, such as near-death experiences, out-of-body journeys, and the various types of spiritual phenomena we'd studied during the past eighteen years. As a result, you may find portions of our commentary to be quite challenging or provocative.

We are not expecting you to necessarily agree with all our conclusions. In fact, you may arrive at very different interpretations of these experiences and form equally valid opinions of your own. We respect you for that and look forward to receiving your letters and learning your points of view.

We've often been asked, "How many people have had an ADC experience?" Based upon our research, we conservatively estimate that at least 50 million Americans, or 20% of the population of the United States, have had one or more after-death communications. The percentages increase dramatically among bereaved parents, the widowed, bereaved children, and all others who have grieved the death of someone they love.

To place after-death communication experiences in perspective, polls estimate that 10 million Americans, or 4% of the population, have had a near-death experience. This means that the field of ADCs is at least five times larger than that of NDEs.

Near-death experiencers were at the threshold of death, and many claim they visited a spiritual world before returning to their physical body. In contrast, all of the communications in this book are from people who actually died and completed their journey into the light. Presumably, they have a deeper understanding and broader viewpoint of life on earth and our purpose for being here.

ADCs are very common in other parts of the world, where they are socially accepted as real communications from deceased loved ones. The people who have these experiences are able to share them freely and joyously with others, and everyone gains from discussing these events openly. We believe after-death communications deserve the same degree of public awareness and acceptance in our culture.

Our presentation begins with an in-depth study of the twelve most common types of after-death contacts, including the comfort and emotional healing they provide. Then we'll examine "fearful" ADCs and two other special topics. The next six chapters will offer persuasive evidence these experiences are genuine communications from deceased relatives and friends. Chapter 22, *A Necklace of Pearls*, features accounts that are the "best of the best" from our files, and the final chapter explores a few of the many far-reaching social and spiritual implications of our research.

CHAPTER 2

Sensing a Presence:
Sentient ADCs

We are not human beings having a spiritual experience,
we are spiritual beings having a human experience.
—*Dr. Wayne W. Dyer*

According to our research, there are twelve major types or forms of after-death communication. Sensing or feeling the presence of a deceased family member or friend is one of the most common types of contact. We call these sentient ADCs.

People reported having an intuitive awareness or inner knowing that their deceased loved one was with them in the same room or area. It was a distinct, almost physical sensation that he or she was nearby. The presence felt familiar and conveyed the identity and personality of the one who had died. As one woman, a psychologist, explained, "Everybody has an essence or a personal energy pattern which is as unique and individual as their fingerprints."

Many people state they can sense the emotions and overall mood of their deceased loved one while they are having a sentient ADC. And some may receive nonverbal messages this way.

Though sensing someone's presence is the least tangible and most subtle form of ADC contact, each experience has a definite beginning and ending. The experiencers are aware when their deceased relatives and friends arrive and when they depart.

The first five accounts in this chapter are typical descriptions of sensing the presence of a deceased loved one.

Diane is a 53-year-old hospice nurse in Ohio. She received a loving visit 18 months after her grandmother died of cancer:

> As I was standing at my kitchen sink, I felt this warmth, this presence. It wasn't physical but more like a presence standing around me, enfolding me. I knew it was my grandmother!
>
> Nothing special was going on in my life at the time, and I hadn't been thinking about her. Bells didn't ring or anything. I just had a sense Grandma was there with me. Then, in less than a minute, it stopped.
>
> I remember feeling very cherished and loved. It was a really nice thing to have happen.

Our research indicates no special preparations are necessary for having a sentient or other type of ADC. When people have such experiences, they are usually engaged in ordinary and mundane activities and not even thinking about the one who has died.

Marjorie, a 59-year-old homemaker in Florida, had this tender ADC about 2 years after her mother died of pneumonia:

> I was sitting on the couch reading a mystery book. All of a sudden, I felt my mother sitting next to me on my left side. I couldn't see her or hear her, but I knew she was there. Her individuality was as real as when she was alive.
>
> She was content just to sit next to me. Nothing had to be said – it was just a joining of our spirits. It was a warm feeling, a very pleasant, friendly feeling. This lasted probably three or four minutes, and then she left.
>
> I was very grateful for our time together.

Sentient ADCs may be quite brief or last for several minutes. Regardless of their duration, the experiencers often feel they have been embraced with emotional warmth and love.

Jeffrey, age 36, is a teacher and freelance writer in California. His grandmother contacted him just a few hours after she died of congestive heart failure:

> I was sitting in my living room looking at a picture that was always my grandmother's favorite. It's *The Good Shepherd*, where Jesus is holding a lamb.
>
> Suddenly, there was a real feeling of softness – an extreme feeling of peace that was unexplainable. I felt my grandmother was in the room. It was a very natural, warm feeling that she was present.
>
> I could feel her spirit, as if she was reassuring me that she was happy and at peace. It was almost like she was saying good-bye one last time before going on.
>
> This lasted about twenty minutes and then the peace gently faded. It was a comfort and reassurance that Grandma was okay.

Throughout our research, numerous people reported feeling an all-encompassing peacefulness and deep comfort during their ADC experience. And some, including the newly bereaved, compared this feeling to "the peace that passes all understanding."

Lynn, a 38-year-old hairdresser in Florida, had a light-hearted experience with her boyfriend, Fred, after he died of a heart attack:

> One afternoon, I was watering plants on the porch. Fred and I loved plants – that was something we shared. As I was watering them, I came to one plant that meant a great deal to him. It was really looking ratty, and I wasn't crazy about it.
>
> As I was standing there thinking how badly the plant looked, I had this sensation Fred was right there with me. I felt him very, very strongly.
>
> I knew that Fred was behind me. I felt if I were to back

up two steps, I would bump into him! It gave me a nice feeling, and I kind of laughed and went on.

The presence of a deceased loved one generally feels distinct, and his identity is easily recognizable. This is because he seemingly returns with every aspect of his being except his physical body.

Ken is a 58-year-old advertising executive in Florida. He had a surprising encounter after his friend, Oscar, died of a stroke:

I always had a great deal of admiration for Oscar, although I never saw him very often. I really didn't spend a lot of time thinking about his death. Just that he was gone, and I was going to miss him because I couldn't talk to him – and things like that.

A couple of months after he died, I was walking down the hallway in my office as I did a thousand times a day. All of a sudden, I felt Oscar! I wasn't in a reverie or even thinking about him. In fact, I was walking to the reception area to meet a client.

I felt his presence – it was all around me. It was like I had been immersed in a bubble of his energy. I got a sense of joy. It was like seeing Oscar again! But I just kept walking as I said something to him silently, and then he left.

After-death communications can happen anywhere. Sentient and all other types of ADCs may occur at home or at work, indoors or outdoors, and when we're alone or surrounded by other people.

As the next five accounts demonstrate, sentient ADCs may occur immediately or long after the death of a loved one.

Edith, a bereavement counselor in Florida, enjoyed a special moment with her 65-year-old patient, Howard, who had ALS, also known as Lou Gehrig's disease:

I was at home when the nurse from hospice called to tell me Howard was actively dying – a process that can go on for hours. His wife was having a real difficult time and wanted me to come over and be there with her. I said, "Of course," and went to change my clothes.

I was in my walk-in closet, when all of a sudden, I experienced Howard's presence. He was there on my right side. There was a lightness of being – a joy and a sense of freedom.

It was like I heard in my heart his good-bye and a thank you for being there for him as I had been. He wasn't there long, probably about thirty seconds.

When I stepped out of the closet, I looked at our digital clock, which said 4:23. I proceeded to get dressed and drove to Howard's house. When I walked in, they told me he had passed on at 4:23.

Edith had this visitation before she learned her patient had died. The time of her experience with Howard and the actual time of his death correspond precisely, supplying additional evidence for the reality of her ADC. Later in this book, an entire chapter is devoted to after-death communications that occurred before the living person was informed of a loved one's death.

Lori is a young homemaker in Texas. She had this poignant experience about 3 months after her 2-year-old son, Kevin, died of AIDS:

I was driving in my truck to a City Council meeting to ask for more funding for AIDS services. It was the first time I ever went to speak before such an audience, and I was a little afraid.

I turned on the radio and heard this song for the first time. It was Eric Clapton's "Tears in Heaven," which he wrote for his four-year-old son who died.

While listening to the words, I had the sense of Kevin's presence. Tears welled up in my eyes, and I started cry-

ing. I felt his presence the whole time the song was playing and had an overwhelming sense of peace. Then
Kevin's presence wasn't there anymore.

After this, I was able to get up my strength to make my
presentation because I knew I wasn't doing this alone.
And everything I asked the City Council for has been
done!

Ever since she had this ADC with her little son, Lori has
been inspired to speak out about AIDS at many high schools
and clubs. Her personal ministry gives greater meaning to
Kevin's short life.

Irene is a self-employed craftswoman in Virginia. She had
this jubilant reunion 6 months after her 22-year-old daughter,
Tracy, died in an automobile accident:

About 5:30 in the afternoon, my husband and I were
out in our field. We had been working very hard and were
down by the pond. I was walking fast, as I usually do,
back to the tractor to get something.

Suddenly, I knew Tracy was there by my side! She was
striding right in step with me – we were walking fast and
strong together. I was enveloped in a feeling of overwhelming love and joy. It was incredible! It was like a
deep breath of happiness.

It is like you are walking with someone and looking
straight ahead. You know they're there. You feel, and your
body feels, their presence next to you. That's what I felt.

Then suddenly, I was aware I was alone in the field. I
felt incredible joy for having this experience – and yet,
sadness too, that I couldn't take Tracy's hand and run
with her again.

The wonder and delight of an ADC is that we may have one
completely "out of the blue," for no apparent reason or special
occasion. These spontaneous moments of spiritual reunion with

a deceased loved one can fill us with immediate joy and leave us with an inner knowing that lasts a lifetime.

Betty, a 56-year-old homemaker in Florida, didn't expect her mother to come back 3 years after she died of polycythemia:

I was driving down the road – just my normal, every-day drive home from work. All of a sudden, my mother was with me in the car! She was just there with me.

I felt her presence, the essence of my mother, as though she was really there. It was almost as though if I had reached out, I could have touched her!

I felt a tremendous sense of warmth, a loving warmth and comforting. It was as though my mother wanted me to know she is always there for me.

It was a beautiful experience. It lasted just a short while and left me floating, feeling so happy.

You may be surprised, just as we were, that some people have had ADCs while driving a motor vehicle. This may seem like an unusual time and place for such an experience, but you will read a number of similar accounts throughout this book.

Lawrence is an Episcopalian minister in Virginia. He was only 28 years old when he became aware of his grandmother's devotion to him 8 years after she had died of a stroke:

This experience goes back to when our elder son was born. My wife had been in labor for a very long time. They ended up having to do a cesarean. The nurse came down to tell me that everything was fine.

As I got on the elevator to see my wife on the fifth floor, I was thankful that everything had turned out all right. Going up in the elevator, it was very peaceful and quiet. I was by myself – at least I thought I was!

Suddenly, there was a presence, and I could feel my Grandmother Anna was there with me. It was rather calming. I felt she was watching over what was going on. I told her, "It's all right, Grandma. They're both fine. It's a boy!" This was her first great-grandson to carry on the family name.

It's very comforting to know there is a connectedness that doesn't cease. The Christian church talks about life after death, and this experience re-emphasized for me that this is so. What the Lord said is true.

It's heartwarming to consider the possibility that our deceased loved ones are able to participate in our celebrations of life. This sentient ADC implies they have an ongoing interest in our affairs and continue to watch over us with loving care and concern.

Having a series of ADCs is fairly common. The next three accounts are examples of people who have had more than one sentient experience with the same deceased family member.

Susan, a 48-year-old homemaker in Florida, began sensing the presence of her father-in-law shortly after he died of cancer:

It was very late at night, and I was sitting at the dining-room table paying bills. I suddenly had the feeling I wasn't alone. I very strongly felt the presence of my father-in-law.

At first, I felt surprised and kind of confused. But that went away quickly because he came with such peace and warmth. I was really excited that he was there!

This happened about three times, always late at night. He seemed curious and concerned for our welfare, and I felt his visits were to check on us.

Then he didn't come anymore. I felt his questions had been answered and that he was really happy once he realized the family was together and united.

It is usually the bereaved survivors who need comforting after the death of a loved one. But in this case, it seems Susan's deceased father-in-law made a series of friendly visits because he wanted to be reassured of his family's well-being.

Tom, age 48, owns a chain of hair salons in the Southeast. He was given ongoing support from his deceased mother during a very stressful period in his life:

My wife, Marilyn, was dying of cancer. During her illness, I felt the presence of my mother drawing very close, time and time again, to give me understanding and to comfort me.

I just sensed her presence. It was no more than a feeling, but I knew she was there. I felt the love of my mother and knew I wasn't by myself.

The day my wife died, I was stunned. I was numb. I just collapsed. I woke up about sixteen hours later and felt the presence of my mother again, so strongly, as if she was grieving with me. And, in some respect, that she was welcoming Marilyn.

It appears that our deceased loved ones can still be there for us when we need them most. They can often be a source of comfort and strength to draw upon during our most difficult life situations. ADCs like these affirm their enduring love for us.

Eleanor is a psychotherapist in Washington, D.C. She had a series of visits from her father after he died of a heart attack when she was a senior in high school:

My father was a very kind, sensitive, and intelligent man. I loved him very much. But he suffered a lot of pain in his life.

For some years after he passed away, I would become aware of his presence. I felt the depth of his presence, the whole sense of him. It was the feeling of the way he was when he was alive and well. The feeling of him was very distinct, very warm, and very supportive.

My father was encouraging me to go on with my life and not to be upset with his death.

Having multiple ADCs with the same deceased loved one can truly be a blessing. They will generally reduce our grief and speed up our healing process dramatically.

Some ADC accounts reported sensing the presence of two or more deceased loved ones at the same time. When this occurred, the experiencer was able to identify each of the individuals.

Nancy is a nurse in Alabama. She needed encouragement and inspiration 2 years after her 9-year-old son, Jason, died of leukemia:

> I received an urgent telephone call from my sister saying that Brandon, my 8-year-old nephew, had been killed by a car while he was riding his bicycle. So I left for North Carolina the next day to attend his funeral.
>
> I brought a poem that was given to me when my son, Jason, died – it had helped me through the darkest times. My family wanted me to read this poem at Brandon's graveside. But I was very uneasy because I didn't know if I could make it through the service. I did a lot of soul-searching and praying, asking for guidance and strength.
>
> As I read the poem, I suddenly felt the presence of Jason and Brandon. Jason was on my left side and Brandon was on my right. I know they were there!
>
> I had an overwhelming sense of love and caring, and a very calm and serene feeling. Intuitively, I felt they were helping me get through this difficult time.

The boys' support not only uplifted Nancy and enabled her to fulfill her commitment at the funeral service, but later she was able to relate her experience to Brandon's parents. One ADC, when it is shared with others, can become a source of emotional and spiritual healing for many people.

The final account in this chapter suggests that time, space, and death are not limitations to the expression of love and compassion by a deceased family member or friend.

Sandy is a 49-year-old nurse in Washington. Her life was changed forever 5 years after her father died of cancer:

> I was an operating room nurse in Vietnam. This happened two or three weeks after I arrived there in 1968. Shortly after I got into bed, the hospital was attacked by a barrage of rocket fire. The earth was shaking and the noise was deafening!
>
> I crawled under my bed onto the concrete floor. I was very cold, uncomfortable, and frightened. All of a sudden, my father was with me! I felt his presence and his emotional warmth – my father's caring and love enveloped me.
>
> I felt wrapped in the security of his strength and had an overwhelming sense of peace. He assured me that it was going to be all right. He was there several minutes, and then he left.
>
> This experience strengthened my spirituality and took away my fear of death.
>
> Throughout my tour, I dealt with a lot of young men who were severely wounded and others who went on to die. The war didn't stop – the casualties just kept coming.
>
> I sat with many who were dying because I couldn't imagine them dying alone in a foreign country. My experience with my father contributed to my ability to do that.

Even though Sandy received this communication from her father without the benefit of language, his message was delivered clearly. Not only did he give his daughter what she needed in that moment, but he also gave her a gift for a lifetime, one she was able to share with an endless line of wounded and dying young men and women who served with her in the Vietnam War.

As you've already learned, a sentient ADC experience often provides us with feelings of love and comfort and warmth. These can be the fruits of directly experiencing the personal essence and the spiritual consciousness of a deceased loved one.

How would you feel if you heard the voice of deceased loved one and were given a verbal message during an ADC? This and more will be discussed in the next chapter.

CHAPTER 3

Hearing a Voice:
Auditory ADCs

There should be no fear of death, for the death of
the body is but a gentle passing to a much freer life.
—*Helen Greaves*

Receiving a verbal message, by hearing the voice of a deceased family member or friend, is also a very common type of after-death communication. We call these auditory ADCs.

Some people reported hearing an audible voice that was from an external source. They heard the voice through their ears the same way they would hear any other person talking to them.

But most people stated they heard a voice internally, inside their head or mind, and they were equally certain the voice originated from a source that was outside of them. This is called telepathic communication. Telepathy is also known as mind-to-mind contact, mental communication, and thought transference.

Whether they heard their deceased loved one externally or internally, the speech pattern and other characteristics of his or her voice sounded familiar. Either way, they easily recognized whoever was speaking to them.

Generally the messages that are received during auditory ADCs are brief and to the point. They may be compared to telegrams, which typically contain twenty-five words or less.

The first three examples in this chapter are external auditory ADCs in which the experiencers reported hearing an audible voice through their ears.

Alfred is a retired farmer and factory worker in Nova Scotia, Canada. He became a bereaved father when his 11-year-old son, Trevor, died of cancer:

> Trevor died at 4:00 in the morning. As my wife and I were starting to leave the hospital and come home, the sun was coming up on the horizon. My sister was with us in the car and she said, "I have never seen such a beautiful sunrise in my life."
>
> Just as I looked up at the sun, I could hear Trevor's voice saying, "It's all right, Dad." It was his voice, just as clear as could be. It came to my ears, just as though he was sitting in the back seat.
>
> Instantly, I had this peaceful feeling I had never had before, which lasted probably ten or fifteen seconds. I then knew Trevor was with God, and this must be the peace he was feeling.

Though he received just a brief message, "It's all right, Dad," Alfred was immediately comforted by his experience. Hearing those four words so soon after his son's death made all the difference.

Philip is a psychiatrist in Kentucky. He was caught off guard when he heard from his 15-year-old daughter, Tina, after she died in an automobile accident:

> Tina had friends all over the city. We didn't realize how involved she had been with so many kids. She was quite a force for good in the community.
>
> She had told one of her friends from Sunday school that if she should die, she would like everyone to have a party for her and not to mourn. Her friend reminded us of this statement.
>
> So the night of Tina's funeral, we had a very large gathering at our home with 200 to 300 kids, some with their parents. It was wall-to-wall people!
>
> I was passing through the hallway downstairs when I

heard Tina say, "I love you, Daddy!" I wheeled around because this was an audible, external voice.

I am a board-certified psychiatrist, and I'm not given to hearing things that are not there. Having lived my professional career as a pretty hardheaded scientific person, I really hadn't expected this.

However, this experience took a good bit of the sting out of the loss because you know you really haven't lost them.

Philip recognized Tina's voice despite the large number of people who were in his home at the time. What words could be more meaningful to any bereaved father than the ones his daughter chose, "I love you, Daddy!"

Sherrie, a 31-year-old corporate recruiter in Washington, was widowed when her husband, Scott, died from a cerebral aneurysm at age 37:

About three weeks later, on Christmas day, I was asleep in the living room of a friend's house. It was about 3:00 to 4:00 in the morning. A sound woke me up.

It was Scott's voice, just as clear as ever! I recognized his voice and his speech manner. It was an external communication that was totally outside of me.

He said, "Don't ever be afraid. You will always have the people around you that you need." He said that with such conviction that it seemed he knew more about things than I did. This statement made me feel like everything was going to be okay, even though Scott was gone.

That experience really changed things around for me. A big burden was lifted off me.

Scott's voice was so strong and real that it literally awakened Sherrie from her sleep. And he spoke with such authority that his message gave her the emotional support she needed to go on with her life.

•　　　•　　　•

The next three accounts are from people who reported having an internal auditory ADC. That is, they heard the voice of their deceased loved one by telepathy. Notice how they all received the message mentally rather than through their ears.

Donald is an English professor at a university in New Jersey. He had this playful experience with his 27-year-old son, Jeff, who died nearly 3 weeks after being hit by a drunk driver:

> One morning, two to three months after his death, I was lying in the dark thinking about Jeff's last hours and minutes of consciousness. I was speaking aloud, "How did it go? How did it go?" It was my whole fatherhood speaking to him.
>
> There was a long silence. Then I heard very clearly my son's voice in my head reply in a Minnesota accent, "Ooo-key."
>
> I felt an immense relief! Jeff's minimum amount of verbalization was right to the point!
>
> In my academic career, we moved around the country a bit. Local dialects had become a point of humor for our family for years. We all listened to Garrison Keillor's *A Prairie Home Companion* and had a lot of fun with the Minnesota accent.
>
> The spirit, the sense of fun, and the memory of old times made this something I was very happy to hear. The fact that Jeff could be free enough to kid in a way that would be instantly shareable made the contact with him all the more valuable.

This ADC illustrates the power even one brief message can communicate. Jeff cleverly chose for his father the perfect word and style of delivery that would convey the greatest meaning. He must have known his father would recognize his fully restored sense of humor and associate it with their many fun-loving times together.

Karen is an assistant professor at a college in Hawaii. Her grief lifted when she heard the voice of her 41-year-old brother,

Walt, after he was killed by a drunk driver in a head-on collision:

> Five months after my brother's death, I was driving home from teaching a night class. I wasn't even thinking of him.
>
> All of a sudden, out of the blue, I heard Walt's voice inside my head. It was telepathic – it was his tone of voice.
>
> He said, "Hey, little sister! Quit worrying about me. Everything is okay."
>
> My immediate response was, "Walt! Walt, is that you?" It was so quick that I thought I must have imagined it.
>
> Then again, maybe a minute or two later, I got the message, "My accident doesn't matter. It's not important. Quit worrying."
>
> This was the answer to many of my fears. I had been worried about Walt because his was a sudden, violent death.

You may be wondering why ADCs occur so frequently in automobiles. It's probably because we become very relaxed when driving, especially if traffic is relatively light and we're alone in the vehicle. Mentally, we're operating on "autopilot" while we perform a familiar, repetitive activity, allowing us to enter a semi-meditative state of consciousness. At such times, we're more likely to be open and receptive to having an ADC experience.

Carla is a schoolteacher in North Carolina. She had this telepathic ADC 18 months after her 5-year-old daughter, Amy, died of a brain tumor:

> I usually stop at my daughter's grave as I drive by. It was Valentine's Day, and I was feeling a little badly because I hadn't brought anything to put on Amy's grave. So I decided I wouldn't stop – I just tried to put it out of my mind and go on home.

But as I passed by, I was aware of this very strong voice. Although it wasn't audible externally, I was definitely able to hear it. Amy said, "Don't worry, Mom. I'm not there. I'm fine. I'm with Grandpa and the other people who have died before me."

My daughter didn't want me to feel guilty because of trivial things like placing flowers on graves. She let me know it was okay and that I didn't need to worry about her. This experience brought me a lot of peace.

While Carla regretted having nothing to offer her daughter on Valentine's Day, she was the one who received an invaluable gift from Amy. Many bereaved parents and others are given the same basic message. They are told their deceased loved one continues to exist in a new life and that only an empty, discarded physical body is buried at a cemetery. They also receive the comforting knowledge that their loved one is now with others who have died earlier, just as Amy stated she is with her grandfather.

From this point on, many of the accounts throughout the book will be more complex because two or more types of after-death communication were experienced at the same time. We call these combination ADCs. For instance, in the next six reports an auditory ADC was combined with a sentient ADC. The experiencers not only received a message from their deceased loved one, but they also felt his or her presence.

Patricia is a customer service representative for a bank in New York. She was contacted by her husband, Herbert, after he died of emphysema at age 59:

When Herb passed away, I cried every day for a whole year because I missed him so much and worried about him. He wasn't only my husband, he was also my very best friend.

A little after the first anniversary of his death, I was sleeping, and Herb's voice woke me up. He called, "Patsy. Patsy." I heard him through my ears.

When I was fully awake, I heard him say, "I'm all right.

I'm okay. I feel fine." I had the distinct feeling he was trying to tell me not to worry about him.

I felt Herb was right there and that by some grace he was able to communicate. I heard his voice so clearly. There was no labored breathing – just his normal, healthy voice, like before he got sick.

There are no words to describe the calmness that came over me. It was a blessing and I felt so good.

Those who both hear the voice and feel the presence of their deceased loved one during the same ADC experience gain additional information about his current well-being. Because Patricia heard Herb's voice, she learned he was completely free of emphysema.

Vicki is a 36-year-old office manager in Florida. She was consoled and renewed by her father after he died suddenly of a heart attack at age 66:

I didn't get to see my father when he passed away, so I guess I took it harder than everyone else. I was given a two-week leave of absence from my job to recuperate.

After my first day back to work, I was driving home and the dam burst. I started crying and crying and had to stop on the side of the road. I bowed my head in my arms on the steering wheel and cried uncontrollably.

About two minutes later, I felt a presence right there in my car. I felt encapsulated in a cloud of love and heard my father's voice as clear as a bell. He sounded elated and said, "I am fine! I am happy! Just take care of your mother." I heard him through my ears.

It was a miracle, a blessing! In that one instant, I was filled with so much love and joy that it completely took all my hurt away. I knew my father was totally at peace, and I was a different person from that point on.

Vicki's father responded to his daughter's needs when she was most emotionally distraught. Her ADC reflects the love and devotion our deceased loved ones continue to have for their family members and friends who are still alive on earth.

Warren is a 55-year-old swimming coach in Texas. He had this reassuring experience with his father:

> My pattern for thirty years has been to get up at 4:30 in the morning to go swimming. I was doing my laps, and when I got to the end of the pool, I felt my father say, "I am in heaven now. Don't worry about me. I feel fine. I'm really happy. All the burdens and problems that were on my shoulders are gone."
>
> I realized Dad was speaking to me internally. I lay back in the water and paused for about five minutes. It was like my father was encompassing me totally with his spirit. It was such a peaceful and positive experience that I can't even describe it.
>
> When I went back to my house, my sister called to let me know Dad had died at 3:44 that morning of respiratory failure.

Warren's account is yet another example of someone who was engaged in a routine and repetitive activity, such as swimming laps in a pool. This allowed him to enter a semi-meditative state and be more receptive to hearing from his father, whom he was unaware had already died.

Peggy, age 50, is a newspaper reporter in Arkansas. She was asked to deliver a message after her grandmother died of old age:

> My grandmother insisted on living with her sister, and they were both in their nineties. When they couldn't take care of themselves anymore, my mother moved them into her house. Mother did everything in the world for them.
>
> But those last six months of my grandmother's life were full of complaints. Nothing suited her – not her food,

not her clothes, nothing. My mother was getting exhausted and just couldn't take care of my grandmother any longer. So she very reluctantly put her in a nursing home where she died about a month later.

My grandmother came to me the day after she died. I was sitting in my living room, when suddenly I was surrounded by her whole presence, like a pink cloud of love. It was so beautiful!

She said telepathically, "I want you to tell your mother how much I really appreciate everything she did for me. I want her to know how grateful I was, even though I wasn't able to express it while I was alive. I want you to tell her that."

Grandma was so lovely! This was a totally different personality from the one we had known – the old lady with the aches and pains that nothing would please. This was a completely different side of my grandmother, once she was out of her body.

So I gave my mother the message, just the way my grandmother told me. And she got real teary-eyed.

Peggy's ADC is an example of someone completing "unfinished business" after he or she has died. We have a number of accounts in our files in which deceased relatives and friends returned to express gratitude or to offer a sincere apology when they had not resolved their affairs before death occurred.

Mario, age 87, is a retired sugar merchant in Florida. His beloved wife, Nina, returned to him after she died of emphysema:

Nina and I were fifty-seven years married. We met in a very romantic manner, and two hours later we were irretrievably in love, completely and forever.

One night after she died, I was sound asleep in our bedroom. Suddenly, I felt my Nina standing next to the bed. Then I heard her voice inside my head say, "I am now in heaven, whether I deserve it or not. My great love for little children all my life made up for my other sins. I got permission to return to tell you that I am waiting patiently for you to join me.

"Time is meaningless here, so don't be in a hurry. Take as long as you want before you leave the world. I will wait patiently until the day comes when you will join me here. Then we will be united in an eternal embrace." And with that, she faded from my consciousness.

I felt a liaison, a satisfying confirmation that death would not part us, that Nina and I would be united again.

Nina's joyous promise is one of many in this book that implies we will be reunited with our deceased loved ones when we die. This seems to be the underlying message, the essence of nearly all ADCs.

Rhoda is a classical musician in Texas. She was 19 years old when she had this transforming encounter with her grandfather, who had died from a heart attack:

Just forty-eight hours after his death, I was awakened. I peeked at the clock and it was 2:10 a.m. I knew my grandfather was there! I felt he was standing at the foot of the bed.

He started talking to me and said, "I want you to know that everything is fine over here. Please tell everyone not to worry about me. I'm happy. I did everything I needed to do on earth, and I want you to tell that to everybody. And tell them that I love them."

It wasn't a voice I heard – it was ideas and thoughts. It was truly telepathic and I simply let it come. It was such a peaceful feeling – I felt flooded with peace all over.

Grandpa was really saying good-bye. I feel he needed to do that as much as I needed to hear it.

It was the most powerful message I could have ever had of life after death. It catapulted me into a deeper search for the meaning of life.

Rhoda's account shows that some people don't actually hear a voice, either externally or internally. Instead, they mentally receive thoughts that they are certain originate outside and independent of their own mind. This is known as thought transference.

The next two ADC accounts include two-way communication. It seems our deceased relatives and friends are able to read our minds and respond telepathically to our innermost thoughts.

Beth, a 56-year-old writer in Florida, had this informative ADC after her father, Norman, died of congestive heart failure:

> The night my father died, I was lying in bed, and lo and behold, I sensed his presence. He said, "Hi, honey!" I said, "Daddy! You're okay!" He said, "Honey, there's nothing to it. Dying is as easy as falling off a log!" I was so overcome that I really didn't know what to say.
>
> My father continued, "I just stood up and there was Carl! He shook my hand and said, 'Hello, Norman. It's good to see you.' Carl and I used to play together when we were little kids, but I hadn't seen him in years. All these other people were there who I hadn't seen in ages, and Carl introduced me around."
>
> I was lying there crying with joy and said, "Oh, that's wonderful!" Then my father said, "I just wanted you to know. Don't worry about me." I said, "Thank you, Daddy." It was all telepathic and that was the end of it.
>
> I fell asleep very, very happy. I wanted to share all this with my family, but I knew they would think I was crazy. So I just used it as support and let it warm me inside.

Beth's account indicates that "death" may be the beginning of a journey of "going home." If this is so, upon arrival we can expect to meet again the deceased loved ones of our entire lifetime.

• • •

Sam, a 90-year-old writer and artist in Idaho, has had multiple communications with his wife, Grace, who died from an aneurysm:

> I have been contacted by my wife, Grace, many times. I have had long conversations with her. I ask her questions, and her words come into my head.
>
> For example, I was standing by the stove one day and felt her right beside me. I asked her, "Do you have any advice?" And she said, "Clean up the house now!" It was like an order. So I said, "Okay, I will."
>
> I started picking things up, and just as I got through, the doorbell rang. Three of her Delta Kappa Gamma sorority sisters came to visit me. One was the president of the whole outfit!
>
> I know very well that Grace knew they were coming and gave me that warning. I was amazed when this happened!

Like Sam, some people are able to have ongoing telepathic conversations with a deceased relative or friend. Because of this, they are often able to receive advice, not only for the important occasions of life, but for the ordinary, day-to-day situations as well.

The remaining five accounts suggest that our deceased loved ones continue to take an interest in our lives and are able to help us in a variety of ways.

Norma is an office manager in Kansas. She had this forceful visit from her husband, Earl, shortly after he died from a heart attack at age 54:

> We lived on a little acreage at the edge of town. My mother and my dad had been living with us when my husband died, and then they left and went back to Nebraska. I had never lived by myself.
>
> That night, we had a really bad snowstorm. The old

wind was really howling! Something banged on the house and I was petrified! I was so scared. I was just tied up in a knot.

All at once, it seemed like my husband, Earl, stood by my bed. I didn't see him, but I felt him. He said, "There is no use in being afraid because nothing is going to hurt you." I heard him with my ears.

I just calmed right down and relaxed then. I went to sleep and never was scared again.

Norma was able to regain her composure immediately after her deceased husband intervened. This story, once again, demonstrates the lasting healing power of an ADC.

Lois, a homemaker in Nebraska, was fortunate to hear from her husband, Ray, after he died unexpectedly of a stroke at age 33:

On the morning after Ray died, I heard his voice say, "I forgot to bank that money! It's in my coat pocket. You better get it and put it in your purse now." It sounded like he was standing behind my right shoulder.

I went and looked in his coat pocket, and there was the money! It was three hundred and some dollars cash! That came in very handy right then.

We had sold my station wagon the afternoon before he died. Ray had put the money in his pocket and was going to deposit it. But I didn't know he hadn't gone to the bank yet.

This account is an example of an evidential ADC. That is, Lois learned something she didn't know and couldn't have known until her deceased husband told her where to find the much-needed cash.

Martha is a physician in the Southeast. She received important guidance from her husband, Alan, who had been an ophthalmologist before he died of cancer at age 56:

About two years after Alan's death, I was having severe headaches almost daily, which was very unusual for me. I wasn't sick – I just had frequent headaches.

One day, I was sitting on the sofa reading. Very clearly, I mentally sensed Alan's voice saying "No wonder you have headaches. Your glasses are crooked! Go see Dan King and have them straightened."

Dan King is a very good and competent optician and a personal friend. The next day, I went to his office and told him about my headaches.

He looked at me and said that one lens was higher than the other because the frame was bent. He straightened my glasses, and my headaches cleared up.

I was relieved that Alan had an answer to my problem!

Alan's intervention is the first of several ADCs in which the deceased made an accurate diagnosis and recommended appropriate medical treatment. Other examples will be given later in the book.

Ruth is a homemaker in Florida. She gladly accommodated the wishes of her 18-year-old grandson, Thomas, almost 11 months after he died in an automobile accident:

One day my daughter, Sally, said, "Mother, I don't want anything for my birthday. Please don't do anything for me. All I want is Thomas, and I can't have him."

At 7:45 on the morning of her birthday, I thought I would ride down to Sally's office and at least give her a card. Within blocks of her office, I heard Thomas's voice in my head say, "Grandma, would you please get my mother a red rose for her birthday?"

I said, "Oh, Tommy!" Then I started to cry and said, "Of course I will get her a rose." He said, "And tell Mom I love her."

So I went to a flower shop. but it wouldn't be open until 9:00. I went to another one – then another and another. None of them were open yet.

It was only 8:15 and Thomas spoke again, "Please, Grandma, get me the red rose for my mother!"

I started driving south. He said, "Turn the car around. Go north." I did, and within ten blocks I came to a sign, "Florist." This was one I didn't even know about because it was off the main road.

By this time it was 8:25, and there was a lady putting a key in the door – even though the shop wasn't supposed to open until 9:00. The front door had a big sign on it – "Special! Red Roses! $1.00 each." I bought the red rose, and then Thomas was gone.

I walked into Sally's office and handed her the rose. I had written "Thomas" on the card. She looked at me and we both cried. I said, "Thomas asked me to do it. He even showed me where to buy it." My daughter was just thrilled!

Every now and then we may be asked to do a personal favor for a loved one who has died. Because Ruth had the courage to act upon the message she received from her grandson, she not only fulfilled his request, but she was also able to deliver a special gift to his mother on her birthday.

The final account in this chapter is from Debbie, a 36-year-old flight attendant in Florida. She was given a crucial warning just a week after her mother died of cancer:

I was staying in Virginia with my best friend, Donna, who had a six-month-old daughter named Chelsea. Donna had put her daughter down for a nap, and I was going to run to the store to pick up some groceries.

When I started to walk out the front door, telepathically I heard my mother's voice very distinctly say, "You need to check on the baby!" I told myself I must be grieving and just blew it off.

As I started to walk out the door again, I heard my mother repeat, "You need to check the baby!" Her voice was crisp and clear.

I turned around and walked back to Chelsea's bedroom and opened the door. I almost fainted! The baby was starting to turn blue! Somehow, she was all wrapped up in the blanket that had been covering her and in another blanket she had pulled off the side of the crib.

I picked Chelsea up and thought I was going to have to do rescue breathing. But she just took a big gasp and let out a blood-curdling scream! I remember sitting down on the floor with her and crying, saying, "My God! Thank you so much, Mom!"

It was fortunate that Debbie's mother persisted in alerting her daughter to the situation. Later an entire chapter is devoted to ADCs for protection, ones in which a person's life was protected or even saved by having an after-death communication experience.

Auditory ADCs help us maintain a sense of connection with our deceased loved ones. Whether we receive a message of emotional support, practical advice, or a warning of danger, hearing their voice assures us of their ongoing concern for our welfare.

What does it feel like to receive a caress, a kiss, or even a hug from a loved one who has died? The next chapter focuses on the comfort people experienced when they felt the touch of a deceased loved one.

CHAPTER 4

Feeling a Touch:
Tactile ADCs

Death is just a change in lifestyles.
—Stephen Levine

This chapter contains accounts from people who reported feeling a physical touch by a deceased family member or friend. Overall, they are a relatively less common type of after-death communication. We call them tactile ADCs.

These experiences were usually felt as a light tap, a gentle touch, a soft caress, a tender kiss, a comforting arm around the shoulder, or an all-embracing hug. Each one was a loving way to express emotional support and reassurance. Regardless of the form, the experiencers easily recognized their deceased loved ones by their familiar and distinctive touch.

Feeling a touch is a very intimate kind of after-death contact, and it seems tactile ADCs take place only between people who have had a very close relationship. The deceased relative or friend returns for the purpose of conveying affection and providing encouragement to the experiencer.

While tactile ADCs may be experienced just by themselves, they occur more frequently in combination with other types of after-death contact, such as sensing a presence, hearing a voice, or both.

The first four accounts in this chapter are typical examples of tactile ADCs.

Joyce is a homemaker in New Brunswick, Canada. Her young daughter, Megan, was almost 4 years old when she died following open-heart surgery:

> Several weeks after Megan's funeral, I was really upset one night and went to bed early. I was just lying there crying. All of a sudden, I felt a little hand gently touching my cheek.
>
> I thought, "Oh, my God, that's Megan!" Her little fingers felt soft and smooth on my face. A tremendous sense of peace and calmness came over me. I felt Megan was telling me she was all right.

Sometimes the smallest hand can provide the greatest comfort. Is there any way a little girl could console her grieving mother more simply and directly than Megan did?

Barbara works in community relations for a large corporation in Illinois. She had this good-natured visitation after her 19-year-old friend, Brian, died in an automobile accident:

> One evening, about two weeks after Brian's death, I was feeling very sad, thinking of him. He had been like a brother to me.
>
> Out of nowhere, I felt a hand tousle my hair, just like Brian was inclined to do when he was alive. This jolted me, as I was home by myself – no one else was there.
>
> I felt Brian was trying to console me and bring me out of my sorrow. I smiled and said, "Okay, Brian. I'll try to snap out of this." And I did.

Because Brian chose a familiar and playful expression of affection, one in keeping with their relationship, Barbara intuitively understood his message. He gave her the perfect signal to encourage her to move beyond her grief and go forward with her life.

Mike, an executive for a construction company in California, is a bereaved father. His 15-year-old daughter, Laura, was killed in an automobile accident:

Two days after my daughter was killed, I lay down on the couch in the family room and fell asleep.

About ten or fifteen minutes later, I was awakened by Laura's kiss. I knew she was there. She kissed me on my lips – I felt her kiss me!

I knew without a doubt in my mind that my daughter was giving me a kiss to assure me she was okay. Everything Laura needed to say was in that kiss.

It was real comforting to me – I felt such joy! It was absolutely the most wonderful thing that ever happened to me.

Laura's affectionate kiss spoke directly to her father's grieving heart. This experience illustrates that even a brief tactile ADC can bring about profound emotional healing.

Dot, age 57, is a family therapist and educator in Washington. She had a completely unexpected visit from her father 5 years after he died of cancer:

I was sitting at my desk in my office. It was an ordinary time of my workday, and I was concentrating rather deeply.

Suddenly, I thought, "What was that?" Then I realized, "It was Daddy!" His cheek had pressed against my cheek, which was his characteristic way to kiss his children, especially when we were young. It was so real, there was no question it was him!

I remember laughing and saying, "Oh, that's so I'd know for sure it was you!" It was a very pleasant experience, very tender and sweet. It was wonderful and I savored it!

Our deceased loved ones are very practical in selecting the best means to convey their sentiments to us. Dot's father chose a way he had used repeatedly with his children, making his manner of touch unmistakable to his daughter even five years after his death.

• • •

As you read the next two accounts of tactile ADCs, notice that each of the women described feeling an emotional warmth that was almost tangible.

Carol is a 43-year-old cosmetologist in Florida. She had this uplifting experience with her mother, who died of cancer:

> Nine years after my mother's death, I was contemplating my relationship with my son, my job, and my life as a single woman. Plus I was feeling financial stress. I felt extremely alone, as if I had the weight of the world on me.
>
> At that point, I felt Mother's familiar tap on my shoulder. I turned around expecting to see her, but there was no one there. I had no doubt in my mind that it was her. It was just a loving, gentle tap on the shoulder to get my attention.
>
> Then I felt a warm, comforting feeling. The pressures of the world were released at that point. I knew all I had to do was ask enough people for help, and help would come. I knew I was not alone with my problems – I knew I was loved.

Carol's tactile ADC left her with a "warm, comforting feeling." This point will be discussed further after the next account.

Rosemary, a nurse in Ontario, Canada, felt a distinctive touch after her 12-year-old son, Mark, died from a playground accident:

> The summer after my son died, I was standing at the patio door looking out at our backyard. I was reflecting on a time when Mark was quite young.
>
> All of a sudden, Mark put his hand on my left shoulder. It was a very light, gentle touch. I had a sense of being enveloped in something warm and comfortable. I got a very serene feeling. It was the first time I almost felt at peace since he died.

The feeling lasted for a good five or ten minutes. I just stood there because I didn't want to let it go.

I knew Mark was okay and was looking out for me. It confirmed for me that my son still exists – somewhere.

Like Carol, Rosemary felt "enveloped in something warm and comfortable" as soon as her son placed his hand on her shoulder. It seems both women received a direct infusion of spiritual energy that lasted beyond the initial touch of their deceased loved one.

The next four accounts are combinations of tactile and sentient ADCs. The people who had them reported feeling a physical touch while sensing the presence of their deceased family member.

Evelyn, a former kindergarten teacher in Florida, was having difficulty coping after her 35-year-old husband, Charles, died of rheumatic heart disease:

A year after my husband's death, I went out to the cemetery. I was really upset and stood there crying, involved in my own feelings. I felt so alone and bereft with three kids to raise.

All of a sudden, I felt Charles standing next to me on my left. I felt his presence, the closeness of him. It startled me because I could feel his arm around my back and his hand resting on my right shoulder. I could feel him there comforting me.

This lasted maybe five seconds at the most, but it made me feel so much better. It pulled me together, and I was able to go home.

Many widows feel abandoned, overwhelmed, and even angry after the death of their husband, especially when they have young children to care for. Although Evelyn's ADC lasted only a few seconds, Charles's supportive embrace communicated the important nonverbal message "You are not alone. I am here for you." This was the emotional understanding she needed at that moment.

Cathy works for a mental health center in New Hampshire. She had this comforting moment with her 15-year-old daughter, Theresa, who died in an automobile accident:

> Throughout the ensuing months, my heart ached and my body ached – I didn't know how to go on.
>
> One day, I lay on my bed facing the wall. I was just wishing to die. Suddenly, I felt Theresa sitting behind me on the edge of the bed.
>
> She began stroking my forehead and hair, just as I had so often done for her. I could definitely feel her presence sitting there – I could feel her energies. This lasted a minute or so, and then she gradually went away.
>
> I was totally joyful to have this contact, and it actually kept me going.

This ADC created a role reversal for Cathy when her grief had nearly destroyed her. Just as she had demonstrated her affection for Theresa so many times, she now became the receiver of the same nurturing expression of love from her deceased daughter.

Paul, a former sergeant in the U.S. Army, lives in Florida. He received gentle reassurance after his 14-year-old son, Keith, died in an automobile accident:

> After my son's funeral, we started to leave the cemetery. My mother was driving the car, and my wife was sitting alongside of her. I was sitting alone in the back seat.
>
> I felt Keith's presence at my left side. He put his arm over my shoulder and kept it there as we rode all the way back to our house. I could feel his body pressing up against me, and I could feel his warmth beside me. I detected that everything was all right. I got a peaceful, quiet, and comforting feeling.
>
> This lasted about twenty minutes, until we got to the driveway, and then Keith was gone. I have no doubt whatsoever. I'm absolutely sure that this happened!

There is no lonelier ride for newly bereaved parents than the long trip home after their child's funeral. For some, there is a feeling of finality and desolation because they believe their son or daughter has been left alone and unprotected in a grave. Having an ADC experience may soften the sharp edges of such profound grief.

Linda, age 45, is a hospice social worker in New York. She had this soothing ADC with her mother, who died of cancer:

My mother and I had trouble getting along, and I always felt the pain of that. It was only during the last few months of her life that we got along well. When she died, I was feeling a lot of sadness for not having had a good relationship with her all those years.

After her funeral, I found myself in the living room curled up in a ball, really mourning my loss of her. All of a sudden, I sensed my mother hovering in the room, on my right side. At first, I thought I was hallucinating.

But then I felt her putting her arms around me, comforting me. She wrapped herself around me like a big, cushiony, warm cloud, rocking me as if I was a scared little girl.

I had been really crying a long time, and she calmed me down. There was a feel about her hug, a nurturing energy, and it seemed it lasted about fifteen minutes.

I knew it was my mother. I just knew it! And I'm very grateful she was there to help me through my pain.

Mourning the loss of something we never had, like a mutually satisfying parent-child relationship, is extremely difficult to resolve after a death. An ADC experience may offer us an opportunity to finally achieve reconciliation with the one who has died. Additional examples of such healings appear throughout this book, and some took place many years after a parent or other relative passed on.

• • •

The next two accounts are combinations of tactile and auditory after-death communications, ones in which the experiencer felt the touch and heard the voice of a deceased loved one.

Janice is a 38-year-old spiritual counselor in Florida. She felt an expression of tenderness from her grandfather 10 years after he died of heart failure:

> I got up in the middle of the night and went to the living room. It was around 3:00 in the morning, and I lay down on the couch and started crying because I was undecided about my life. I was questioning my goals and some of the things I was doing. I was feeling self-doubt and confusion.
>
> As I was crying, I felt a touch on the left side of my face – I felt my cheek being pinched! It was an affectionate little gesture that immediately reminded me of my grandfather. Frequently when I was a child, Grandpa would come up and pinch my cheeks. It was a very typical, loving gesture of his.
>
> At the same time, he said to me, "Everything's going to be all right. Go back to bed." This was very real to me. It was not something I doubted or was looking for to happen. In that moment, I felt very reassured and comforted. I felt a renewed confidence, and I immediately went back to bed.

Only one person in Janice's life ever gave her that special little pinch. Even ten years after her grandfather's death, she immediately recognized his unmistakable yet affectionate mannerism.

Sarah is a dental hygienist in Colorado. She and her family experienced a heartwarming reunion soon after her 24-year-old son, Andrew, was killed in a motorcycle accident:

> I was standing in our kitchen before Andrew's memorial service. Kyle, our other son, came over and put his arm around me. Then my husband, Doug, came over to us, and we opened into a three-way hug.

As we stood there silently with tears rolling down, we felt a light pressure, a light caress on our shoulders. In my heart I knew it was Andrew – and Doug and Kyle did too. We all felt the warmth of his embrace and his love. And mentally I heard Andrew say, "Hey, guys, it's okay."

This lasted no more than thirty seconds, and then the warmth and the pressure were gone. But Andrew's hug had made us a complete family one last time.

This is an example of three people who participated in the same after-death communication experience. Later in the book, there is an entire chapter of accounts in which two or more people shared an ADC when they were together at the same time and the same place.

The next two accounts are combinations of tactile, sentient, and auditory ADCs.

Ellen is a homemaker in Oklahoma. She became a widow when her husband, Harry, died of a heart attack at age 60:

Just a week after Harry died, as I was going to sleep, I thought I felt our collie getting on the bed. So I reached out to push her off. But all of a sudden, I realized it wasn't the dog. Then I said, "Harry?"

I felt my husband lie down on the bed beside me and put his arms around me. Then he laid his head on my shoulder. I was filled with an indescribable sense of peace, as I have never known.

He was reading my mind, and I was reading his thoughts and understanding them. Harry was reassuring me. I felt him telling me "I am fine. I remember all the things I was and knew and felt. I will go on being me, learning and building my life. Yet I will be here waiting for you when you come."

It was wonderful! I certainly didn't expect anything like that! I had been wondering how he was and what he was doing. Now it was enough to know Harry was okay somewhere, and I went peacefully to sleep.

Harry's comforting and loving words assured his widow that he is waiting to be reunited with her when she makes her transition. This experience confirmed for Ellen that there is indeed a life after death she can look forward to enjoying with her deceased husband.

Gail is a nurse in Pennsylvania. She was filled with new hope 6 weeks after her two sons, Matt, age 26, and Eric, age 24, were killed together in an automobile accident:

> Every night I would go out and sit on the steps of my front porch and just cry and cry and cry. I was having such a hard time, and I had been doing this for so long.
>
> One night in the middle of October, I was looking at the moon, when all of a sudden, I felt this real warmth. I felt Matt to my left and Eric to my right with their arms around my shoulders. I knew Matt was to my left because he was so much taller – Matt was 6'4" and Eric was about 5'11".
>
> I heard them saying, "Mom, it's all right. We're fine. Just don't worry. Everything's going to be okay." I felt a peace that I hadn't felt since their deaths. It just lifted me so.
>
> I felt a real relief when they said they were okay and that I shouldn't grieve so much. That was a turning point for me, and I gradually began to sleep easier.

Few people can imagine the utter despair of a bereaved parent who has endured the death of two or more children. Gail received a triple blessing when she learned both her sons had survived physical death, were still together, and were all right. This ADC gave her some inner peace because so many of her questions were answered.

The final account in this chapter illustrates that age is not a limitation when making after-death contact with a living person. Mary is a 30-year-old respiratory therapist in Florida. Her life was brightened by her little patient, Nicole:

I was working in the neonatal intensive care unit, and Nicole was with us for nine months. She had chronic lung disease and had a lot of special needs. I became very attached to her. I had gone through a personal loss myself, so I really focused on Nicole and became her primary caregiver. I also became pretty close friends with her mother.

Nicole had a series of chronic illnesses, and the more they looked, the more they found. Her mother allowed me to be real close to her and Nicole through all that time. We both held her in our arms the night she died.

When I came home, I felt very upset. I was lying in bed tossing and turning, wide awake. Suddenly, I felt a peace come over me – a tremendous peace. And I felt Nicole's presence – I felt it in my heart.

I had a feeling Nicole was touching me, giving me a hug, like a big bear hug. She was telling me she knew who I was and that she knew I had been there for her. And she told me that she loved me too.

Nicole gave me that peace. I feel she was comforting me, even though she was just a baby. I felt lifted up, and I was reassured that she is in a better place.

Professional and volunteer caregivers may become emotionally involved with their dying patients. An ADC can provide a sense of completion, renewing them in their devoted service to others.

The familiar touch of our deceased loved ones is more tangible and intimate than other forms of after-death communication. Tactile ADCs serve as lasting reminders of their love and affection.

Have you ever smelled a fragrance that you associated with someone who has died? The next chapter contains accounts from people who smelled a scent and intuitively knew a deceased loved one was communicating with them.

CHAPTER 5

Smelling a Fragrance: Olfactory ADCs

A rose will still be a rose in heaven,
but it'll smell ten times sweeter.
—*Meg Woodson*

The accounts in this chapter involve smelling a fragrance that is associated with a specific deceased family member or friend. They are a relatively common type of after-death communication, and we call these olfactory ADCs.

Typical scents include the fragrance of a perfume, cologne, or aftershave lotion; the essence of roses or other flowers; and the aroma of a food, beverage, tobacco, or commercial product. The variety of odors that can be identified is virtually unlimited.

During an olfactory ADC experience people reported smelling a fragrance that was clearly out of context with their surroundings. The room or area they were in was suddenly filled with a particular aroma, but it had no physical source.

Occasionally, two or more people who are together in the same place at the same time can smell this scent. In fact, an olfactory ADC is the one type of after-death communication that is most often shared by a group of people.

Anyone may have an olfactory experience by itself, or it could be combined with a sentient, auditory, or tactile ADC.

In the first four accounts the experiencers smelled a familiar fragrance and intuitively associated it with a deceased loved one.

Kathryn, a homemaker in Virginia, received a demonstration of caring from her mother, who died of cancer at age 75:

> One afternoon, just a couple of weeks after my mother died, I was lying on my bed sobbing. Suddenly, my room was flooded with the scent of green apples. I stopped crying in a flash and sat up in bed, sniffing the air like a bird dog.
>
> It was no little maybe, maybe not kind of thing. My whole bedroom was permeated with this wonderful aroma! The green apple smell just filled up the room and it didn't go away. It lasted for a full minute or possibly longer.
>
> My mother had a wonderful air freshener she used at home that was the fragrance of green apples. I never smelled it anywhere else. I loved it and always made a big to-do over how marvelous it was.
>
> It is the only scent that I identify with my mother – and absolutely no one else. I knew this was a signal from her to help me get my act together. I was so grateful for the contact, as it helped me enormously.

Aromas have a strong effect on our emotions and can produce a marked change in our mood. Kathryn's mother chose the one scent her daughter associated exclusively with her, and it quickly achieved the desired result.

Brenda works for a social service agency in Virginia. Her husband, Russell, was 42 years old when he died of a heart attack:

> Russell and I had always said whoever went first would find a way to communicate back to the other one. And he did!
>
> Three or four weeks after Russell died, I was sitting at my desk at work. I suddenly had this fantastic aroma of roses! It was as strong as if there was a bouquet of roses on my desk, right under my nose. I knew it was from Russell!

I looked around the office, and there were no roses anywhere. Nobody else smelled them – only me. The aroma stayed for quite a while, and I felt a total, profound peace.

Russell used to delight in sending a bouquet of roses to me at work for my birthday, anniversary, or sometimes just because. I intuitively knew he had sent them again as his way of communicating his love for me.

Brenda's account mentions an agreement that she and her husband had made before he died, that the one who died first would try to return to contact the survivor. This is called a "compact," which is frequently made between husbands and wives, as well as with other close relatives and friends.

Doris operates a business in her home in Florida. She was widowed when her husband, Nadeem, died of a heart attack at 40:

When my husband and I came to Florida, my big decision was what to do because I had been a well-paid secretary in New York. After we purchased a brand new house, I said to Nadeem, "You know what would be a very profitable business for me? Baby-sitting young children in our home!"

Nadeem became very angry. He said, "No, no, no! I can just imagine crayons on the wall and spilled apple juice on the carpet." He went on and on – he was quite adamant.

But after Nadeem died, I had to supplement my income somehow because he had let his life insurance lapse. So about a year later, I started a daycare business in my home.

That first morning, something woke me up – it was an extremely strong aroma of coffee! I walked through the house because I thought maybe I had left the coffeemaker on. But when I walked into the kitchen, it was off. Yet the aroma of coffee lasted for a long while.

When Nadeem was alive, being Lebanese, he really

liked very strong coffee that would make your nostrils turn
upside down in the morning. When I smelled that aroma,
I knew Nadeem was finally giving me his approval!

It appears Nadeem changed his mind after his death regarding his wife's new business. What simpler way to convey his
approval than to contact her on its opening day by utilizing an
aroma she would immediately identify with him.

Many people can be rather closed-minded and controlling
during their lifetime, especially concerning the plans of their
spouse and children. Hopefully, they will gain a larger perspective after they die and develop more acceptance for the
opinions, values, and goals of others. Their new awareness
could help them achieve more tolerance and compassion for
everyone, including themselves.

Pat is a realtor in British Columbia, Canada. She became a
bereaved mother when her 21-year-old son, Bryce, was killed
by a drunk driver while he was out walking:

About six months after Bryce died, I was sitting in the
kitchen reading the paper. All of a sudden, I got this immensely strong smell of flowers!

My first thought was that somebody had brought
flowers into the house. I looked around, but nobody was
there, and I knew I didn't have any flowers at the time.

The scent of flowers all around me lasted a good five
minutes. I couldn't pinpoint the source, but wherever I
went I could smell them. It was the fragrance of lily of the
valley.

Then I realized, "It's Bryce!" It was Mother's Day, and
this was a gift from my son. It was his way of saying,
"Mom, I'm still here. I'm close to you. I'm remembering
you, particularly on Mother's Day."

This is one of many examples of having an olfactory or
other type of ADC on a special date. These experiences demonstrate the continuing love and concern our deceased loved ones

have for us, particularly on those days we are feeling saddest and missing them the most.

Other significant days may include our birthday and wedding anniversary, the birthday and death day of our deceased loved one, Valentine's Day, Easter, Father's Day, Thanksgiving, Christmas, and other holidays and special anniversary dates. Of course, any day we have an ADC experience is a cause for celebration!

In the next four accounts the experiencers reported smelling an aroma and feeling that their deceased loved one was nearby.

Cheryl, an employment counselor in Georgia, had this joyful ADC after her son, Derek, died in an automobile accident at age 21:

> It was about eight months after Derek died, and I had just come home from shopping. As I unlocked the door to the house, I could smell Derek's aftershave – it was very strong. He used Old Spice, which has a very distinctive aroma – it was unmistakable! The fragrance was right in the doorway, like he was waiting for me.
>
> I knew immediately it was Derek. But just to make sure I wasn't hallucinating, I went into his room and opened a bottle of his Old Spice that I still had, and it was exactly the same smell! I also wanted to make sure that the bottle hadn't fallen or broken and that the lid was still sealed, which it was.
>
> I couldn't see him, and I couldn't touch him, but I knew Derek was there. I had the strong sense that my son was sending me love.

During an olfactory ADC, men are most frequently identified by their aftershave lotion or cologne. While many different brands of men's fragrances were reported, "the bottle with the ship on it" was specified more frequently than all the others.

Elizabeth is a private investor in the Southeast. She had this engaging encounter 8 years after her grandmother died at age 98 of natural causes:

I was sitting in a chair nursing my baby. All of a sudden, I felt a cool breeze brush by me. My grandmother always wore this perfume called Blue Waltz – a really old brand.

The room filled up with that fragrance, and I knew she was there. I had an overwhelming sense of feeling her love.

My little boy stopped nursing and opened his eyes. He turned to look where I felt my grandmother was standing and made little cooing sounds.

She was there for probably fifteen minutes. I told her that I was happy and healthy and how much I appreciated her coming. I knew she was really excited because this was her first great-grandbaby.

Many women wear a favorite perfume or cologne for years, which might be called their "signature scent." This makes it very easy to recognize them when they return, just as Elizabeth was able to do when her deceased grandmother stopped by for a short visit.

Elizabeth's infant son may have detected the presence of his great-grandmother too. While we can't know this for certain, several other accounts in our files strongly suggest that very young children are aware of much more than is generally considered possible.

Sharon, age 34, works in community relations in Florida. She had this charming visit from her grandmother, who died of old age:

My grandmother had a very particular scent about her – it was her very own. Sometimes elderly people just have their own scent.

Hers was lovely – it was not offensive at all. It was a nice, comforting, grandmotherly smell, and there was some lavender associated with it too. She always used lavender soap for bathing and kept bars of it in drawers with her clothes. I hadn't smelled that scent since I had last seen her.

The following spring, about a year after my grandmother's death, I was walking up the stairs in my town house. Her scent was just everywhere! It was very clear and very real to me.

I sat down on the stairs and started to giggle. I said, "What are you doing here, Grandma?" There was a humor in the air and a kind of "Hello!"

Most people have a pleasant personal scent that can be enhanced by the fragrance of soaps, bath powders, shampoos, lotions, and assorted toiletries and cosmetics. Their clothing may also retain the odor of cedar chests, mothballs, or sachets.

Nearly every mother can identify the personal scent of her own child. And many bereaved parents report smelling a variety of baby products when they have an olfactory ADC with their infant.

Vera is a hairdresser in Arizona. She was given a dramatic new appreciation for life from her father about 15 years after he died of cancer at age 40:

I was in the hospital to have our first child. We were thrilled because we had wanted a baby and had waited so long to finally have one.

Suddenly, I was in a lot of trouble! My contractions were strong, yet I stopped dilating, and nothing was happening. The doctor said they had to do an emergency cesarean.

On the way to the operating room, we stopped at the blood lab. I was alone in the corridor when suddenly I could smell the aroma of my father!

He had been a furrier by occupation. His aroma was the combination of animal skin and tannic acid he had used to tan hides. It's a very distinct odor – there's no other smell like it. It's a very clean fragrance and was very much a part of my father.

I could feel my daddy was there with me, and I relaxed. A peaceful feeling came over me, and I knew everything was going to be fine. My son was born easily – the whole thing proceeded like a piece of cake!

Many industrial and occupational odors are absorbed by those who work with foods and chemicals over a long period of time. Vera's father acquired an unusual yet pleasant personal scent that was related to his profession. Even fifteen years later, Vera was able to easily recognize this familiar, unmistakable fragrance. Additional accounts of ADCs that occurred five or more years after the death of a loved one are examined in Chapter 17, *Expect the Unexpected.*

These next two experiences are combination ADCs that include smelling a fragrance and sensing a presence.

Kenneth is a retired credit manager in Washington. He had a series of encouraging contacts from his wife, Roberta, after she died of cancer at age 69:

One evening about a month after Roberta passed on, I went to our bedroom to get ready for bed.

I suddenly felt her presence and smelled her after-shower splash, Jean Naté. That's what she used all the time. It was very, very strong and lasted for seven to ten minutes, and then the aroma was gone.

Exactly the same thing happened three times in the past one and a half years. There was no Jean Naté in the house because I had my daughters go through Roberta's fragrances and give them all away.

Each of these experiences lessened my grieving for her. I think she was trying to tell me that she is okay and is waiting for me when I pass on.

The initial value of having an ADC experience is that it will nearly always reduce the intensity and shorten the duration of our grief if we are bereaved. These results affirm the remarkable healing powers of after-death communications.

Tara is a 39-year-old artist and designer in Rhode Island.
Her cousin, Larry, fulfilled his promise after he died of cancer:

> My cousin, Larry, and I grew up together, and we knew
> each other all our lives. We made an agreement that, if
> we could, whoever died first would communicate back to
> the other. We didn't know how we would do it – except
> we would, somehow, someway.
>
> Three days after he died, I went into my bedroom. All
> of a sudden, I felt Larry's presence! Then the room filled
> up with the scent of English Leather, which was his fa-
> vorite cologne – that's all he ever used. I don't have any
> perfumes because I have allergies, and my husband
> doesn't wear any cologne.
>
> I said, "Oh, my God, it's Larry!" So many emotions
> were going on inside me at once. Larry was keeping his
> pact! I knew he was telling me there is something after
> death.
>
> Then the scent and the feeling of his presence were
> completely gone. But I knew he had been there. And I re-
> alized, "We did it! He contacted me! We really did it!"

A large number of compacts are fulfilled by those who made
these agreements before they died. Imagine the excitement you
would feel if your deceased loved one was able to keep his
promise to communicate with you after his death. It would either confirm your existing faith in an afterlife or challenge you
to seriously reexamine your denial of the possibility of life after death.

The next two olfactory ADC accounts contain the additional
feature of hearing a voice.

Natalie, a 40-year-old counselor in Florida, had this notable
experience with her mother, who had Alzheimer's disease:

> I was in Japan sleeping in my hotel room. Around 3:00
> a.m., I woke up with a start and smelled this beautiful

scent of lilacs. The smell overwhelmed me – it just filled the room! A feeling of great love and warmth came over me, and then I went back to sleep.

Three hours later the phone rang – it was my husband calling from the United States. He said the nursing home had just called him because my mother had died three hours earlier. When I calculated the time difference, 3:00 a.m. in Japan was the exact moment of her death in Connecticut.

As I was crying, the smell of lilacs came again! Lilacs had been my mother's favorite flower. I then realized my mother was there and said, "Mom, it's you! I'm really sorry I wasn't there with you when you died." She said, "I understand. Everything is all right. Don't cry for me. It's better on the other side."

An unusual element of Natalie's ADC is that her mother was persistent and came a second time the same night. This experience implies that our deceased loved ones can locate us instantly, anytime and anywhere in the world, whenever they want to contact us.

Hazel is a homemaker in Florida. She needed help with a painful emotional concern 12 years after her father died of a cerebral hemorrhage at age 57:

My twenty-three-year-old nephew, Brett, died suddenly of a heart attack. He was a dedicated young man in premed who had been married just eleven days. It was a very hard thing for me to accept, and I was very resentful and bitter toward God.

Three weeks later, I was out working in my garden, planting flowers on a Saturday afternoon. All of a sudden, I could smell the tobacco from my father's pipe! It was a special blend made up for him at a tobacco shop – it had a very sweet, spicy aroma.

My father said, "You've been terribly unhappy, and I've

come to set something straight. Don't worry about Brett, he's here with us. He's happy and he's well. Don't concern yourself. Let it go."

It was just like somebody had poured warm sunshine on me. I had this absolutely peaceful feeling, and I could let go.

Just one ADC message can heal our resentment, anger, and bitterness. This was true for Hazel when she learned that Brett was alive and happy in his new life.

The remaining three accounts are examples of olfactory ADCs that were shared by two or more people who were together in the same place at the same time. We call them ADCs with a witness.

Peter is a salesman in Florida. He and his wife, Vivian, had a series of olfactory ADCs shortly after their 20-year-old daughter, April, died of a brain hemorrhage following an automobile accident:

Vivian told me she had been in April's bedroom and smelled an overwhelming fragrance of roses. As she told me that, I thought, "Well, honey, whatever is going to help you get through this – great." But I knew neither we, nor our neighbors, nor anybody else around us had roses.

The following day we were in April's bedroom together. Vivian was standing on one side of the bed, and I was on the other side. We were talking and grieving and crying and asking, "Why? Why did this happen? How are we ever going to get through this?"

Then I had the most overwhelming fragrance of roses you can imagine! You cannot stick your nose in a rosebud and smell the intensity of that fragrance. I took this as a sign from April, "Hey, I am in a better place!"

For the next six to eight weeks, though the fragrance wasn't there constantly, sometimes when we went into April's bedroom we would smell a powerful scent of roses.

At those times we would say to our daughter, "Hi, April. We understand. We both smell the roses. Thank you for letting us know that you're in a better place."

Some people in our culture tend to be a "doubting Thomas" about another person's experience until they have a similar one of their own. And many men who have already had a significant ADC are reluctant to reveal it because they fear what others might say about them.

It seems wherever we presented our workshops, at least one man would quietly approach us afterwards. He'd tentatively begin by saying, "You're probably going to think I'm nuts, but ..." or "This may not be what you're looking for, but...." Then, invariably, he'd share a detailed and poignant ADC, often concluding it with "I've never told this story to anybody else."

Emory, age 36, is a legal secretary in New York. He had this impressive group experience after his foster father died of cancer:

There is a tradition in the Jewish faith of saying the Kaddish on the anniversary of a person's death. It is a prayer recited by mourners after the death of a close relative.

Since my foster father didn't leave any children behind of his own flesh and blood, I had taken it upon myself to say the Kaddish for him every year.

Not being Jewish, I am not part of a synagogue. However, I can go on the anniversary of Dad's death and say the prayer. This particular time, my wife and a friend went with me.

On the way down from the sanctuary, we all smelled pipe tobacco in the elevator. It smelled like an apple pie out cooling on a window sill.

Later, I asked my foster mom about it. I knew that Dad had given up smoking cigarettes, but I didn't know he had become a pipe smoker before he died. When she told me that his tobacco smelled like apple pie, I was about ready to pick my jaw up off the floor!

Since Emory had two witnesses who also smelled the aroma of pipe tobacco in the elevator, he could be certain his experience was real. This is also an evidential account because Emory learned his father had been a pipe smoker, which was something he hadn't known before.

The final account is from Lorraine, who is employed by an optometrist in New York. Her daughter, Tammy, was 25 years old when she was killed in an automobile accident:

When my daughter, Tammy, went to the Bahamas, she bought me a bracelet and a necklace. The night that she died, she had the bracelet on and it was destroyed. For over two years since the accident, I had been trying to find a new bracelet to match my necklace. I would have paid anything for it!

It was nighttime, and we were coming out of one of the attractions at EPCOT Center at Walt Disney World. My other daughter, her friend, and my husband were with me.

My daughter turned to me and said, "Ma, do you smell that?" I said, "Oh, yeah!" We were smelling the Gloria Vanderbilt perfume that Tammy always wore!

But as we looked around, there was nobody near us. Her girlfriend smelled it too and said, "Why don't we go in here?"

So we all went into the store, and I began browsing in the front. My daughter called, "Ma! Ma! Come back here!" I went to the back of the store, where they were selling jewelry. And there was the bracelet – the exact match to my necklace from Tammy! It was unbelievable!

It seems reasonable to assume that Tammy wanted to replace her mother's bracelet and found a clever way to provide guidance to her family. Her choice of time and place to contact them indicates she probably knew in advance that they could discover the priceless bracelet in the nearby gift shop.

Spontaneously smelling a fragrance that you associate with a deceased loved one may trigger a flood of warm, loving memories of that person. And having an olfactory ADC at a special time or place can provide much comfort and support when you realize you are still in the thoughts and in the heart of the one who has died.

What would be your response if you saw a deceased loved one who returned to visit you? The next two chapters examine reports of partial and full appearances that were made by deceased relatives and friends.

CHAPTER 6

Partial Appearances: Visual ADCs

> I am quite confident that the most important part of a human
> being is not his physical body but his nonphysical essence,
> which some people call soul and others, personality....
> The nonphysical part cannot die and cannot decay
> because it's not physical.
> —*Rabbi Harold Kushner*

Seeing a deceased loved one who has returned for a visit is a very dramatic yet quite common type of after-death communication. These accounts are so exciting and numerous that we divided them into two chapters, *Partial Appearances* and *Full Appearances*, to study them fully. We call both forms of contact visual ADCs.

This chapter contains reports from people who perceived a partial appearance of their deceased loved one. That is, they were able to see only part of the body, or if they saw the entire body, it appeared to be less than solid.

These accounts describe seeing a deceased relative or friend in one of the following ways: as a bright light, as a face in a bright light, only the upper portion of a body, or as a complete body ranging in solidity from a transparent mist to not quite solid. Regardless of the form the experiencers saw, they received a great deal of comfort from their visual encounters.

Partial appearances may include any of the types of ADCs that were introduced earlier: sensing a presence, hearing a voice, feeling a touch, or smelling a fragrance.

In the first five accounts the experiencers described seeing a deceased loved one as a very bright light, but the brilliance and intensity of the light did not hurt their eyes.

Phyllis, age 40, is a teacher in Texas. She had this extraordinary visual ADC with Joshua, a 9-year-old boy who had been born with Down's syndrome:

> I had been taking care of Joshua in his home during the summer while I was going to school. He was severely retarded and physically handicapped. Then he went off to a school for handicapped children, and about nine months after that, he died in his sleep unexpectedly.
>
> Three days later I was in my bedroom, and I suddenly became aware of a very bright blue and gold light of tremendous brilliance. There are no words in our language to describe these colors. A sense of the magnitude and beauty of this being was impressed on me as this light.
>
> It became very clear that this was Joshua and that he wished to send a message to his mother. His message was simply that he was very happy and free. Now he could laugh, now he could dance, and now he could sing!
>
> When Joshua was sure that I had received the message in a telepathic way, he was gone.

This account clearly demonstrates the transformation of a young boy, one who had been severely retarded and physically handicapped, into a being of magnificence and beauty. Could it be that during Joshua's lifetime his impaired physical body was merely a disguise of his true spiritual identity?

Sometimes the one who has died is unable to make direct contact with a particular person. He may then seek out someone else he knows, someone he can trust, to deliver his message for him. This was true for Joshua, who asked Phyllis to give a message to his mother, which she did gladly. And what a joyous message Joshua's mother received, saying "now he could laugh, now he could dance, and now he could sing!" At last she had the opportunity to visualize her son completely healed and whole and free of all the limitations of his earthly life.

Edna is a special events coordinator in South Carolina. She too saw a very bright light just a short time after her mother died of cancer at age 66:

> Two or three hours after my mother died, I wanted to be by myself. I went to the garden and suddenly saw an intense bright light. It was about four feet off the ground and three or four feet in diameter. The light didn't have any specific shape, but I knew it was Mother.
>
> She said, "Hello, Edna. I love you. I'm all right, and you'll be fine. It's beautiful where I am now, and I am blissful. I am home." I told her, "I'm so happy for you." And she said, "Take care of your daddy." My father also had terminal cancer at that point.
>
> I said, "Daddy doesn't belong here anymore. He belongs in that wonderful place with you. In fact, I don't want to be here anymore either. I want to be where you are in that extraordinary bliss."
>
> Mother said, "It's not your time. Your task is not yet complete. Stay and live each moment to the fullest. Enjoy the gift of living on this beautiful earth.
>
> "This is my legacy to you. Behold each sunset, flower, and relationship with joy. Let others see that joy, and let love flow through you. Because love is the most important thing there is." Then Mother said, "I'll be with you always." And at that point she just faded away.
>
> It was the most incredible experience I've ever had!

Edna's enduring legacy from her mother was a prescription for living life fully, one far more valuable than any material inheritance. Along with many of the world's religions, this account reminds us "love is the most important thing there is."

Marie is a secretary in Quebec, Canada. She saw more than a bright light during a joyous occasion almost 8 years after her mother died of a heart attack at age 57:

It was my wedding day. While I was kneeling at the altar at the time of my vows, I had an urge to turn my head to the left.

I saw a very bright light, like an illuminated cloud. I knew my mother was there – I felt it. I didn't see her face perfectly, but I saw her smile and her eyes. I think she was in peace.

I was very surprised to see my mother. I felt her warmth and tenderness, and I was very happy that she came. It was just a few seconds, and it ended like a cloud which goes away with the wind.

This is another example of an ADC occurring on a special day. Even though Marie was barely able to see her mother's face during the wedding, her smile was enough to convey her blessings.

Pam, a secretary in Florida, became a bereaved mother when her 20-year-old son, Brad, died in a motorcycle accident:

Ten days after my son's death, a light appeared in my bedroom. I saw Brad's face with his eyes and his smile, and this light was around his face. I wanted to go to him, and I reached out with my arms.

Brad said, "Mom, I'm all right." I knew what he was saying because it was like it went directly into my head. I said, "Son, I want to be with you." He shook his head and smiled, saying, "No, it's not your time, Mom." He had a look of peace and happiness as he went away.

Then I rolled over with a feeling of peace and had the best sleep since Brad had died.

Understandably, bereaved parents are often so devastated by the death of their child that their strongest wish may be to join their son or daughter immediately. But like many who have had a near-death experience, they may be told, "It's not your time yet." This indicates that each of us may have a spiritual purpose for our life and a sufficient amount of time to achieve it. Very simply, if we are still here, we must have more to accomplish.

"It's not your time yet" also implies there is a larger objective and a deeper meaning for everyone's existence than mere day-to-day physical survival. It suggests we are all students in an enormous school or university that provides unlimited possibilities for our spiritual growth.

Wayne is a technical writer in Florida. His father was 66 years old and had pneumonia:

> I was working in Florida when my father became extremely ill. He was living in Chicago. I was called at work and told that he could very easily pass away, so I took time off and started driving to Illinois.
>
> I was driving along somewhere in Tennessee, and it had just turned dark, past the point of dusk. All of a sudden, a pinpoint of light exploded into this great circle of light – right there in front of me!
>
> As this light opened up, I saw my father's face and a little bit of his shoulders, and there was a brightness behind him. His face was natural and three-dimensional.
>
> The thing that impressed me was the smile that he had. My father wasn't gentle in his ways, yet this smile was the sweetest I had ever seen on him. Instantly, I knew that my father had died. I also knew that he was extremely happy.
>
> It all happened so quickly – the light came on, then it collapsed, and it was gone. This was my father's way of saying good-bye. I just knew it.

You may have assumed that having a visual ADC would be a startling event. But as Wayne's account shows, even if someone has such an experience while he is driving a car, he is able to maintain complete control of his vehicle, effortlessly and safely. This story is another example of learning through an after-death communication that a loved one has recently died.

In the next two accounts the experiencers were able to see the entire upper portion of their deceased loved one.

Consuelo is a homemaker in Washington. She had this loving encounter with her father, who died of lupus at age 62. Her family and she are originally from Puerto Rico, where their native language was Spanish:

About a week and a half after my father died, I was sitting up in bed. I had been having a really hard time dealing with his death, and I was crying. I felt like my world was falling apart.

I looked up and saw my father from the chest up, right next to my bed! He was maybe two feet away and looked very clear and solid. He had on a white shirt, with a dark suit, and a gray tie with specks in it. He no longer looked ravaged by disease. I blinked my eyes, and he was still there.

His brow was furrowed, and he looked really concerned. He seemed upset by my distress. I said, "¡Papi!" – which means "Daddy." We spoke in Spanish, our mother tongue.

He said, "¡Mi hija! No te preocupes, tú no estás sola." This means, "My daughter! Do not worry, you are not alone." I heard his words, like he was talking inside my head.

At that point, his face relaxed and his eyes got tender. He turned and kind of smiled a little, like he was telling me he loved me. I felt very comforted by this – I felt wonderful! It was like fifty pounds had been lifted off my chest. Then I blinked and my father was gone.

His visit made me feel like I wasn't alone and that everything was going to be okay. It eased my grieving process. It was like a whole new world opened up for me.

Latinos believe people don't simply die – that there is a continuation of spirit. It's very normal for them to show up and comfort you. When I told my children about my experience, they were delighted.

This is one of numerous accounts in which the experiencers saw their deceased loved ones were healed of the disease that had caused their death. Consuelo's father also conveyed very caring sentiments to his daughter that lifted a great emotional weight from her, again illustrating the strong healing power of ADCs.

Consuelo's account is also an example of a deceased loved one speaking in his native tongue. We have other ADCs in our files that include the following languages: French, German, Italian, Polish, Russian, and Yiddish.

Cindy is the manager of a retirement home in Florida. She had a warm visitation about 2 years after her maternal grandmother died from heart failure at age 82:

> I had just gotten into bed and was relaxing, thinking about the day. I was still awake when a cloud appeared right next to the bed. The cloud was all lit up, and the rest of the room was pitch black.
>
> My grandmother was in this cloud! I could see her from her waist to the top of her head. She was very distinct and solid – I could see everything about her.
>
> She was beautiful! She looked so radiant and so happy. I had never seen my grandmother look that beautiful because she was always a hardworking woman. Her hair was gray, but it was like she had just come from the beauty parlor, and she appeared years younger.
>
> I said, "Grandma!" She didn't say anything, but she was smiling at me and radiating love and peacefulness. It was as if she had come to tell me she was fine and everything was okay, and that she was in a wonderful place.
>
> She was wearing a pink silk blouse I had given her as a Christmas present many years ago. But I had never seen her wear that blouse before. I was really astounded! Then she just disappeared, and I fell asleep.
>
> The next morning, I called my mother in New York and told her, "I saw your mother last night. Grandma came to

me!" When I told her what had happened, she was shocked. But she seemed to be comforted to know her mother was okay.

Cindy's grandmother's appearance spoke volumes! This is the first of several accounts in the book in which an elderly person appeared to be years younger than when he or she died.

In the next seven accounts the experiencer saw the entire body of the deceased loved one, which appeared to be transparent.

Kurt, a 44-year-old counselor in Florida, gained vital insight soon after his father died following a series of heart attacks:

> I had always wondered, "Why does my father hate me?" During my lifetime, he was not a loving man. He was very abusive in his physical corrections and discipline of his children. I had even seen times when he was abusive to my mother.
>
> On the third day after his death, he made an appearance to me. He was just as he looked before he made his transition, except I could see through him. His form was like a gray mist, but he was very easy to recognize. And I could see a bright, white light shining behind him.
>
> My father was crying and asking for forgiveness. He told me that he was sorry for everything he had ever done to me, or to any of the family, or to anybody else. Now he realized that he had been wrong. We needed to understand that as a child he had seen abuse and had been taught that way.
>
> My father also said that he did love me – that he always had – but wasn't able to show it because of his upbringing. And then he was gone.
>
> Right after he left, I cried because I felt like a large weight had been lifted from my shoulders.

Apparently, it is never too late to offer a sincere apology or to ask for another's forgiveness. This ADC affirms that some people may undergo a dramatic transformation shortly after their death, as Kurt's father evidently did in just three days. Perhaps he was able to see his life from a broader point of view, which caused him to experience deep remorse for his abusive behavior.

Rita is a schoolteacher in Florida. She deeply appreciated her father-in-law's thoughtfulness after he died of a heart attack:

My father-in-law passed away at 4:00 in the morning, and we were called very shortly thereafter. Dad and I had been very, very close – in fact, closer than he was with my husband.

I took my husband to the airport to go to the funeral and put him on a plane. I wanted so desperately to go too, but I was pregnant with our first baby, and my doctor wouldn't let me.

When I came back to the house, I was especially tired and lay down on the bed, trying to get myself together. Over in the corner, right in front of the closet door, Dad appeared!

It was a full outline of his body, and there was a glow about him. He was wearing a pair of pants and a white shirt open at the neck, but he was transparent.

Dad said, "I am all right. I am fine. It's okay that you can't go to my funeral." It was as though he wanted me to know he was very happy and very much alive. I felt a whole lot of love from him – this loving feeling was so strong.

I never had anything like this happen to me before, but I had no fear at all.

We may be feeling remorse for not having said "good-bye" to someone before he died. Or we may be regretting that we weren't present at the time of his death, believing we neglected him at that most sacred moment. Or we may be feeling guilty for not having attended our loved one's funeral.

Rita's experience with her father-in-law is one of several ADC accounts in which deceased loved ones assure us they are aware of our love for them, whether or not we were there when they made their transition. According to our research, they generally tend to make light of these occasions, including their own funeral.

Ben is a probation officer in Florida. He had this supportive ADC 16 years after his father died of cancer at age 75:

> My second marriage was a real mistake, and it only lasted about four months. I was extremely depressed about what I was going through. I was so deep in depression that I was just lying there on the bed when my father came to help me.
>
> He was a transparent figure, so the room showed through him. He had a bit of a smile on his face, and he wore a dark pair of trousers and a cream-colored casual sport shirt. He was wearing bright red suspenders and placed his thumbs through the suspenders and kind of flipped them.
>
> My father hadn't been a particularly loving person. He didn't say loving things, but we knew he loved us. So just his presence with a smile meant a great deal to me. He didn't have to say anything – he was there.
>
> My father's presence at my time of need was a real sign of his love. This seemed to be the breakthrough for me to start upward out of the depression – to bring myself back a little bit and get some peace of mind.

Ben's father intervened when he was needed most. Some of us feel uncertain or even apprehensive about what to say to somebody who is depressed, terminally ill, or bereaved. This ADC illustrates that just "being there" can often be enough. It is a way of conveying "You are important to me. I care about you." Holding someone's hand, giving him a hug, being willing to listen to his feelings without judgment, or allowing him to cry are all means of "saying the right thing."

Hal, 55, works in real estate in New Jersey. His father-in-law, Vincent, made an unannounced visit the day after he died of cancer:

> About 2:30 in the afternoon, I was looking through the mail in the dining room. I had an eerie feeling someone was with me and when I looked up, I saw my father-in-law! He was standing in the kitchen looking at me. The hair on the back of my neck literally stood up!
>
> He was dressed in corduroy pants and a loose wool shirt that he wore a lot. I saw him clearly – he was three-dimensional, yet I could see through him to the kitchen wall.
>
> My father-in-law was extremely healthy now and not at all ravaged by cancer. He was gazing at me with that wonderful look he had. My senses rebelled at what I was seeing, but I knew it to be a fact.
>
> There was a telepathic message from him to me that said, "I want you to know that I am all right. Tell them not to worry." I assumed he meant my mother-in-law, my wife, and his other daughter. It lasted no longer than thirty seconds, and then he was gone.
>
> This is as vivid in my memory as if it happened ten minutes ago. It was a very profound experience, a wonderful gift.

Vincent's wife and two daughters may have wondered why he appeared only to Hal. Unfortunately, there can be hurt feelings when one family member is contacted but the others are not. Since some people are more receptive to having ADCs than others, the one who died probably contacts the person who is most open and most likely to deliver a personal message to the whole family.

John is a communications coordinator in Newfoundland, Canada. He was just 24 years old when he had this remarkable experience with his grandmother, who had died of cancer:

I was deeply attached to my grandmother. I grew up in the same house with her through my formative years, and I loved her deeply.

The day after she was buried, it was evening and I was lying on the bed in my room. I was crying a bit and really feeling terrible when my grandmother came to the end of the bed!

She was totally illuminated with light – a white and golden light was streaming from her. It surrounded her and extended about eight inches from her whole body!

Grandma appeared a bit more solid than a hologram. She was wearing her favorite dress, which was green with roses on it. She also had on green earrings, a necklace, a ring, and a gold watch. Grandma appeared to be in robust health! She was the same age as when she died, but her makeup and her hair were done perfectly.

She looked beautiful and was radiantly happy. She had a gorgeous smile on her face as she said, "John, you've got to stop worrying about me. I feel wonderful! I'm all right now, and I'm in a wonderful place." Then she turned and walked five or six feet away from the bed and disappeared suddenly.

I know this happened because I was wide awake with full control of my faculties. This was an absolutely stunning visual communication of an afterlife – it was miraculous! Once I had that reassurance, there was no need for me to grieve for my grandmother anymore.

Even when it's nighttime and the room is dark, our deceased loved ones are usually seen in full detail. In some ADCs, a bright light is visible behind them. In others, they may be the source of the light that extends beyond their body and illuminates the entire room.

The experiencer typically describes seeing a clear white light, though sometimes it may have a golden, yellow, or blue tinge. This is reminiscent of the colorful auras some people claim they are able to see surrounding those who are physically alive.

Trudy is a laundromat attendant in Connecticut. She was only 19 years old when her adoptive father eased her sorrow after he had died suddenly from an allergic reaction to penicillin:

> My mother and uncle came to tell me that my father had died. After they left, I started crying and went upstairs and lay down on my bed. I was very, very upset because I felt Dad would never get to see my child, his first grandchild, who was due in three months.
>
> All of a sudden, the room felt very calm and I opened my eyes. Standing at the end of the bed was my father! He had been dead less than six hours.
>
> Dad wasn't really solid. I could see what he was wearing, but I could also see behind him. He had on a gray pair of work pants and a red plaid, flannel shirt.
>
> I thought this was strange and said, "What are you doing here, Dad?" He was very calm and smiling, and he talked very soothingly to me. He said, "I'm here because you're upset."
>
> I said, "I'm very upset because I know you're not going to see your grandchild." And he said, "Don't worry, I'll see all my grandchildren!" After that, he just faded away and was gone.
>
> I sat up and realized, "He's still with me!" I didn't feel upset anymore and wasn't crying – I felt very good, very peaceful.

Just as Trudy presumed her father would never be able to see her baby, most people assume their deceased relatives and friends can't be present to participate in the special happenings and events in their lives. But, as the next account indicates, perhaps the opposite is true.

Billie, who works at a service station in Florida, observed a sweet moment after her mother died of cancer at age 52:

After we went to the funeral parlor, we came back to my mother's house. I laid my five-week-old daughter, Kelly, on the recliner in the living room, and I lay on the couch.

I was just fixing to put my head down when I saw a glow come through the front door. It took form and became my mother!

She was walking about six inches above the floor. I could barely see through her — she wasn't quite solid. She radiated pure white light and was dressed in a long, flowing white gown. I'd never seen my mother look so beautiful!

She walked over to Kelly and looked down at her. Mom was grinning from ear to ear. She reached out and stroked Kelly under her chin, saying, "You're so cute." She said it twice, and I heard her through my ears.

Then Mom looked over at me and smiled and slowly disappeared. She was gone before I could say anything. I think she came to see her granddaughter because Mom was too ill with cancer to see her before she died.

How often do our deceased parents, grandparents, or other family members come by to pay a loving visit to us or our children? Probably far more frequently than we realize. After Billie's mother was no longer confined to her diseased physical body, she was able to see and caress her granddaughter. But if Billie hadn't been present and aware, she might not have known that her mother had returned to admire the new baby.

In the remaining four accounts the deceased love one was reported to be denser or more substantial in appearance, but still less than completely solid.

Anita, a nurse in Florida, received unexpected news from her grandfather after he died of heart failure at age 87:

This happened the day of my grandfather's funeral. I was lying in bed that evening, when all of a sudden I felt his presence.

I opened my eyes, and my grandfather was standing beside me. He looked opaque, not like a solid person. He looked very healthy and had a glow about him, like a shining golden light was coming from his body.

He bent down toward my head, as though he was going to tell me a secret. He said, "I will be a great-grandfather in the spring. I will have a great-grandson!" Grandpa was born in Hungary and had a very strong accent.

I had an overwhelming feeling of comfort and warmth, and then he was gone. I got up immediately and went into the living room to tell my husband what had just happened.

The next day I had a pregnancy test, and I was indeed pregnant! When our son, Tyler, was born the following May, I kept saying, "Grandpa, you were right!"

This is one of several ADC accounts we received in which a deceased loved one informed a woman she was pregnant. Some of these heavenly birth announcements also revealed the gender of the unborn child, and this information was later proven to be accurate.

Marcia is a 44-year-old manager for a bank in Louisiana. Her 7-year-old son, Elliott, died a short time after he was struck by an automobile:

A month or two afterwards, I was lying there in my bedroom. I looked over at the doorway, and I saw Elliott! He was just standing there smiling, and he waved at me.

He had on a short-sleeved button-up shirt and pants. He didn't look solid, but I couldn't see through him. There were no words or anything, but I knew that he had come to say good-bye and to tell me that he loved me.

It was a very loving and peaceful feeling, and I wasn't frightened at all. I didn't feel surprised seeing him there – I just accepted it. I lay there for a few moments, then I got up and started walking towards him, but he disappeared.

I went back and lay on the bed, and I said out loud, "I love you, Elliott." He appeared for a few seconds more, and then he disappeared again.

I felt peace and love, and afterwards I cried. The experience gave me the ability to close the door because I felt it was his final good-bye.

Marcia's account is very interesting because her son appeared, disappeared, and then appeared to her a second time, which is quite unusual. More importantly, she was given the golden opportunity that bereaved parents so fervently wish for – one more chance to say, face-to-face to their deceased child, "I love you."

Dale is an interior designer in Ohio. He had this profound meeting more than a year after his partner, Robert, died of AIDS at age 38:

It was about 1:00 or 2:00 in the morning, and I was in a dead sleep in my bedroom. My eyes were closed, when all of a sudden what awoke me was this brightness. It was like somebody put a flashlight in front of my face – it was that bright!

When I opened my eyes, Robert was standing over me right by my bed, not even half a foot away. There was this intense, bright white light around his form that was coming from within him that did not hurt my eyes. The rest of the room was pitch black, but I wasn't afraid.

Then a lot of things happened all at once. I could not quite see through him, but he wasn't solid either. There were swirls of vapor totally surrounding his body, and these ripples of vapor were moving. His clothing was like a robe, maybe with a hood.

Robert radiated an intense love that penetrated every bit of me, like a merging of energy. Every fiber of my being felt love. There was total love, understanding, and compassion, totally different than what we experience here. It was very cosmic!

He had beautiful eyes, striking eyes. I touched his right arm with my left hand, and I felt a lot of heat coming from his body. I also felt a high vibration, like if you put your hand on a massager.

Then Robert took my left arm and put it back down by my side and just disappeared. The light went with him – it was sudden, like if you turned a light off.

Of all the gifts Robert has ever given me, this was the most beautiful. It was healing, and now I have no fear of death. It verified everything I had ever read by Elisabeth Kübler-Ross on this subject. I will stand up against any skeptic that this was a very real incident.

It's well known that those who have a near-death experience virtually always lose their fear of death. This is also true for many people who have had an ADC experience, freeing them to embrace life and live it more joyfully.

The final account is from Carolyn, a labor relations manager in Florida. She had this sentimental reunion with her father 2 months after he died suddenly of a heart attack at age 63:

I was living in Colorado. I was out in my garden around 10:30 in the morning digging up some weeds in my salad patch where the green peppers were. I clearly heard my father say telepathically, "Hi, Cricket!" Only two people in the world called me Cricket – one was my dad and the other was my mom.

I turned and my dad was there, sitting on a log with his legs crossed, about three feet away. I could almost reach out and touch him, but I knew I shouldn't do that. He wasn't quite solid – his density was soft, like cotton candy.

Dad looked just like a million bucks! He had the most wonderful smile, and I could see the wrinkles around his eyes. He was wearing his old chinos, a light blue oxford shirt, and his white deck shoes. He looked a little younger, and all of his health was there.

He said, "How are you doing, sweetheart?" I said, "Daddy! I'm so happy to see you! I'm fine." And he said, "I just want you to know that I'm okay, and I'm watching over all of you." Then he said, "I'll see you, sweetheart," and he was gone.

This experience was wonderful because Daddy didn't have a chance to say good-bye to me before he died. It taught me that love is enduring and that my father's love for me continues. This was God's way of showing me that death doesn't stop love, and it doesn't take away relationships.

A sudden death usually denies us the opportunity to be with somebody when he dies, which often causes prolonged, unresolved grief. One of the strongest healing qualities of an ADC is that it provides a second chance to say good-bye and achieve emotional completion, just as Carolyn did with her father.

How would you feel if a deceased relative or friend visited you and seemed as real and lifelike as any other human being? The next chapter is a continuation of this one, except it features examples of full visual appearances.

CHAPTER 7

Full Appearances:
Visual ADCs

Death ... is no more than passing from one room into
another. But there's a difference for me, you know.
Because in that other room I shall be able to see.
—*Helen Keller*

This is the second of two chapters devoted entirely to visual
ADCs. These accounts are from people who reported that a deceased relative or friend had made a full appearance to them.
They saw his or her complete body, which looked absolutely
solid and real.

The deceased loved ones demonstrated they were healed
and whole, regardless of their age when they died or their cause
of death. Nearly all were much happier and freer than when
they were wearing a physical body. Many also radiated a spiritual serenity that is rarely found on earth, and they frequently
expressed far greater love, compassion, and wisdom than they
had before.

A full appearance by a deceased loved one is generally a
very healing event. The experiencers gain a dynamic new mental and emotional portrait, an update, that can replace any old,
painful memories they may have. In fact, these accounts are so
warm and comforting to read that it may be hard to remember
they are descriptions of family members and friends who have
already died.

Full appearances are quite common and may be experienced

in combination with any of the other types of ADCs discussed earlier.

The first four accounts in this chapter are typical examples of full appearances made by deceased loved ones.

Joanna is a librarian in Wyoming. She was widowed when her 25-year-old husband, Ted, died from a brain tumor:

> This was the night after Ted's funeral, and I was staying with friends for a few days. I lay down on the hide-a-bed in the living room by the fireplace and started to doze off to sleep.
>
> I don't know why, but I opened my eyes and looked around. There in a rocking chair beside the fireplace, I saw Ted! He was in blue jeans and a western shirt – what I usually saw him in. He looked solid and appeared in good health.
>
> Ted looked incredibly peaceful and reassuring. He wanted to let me know he was okay and that I was going to be okay too. It lasted for a few moments, and then he was gone.
>
> I felt Ted was watching over me and trying to be of some comfort.

A full appearance can answer so many questions at once about the deceased loved one that often no words are required. The healing power of this ADC is contained in its simplicity and directness. Just being able to see Ted gave Joanna the quiet assurance that he would continue to be there for her.

Eileen is a substance abuse counselor in Florida. She had this thrilling visit the night her sister, Leslie, died from complications of diabetes at age 50:

> I lay down on the bed and was crying. Suddenly, I had a feeling there was somebody in the room, somebody just standing there. I sat halfway up and looked at the foot of my bed, and there Leslie stood!
>
> She looked gorgeous! She was dressed in white, and

her hair was upswept into a beautiful, smooth Grecian coiffure. Her skin was just as smooth as alabaster. I was so taken aback!

She appeared very serene and was half smiling. She looked better than she had ever looked and was very solid and real. It seemed she was about to lean over and say something to comfort and reassure me.

Then I heard a whoosh, and she was gone. It didn't frighten me – it left me with a feeling like "Oh, Leslie's all right! She came back to tell me she's okay." I lay back down feeling very comforted and went to sleep.

When I tell people this experience, they say, "Oh, you were asleep, you dreamed it." But I know I wasn't – I know I was awake. It's every bit as real to me now as it was to me then.

How quickly some people try to discount and explain away the experiences of others! Because many skeptics insist "There is no scientific evidence for life after death," their assessment of ADC experiences often is "They can't be real – therefore they aren't." Instead, they offer psychological and physiological explanations for ADCs, NDEs, and other kinds of spiritual experiences. Yet several people we interviewed admitted they had been ardent skeptics until they had an after-death communication experience of their own.

Anne is the manager of a retail store in Prince Edward Island, Canada. Her son, Justin, 18, tried to rescue his younger brother, Bobby, 17, while they were swimming, and both boys drowned:

It was 9:00 on a Saturday morning about a year later. I was in the kitchen putting some dishes in the dishwasher. All of a sudden, I felt there was someone in the room with me. When I turned, Bobby was standing there leaning on the refrigerator!

He looked very healthy and happy. He had on a brown and white checkered shirt and a pair of brown cord pants he used to wear. He looked very solid and so real that it seemed I could have touched him. There was a bright light where he was standing.

Bobby's blue eyes were glowing – they had such a knowing expression. He gave me the most wonderful smile I have ever seen. I knew his smile was saying, "We are both fine. We're all right. Just get on with things and be at peace with yourself." I realized his message was from Justin too.

I screamed and dropped the glass I had in my hand! I ran over and tried to put my arms around him, but he just disappeared. I knew Bobby had been there, and I started to cry.

Many people weep tears of joy from having an ADC, but for others it may be a bittersweet experience. For instance, a few bereaved parents told us that while they treasure their after-death communication, they cried tears of sadness afterward because it was difficult having to say good-bye to their child one more time.

Molly is a legal stenographer in Missouri. She was delighted when she saw her grandmother, who had died of old age at 87:

My grandmother and I were extremely close – I lived a good part of my life with her. She was crippled from the time she was in her early twenties, so I never really saw her standing straight.

The second night after her death, I was in bed but I was not asleep. My eyes were wide open, and I saw her! She was standing up straight and looked to be about thirty or thirty-five years old. She was solid and lifelike, just like a living human being.

Her hair was cut short, and it was real curly all around her face. She had this sweet smile. She didn't say anything, but I got the idea that she was showing me, "See, now I'm standing straight!"

She was wearing an older style dress with an unusual

pattern – a white background with a red stripe – that I didn't recall ever having seen before. All she did was stand there and smile. I got out of bed and turned on the lights, but she was gone.

I told my aunt about it the next morning. I described my grandmother's dress to her, and she took me to the basement and pulled out some old trunks. She found a quilt my grandmother had made. And there was the same material, that had a white background with a red stripe, sewn into the quilt!

This is another example of an evidential ADC because Molly was able to validate her own experience when she later saw her grandmother's quilt. Then she immediately recognized that the piece of fabric sewn into it was a leftover scrap of the same material that had been used to make her grandmother's dress.

A full appearance frequently includes verbal communication, as the remainder of the experiences in this chapter illustrate.

Stuart, age 85, is a retired patent agent in Pennsylvania. He had this dynamic encounter 11 years after his wife, Gladys, died following a long and debilitating illness:

I was sitting in a chair in my living room when I suddenly realized Gladys was coming down the stairway. I was just dumbfounded when I saw her!

Her appearance was not the same as when she was sick – she was beautiful. The brilliant lighting and the intensity of her was next door to unbelievable! It's impossible to describe the brilliance, absolutely impossible.

Gladys was smiling. She was solid – there was nothing ethereal about her at all. After this intense scene and some brief communication, she disappeared.

I have no question that this was an appearance from another world. I can't answer why Gladys came to me, but it was an exceedingly pleasant contact. Though when you've had a marvelous, unbelievable relationship with a wife for over fifty years, that's a good enough reason.

What a joyous and unexpected reunion for a widower to have with his deceased wife after more than fifty years of marriage! It may well be that Gladys wanted to show Stuart, now in his twilight years, that death is but a gateway to another dimension of life.

Virginia is a nurse in Massachusetts. She was immediately relieved when her 17-year-old daughter, Erica, came back to her after dying in an automobile accident:

> Almost a year later, I woke up one night, and Erica was standing at the end of the bed. She looked at me and seemed to be in a happy mood. She appeared to be in perfect health with no injuries or anything.
>
> It was Erica, in person! She seemed alive and well! She was very vivid. She had on a navy blue skirt and sweater that she used to wear a lot. She seemed solid and looked very, very peaceful.
>
> Erica had a slight smile and said, "I'm fine, Mom. I'm all right. Don't worry about me." It only lasted about twenty seconds or so, and then she suddenly disappeared. A peace came over me at that moment, and I went right back to sleep.

More than any other type of ADC, full appearances assure us that our deceased loved ones continue to exist. Perhaps for the first time in months or even years, we are filled with a profound sense of peace, knowing their well-being is certain.

Gordon, an architect in New Mexico, was contacted by an old friend of the family, Mrs. Tinsley, who died at age 93:

> I went into the viewing room at the funeral home to pay my last respects to Mrs. Tinsley. I was the only person there. As I was standing looking at her body, I heard, "Gordon, it's okay if you cry."

I looked around because it was Granny Tinsley's voice! When I looked up, she was on the other side of the room, maybe ten feet away. It was like she was really there – I could see all of her. Her hands were slightly lifted, and she had on a different dress than she was wearing in the casket.

Suddenly, I had this explosive sob – it was really wrenching! I was really hurting, but I didn't know it. I looked away and cried, and when I looked again, she wasn't there anymore.

I don't think I would have cried if she hadn't said something. I knew I missed her, but I would have just kept it bottled up inside. Since then, I've remembered on occasion that it's okay to cry because Mrs. Tinsley gave me permission.

Mrs. Tinsley taught Gordon the very important lesson that "it's okay for big boys to cry." Presumably she knew that any kind of grief or trauma that isn't resolved fully can surface unexpectedly and destructively later in our life.

Paula is an attorney in Virginia. She acquired a lasting sense of peace when her son, Jimmy, appeared to her about 2 weeks after he died of leukemia when he was 12 years old:

When you're suffering from a massive loss, you have about fifteen seconds or so, as you wake up, before the reality comes back to your consciousness.

The morning sun was streaming into my bedroom. As I woke up, I remembered – and the grief hit me like a great big, cold, furry thing.

Suddenly, Jimmy was standing by the bed with a big smile! I saw his whole body. There was nothing ephemeral about him. He had on a striped T-shirt and blue shorts.

He didn't have any evidence of leukemia! He had a lot of hair, which was strange because he didn't have much for the last part of his life. And he didn't have the scar on the side of his head where he'd had surgery.

Jimmy talked – I heard him! He said, "Mom, I am dead, but it's okay. I'm fine!" He looked exactly like he did when he was alive. He moved gracefully and was clearly happy and well. Then he disappeared.

I was so happy to see him and hear he was okay. I was pretty sure he was, but it was very nice to have him come and tell me. I was elated! It was so wonderfully special, and I smile whenever I think about it.

When we are the primary caregiver to a loved one who dies following a prolonged illness, it can be hard to recall a time when he was healthy and free of pain. And, unfortunately, this may be how we will continue to remember him. But imagine our sense of relief if we see a deceased loved one again in a full visual ADC and he is healed and whole and happy. Now our old painful memories can be replaced by joyful ones each time we recall his new appearance and state of being.

George is a mental health counselor in the Southeast. He was 24 years old when he received a message from his grandmother about 4 years after she had died of kidney failure:

During the middle of the night, I was roused from my sleep as my grandmother entered my room from the hallway. She stood on the right side of the bed.

The room was light enough to see her, but I don't know what the source was. She appeared solid and real, about the same age as when she died. I was able to see her face, and she was very happy and smiling.

She was in a loving, soft mood and spoke directly to me. She said, "I've come to let you know that I love you. Who you are and what you are is right for you. I want you to know that I approve of you. Your life is right for you."

I felt intense happiness and joy, and I remember telling her that I appreciated what she was saying to me. Then she kind of drifted away.

I woke up the next morning feeling a new security and freedom. I felt like a great weight had been lifted off me.

To be quite honest with you, I'm gay. My grandmother came at a time that was a real transition for me. I was struggling with my gay identity and my self acceptance. This experience helped me to move forward with my life.

ADCs will not necessarily occur because we want to have one, even if we are deeply bereaved. Many take place at a later time, such as when we are wrestling with a difficult problem and could benefit from receiving a loving and supportive message.

Eve is a retired secretary in the Southwest. Her husband, Pete, was a career Master Sergeant in the U.S. Marine Corps before he died of cancer at age 59 as a result of exposure to Agent Orange in Vietnam:

After her father died, our daughter, Merri Beth, completely fell apart – drinking for weeks, disappearing for hours, and driving drunk. About a month later, I put her in a recovery center for alcoholism. This was not an easy thing for me to do. I returned home mentally and physically exhausted and went to bed at 11:00 p.m.

About 3:00 a.m. I woke up, and my husband was standing in my bedroom! There was a very bright light behind him, but I could see him perfectly. It was almost as if I could reach out and touch him – he was that close and that distinct.

Pete was in his full dress blues, with his medals and hat on. He looked at least twenty years younger, the way he had been before he got ill. He looked wonderful, strong, and healthy, as if he had never been sick a day in his life!

It was a miracle, and I was in shock for a second or so. Then Pete smiled and said, "You did the right thing, honey. You had no choice. Merri Beth will be all right now." He looked so calm and peaceful, and then he just disappeared. I felt a sense of relief that I had done the right thing.

Merri Beth has not had a drink in over seven years. She has accepted her father's death and is doing well in her job. My daughter and I are closer now than we have ever been in our whole lives.

Once again, an ADC suggests that our deceased loved ones are aware of and take an active interest in the events and situations of our lives. Those difficult occasions when we are forced to exercise "tough love" with our children can be very lonely and uncertain times for parents. Pete's message to Eve provided strength and reassurance, giving her courage to follow through with what was best for their daughter.

Helen is a homemaker in Alabama. Her son, Adam, was killed in a helicopter crash at 27 while he was in the Coast Guard, and her niece, Jessica, died in an automobile accident 5 months later at 20:

After Adam died, I did things because I felt I had to, not because there was any joy in it. I kept the dishes washed and the beds made up – I made the appearance of living a normal life. But inside there was a hole, a void, there at all times.

One afternoon about ten months after my son died, I got a cup of hot coffee and lay down in my bedroom to listen to the radio. All of a sudden, Adam and my niece, Jessica, appeared together before me, holding hands!

They were in perfect health and their faces were shining. They appeared absolutely solid and had on full-length white robes. A soft light encircled both of them. They were so peaceful and happy – they were radiant!

Adam said, "Hi, Mother. I love you. I'm all right. I'm happy, and you will join me one day. Please don't grieve for me, Mother. Release me. Let me go."

Then Jessica said, "Hi, Aunt Helen. I want you to tell my mother to quit grieving for me. I am happy, and this was meant to be." Then they left.

That's when I was able to release my son. I let Adam

go, but not in my memories, not in my love. This experience let me accept the fact that Adam is no longer on this earth, but is just a step away. I learned to have complete faith in God, and now my attitude and general health are better in every way.

When someone we love dies, it's natural to feel a deep sense of sorrow. But it seems our deceased loved ones want us to know that it isn't necessary to grieve for them. This may be one reason they are so eager to show us they are at peace in their new life.

The next three visual accounts include feeling the touch of a deceased loved one.

Sonia is a home health aide in Washington. Some of her many questions were answered about 6 weeks after her daughter, Valerie, died from a brain hemorrhage when she was 9 years old:

Valerie died very suddenly – it was a very traumatic experience. I was frantic, just a basket case. I was questioning, "How do we know there's a God? How do we know there's a heaven? And where is Valerie now?"

I went to bed quite early because I had exhausted myself, but I know I was awake. I was lying on my right side, and I felt someone touch my shoulder. I turned over and Valerie was standing there!

She seemed real to me. She looked exactly like herself and in good health. She was bright, sort of glowing, and was dressed in a sparkling, dazzling white gown.

She said, "Mommy, I love you. My headache is gone. I'm all right, and I don't want you to worry about me." She was very calm and happy and quite beautiful. Then, suddenly, she was gone.

I believe there are times when God sees fit to send someone back to give you a message. I think that's what happened to me. God sent Valerie down to take this dark cloud away, to remove this terrible boulder that was on my shoulders.

It seems our deceased loved ones can choose their own clothing when they appear to us. While some return wearing white or various colored robes, many select their more familiar earthly attire. Perhaps a grandfather comes back in his old bib overalls so that he can be easily recognized. Others apparently feel more comfortable dressed in their "Sunday best," a military uniform, or the clothes they were buried in. No matter what they are wearing, the garments usually convey something meaningful to the experiencers.

Hannah, a homemaker in Utah, had this tenderhearted meeting about 6 weeks after her mother died of a stroke at age 82:

> I couldn't sleep one night, so I got up and did a couple of chores around the house. Then I sat in the chair in the front room. I was thinking about Mother and feeling the loss of no longer taking care of her.
>
> Suddenly, I saw her walk into the room! The first thing I noticed was that she was walking normally. Ten years before the end of her life, she was forced to have both legs amputated above the knee.
>
> Mother had both her legs again, and she walked right over to me and sat on the arm of the overstuffed chair. She put her arm across my shoulder and said, "Hannah, darling, you have been like an angel to me. Don't feel sad. Don't grieve for me."
>
> There was a radiance about her, and she looked so happy. Then Mother got up and walked around to the other side of the chair. She said, "Don't worry about me. Just remember I'm happy." Then she kissed me on the cheek and left.
>
> It was so very real — I felt the touch of Mother's arm on my shoulder and the press of her lips on my cheek. I felt the special love and closeness that always existed between us.
>
> This was a very loving and special occasion for me and something I've kept sacred.

Evidently, our family members and friends don't want us to suffer as a result of their death. Now that they are free of the pain and limitations of their physical body, they know it's unnecessary for us to worry about them. This could be another reason they return, to assure us that they still exist and have been restored to complete health and wholeness.

Richard is a real estate broker in North Carolina. He had this convincing ADC with his father, who died of a stroke at age 66:

Three days after his burial, someone woke me up. I sat up to see who it was, and it was my father! Street lights coming through the window behind me were shining on his face. I could see him very well – there was no question it was him.

He said, "Richard." I knew my father's voice, and I raised up from the bed. He shook hands with me immediately, and his hand was very familiar and warm.

Then he said, "I'm so glad to see you, Richard. Don't worry about anything. I love you." I heard this externally, directly from his lips. His voice sounded clearer than ever.

I couldn't take my eyes off his face. He looked better than I'd ever seen him look in my whole life. Instead of having gray hair, his hair was black. And his skin was smooth. My father looked absolutely great!

There was a smile on his face, and he appeared contented and happy, like there was something much better than I could ever dream of. And then he left.

I was greatly astonished and thrilled. I had been in deep bereavement, and that experience gave me assurance that there is life after death. It was real – there is no question in my mind, no question.

No wonder Richard didn't doubt his ADC experience. What could be more tangible and real than not only seeing your father after his death but actually shaking hands with him too! Although his father spoke to him, it was his visual appearance that communicated an even more powerful message, that he was much younger, happier, and more peaceful than before he died.

The remaining four accounts in this chapter are among the most complete after-death communication experiences in our files. They are examples of full visual appearances that include hearing a voice, feeling a touch, and smelling a fragrance.

Deborah, a medical researcher in Kentucky, felt grateful when her brother, Joseph, returned after he died of cancer at age 44:

> I was a card-carrying skeptic before this experience. I'd had dreams about my brother, but this wasn't a dream.
>
> About three months after Joseph died, I was asleep in bed with my husband. I felt somebody shaking my leg to wake me up. I looked over, and there was Joseph sitting on the edge of the bed with his hand on my leg.
>
> He looked real, like any living person sitting there. He looked great! He radiated a warm, yellowish white light like an aura. He looked very calm and peaceful. He hugged me – I felt his hug – it felt wonderful and warm and loving. And I smelled his cologne too.
>
> Joseph told me, "I am all right, and you shouldn't be unhappy. Everything is all right. It is beautiful where I am." I talked to him with thoughts, and I told him I loved him. Then he just gradually faded away.
>
> I felt relief because I didn't have to worry anymore about my brother being all right.

A number of interviews we conducted began with a statement similar to Deborah's "I was a card-carrying skeptic before I had this experience...." Our research revealed that prior belief in ADCs is not a requirement for having communication with a deceased loved one, as Deborah's special encounter with her brother clearly indicates.

•   •   •

Edward, a sports trainer in Alberta, Canada, had this colorful reunion after his father died suddenly of a heart attack at age 73:

> The night after my father's funeral, I had been sound asleep, and what awakened me was a warm sensation on my right hip. After opening my eyes, I realized my father was sitting on the frame of my waterbed. He was as solid as you and me. He had his hand on my hip, kind of patting me.
>
> I saw everything – his blue eyes, his gray and white beard, and his clothing. He was wearing the orange and white Can-Am motorcycle racing jacket that I had given him. He had his suede hat on that he always wore when he was camping, a white checkered shirt, and his favorite green work pants. My dad was an outdoorsman – his scent was there, a mixture of wood smoke and his body odor.
>
> I asked, "What's up?" He said, "I just want you to know I'm fine, and I'll see you again. I'm sorry I can't stay any longer." He seemed really relaxed, happy, and at peace. Then he stood up, took a step away from the bed, and was gone in the blink of an eye.
>
> I didn't go back to sleep for the rest of the night, but I felt a lot better and knew everything was okay. I felt all the loose ends had been wrapped up, and I went on with my life.

After our loved ones die, nothing dispels the anxiety, worry, and concern we may have for them more quickly and thoroughly than a full visual ADC. Being able to see them and learn they are all right frees us to move forward in our bereavement process and focus entirely on healing our personal sense of loss.

Tanya is a computer systems supervisor in Texas. She had this spectacular experience about 1 year after her lifelong friend, Gina, died in an automobile accident at age 30:

I was on a layover at the Atlanta airport, en route to San Francisco. I was sitting in the airport lounge reading, when I smelled White Shoulders, the cologne that Gina had always worn.

I looked up, and there she was, sitting at the table with me! She looked relaxed and as pretty as she always did, the same as I had last seen her. She had on a red and charcoal gray plaid shirt that I had given her a few years back.

I said, "Gina, what are you doing here?" She smiled and said, "I came to see you." When I looked down, her hand was on top of mine for a brief moment. Her hand was solid and very warm.

I was a little choked for words, and she said, "Just relax. I want you to be happy, and I want you to stop worrying and feeling so badly about my death. I'm fine. I'm not going to visit you again, so I want you to make sure you get all your affairs in order." Then, in the blink of an eye, she was gone, and I sat there absolutely dumbfounded.

When Gina died so suddenly, her affairs were in complete disarray. Maybe that was the lesson she wanted me to learn. Consequently, ever since, I've worked very hard to make sure my finances and my life are in order.

No matter when we die, our kindest legacy to our loved ones will be to have our personal and business affairs in good order. Our thoughtfulness can be expressed by preparing a living will, granting permission for organ donation, leaving instructions for our funeral or memorial service and the cremation or burial of our body, filing a last will and testament, and securing important documents in a safe place. We should also designate a responsible person to carry out all our wishes.

The final account in this chapter is from Leonard, a 44-year-old certified mechanic in British Columbia. He was blessed by having this visitation from his mother, who died following a long illness:

> About six months after Mama died, I went to bed one night. During the night, I was awakened by a voice that said, "Look!" I looked and there was light in my room.
>
> At the foot of my bed was a white, filmy mist, like bright vapor. It seemed like a faint outline of a person, and it became clearer and more distinct as it came closer. Then I recognized the shape, the size, and the walk – I recognized Mama!
>
> She took three more steps toward me, coming completely out of the haze, and I got up and walked toward her. We met halfway and I said a very happy "Oh, Mama!"
>
> She whispered, "Hi, son." Her face had the most beautiful, healthy, loving, and serene look. Her eyes gave off warmth and love. Her cheeks were cherubic and rosy in color. She looked a lot younger, and her hair was a little bit darker.
>
> We just hugged, and I felt an all-consuming joy. It was an enveloping warmth and oneness that made my heart soar! Like how I felt when my kids were born, only greater. It was the best hug and exchange of love I have ever had.
>
> Mama was solid and firm and real. She was her same size and height and weight. She was still a big woman, very warm and homey and protective.
>
> My mother did all the familiar things. She rubbed the back of my neck as she held me. And she stroked my cheek and put her hand over the top of my hair. She always had a very neutral scent, so I didn't smell anything different.
>
> Then she pulled back just a little bit, with her arms still around me, and said, "Be happy, Leonard. Be happy." Mama always wanted happiness for all of us. Then she smiled at me and fairly quickly faded out and just left me standing there.

This was a very loving and rewarding experience, and I know it was not a dream or a figment of my imagination. I think Mama came back to let me know everything is fine and to pass this message along to whoever happens to need it.

No reunion with someone who is physically alive could be any more tangible and real than the spiritual encounter Leonard had with his deceased mother. He can savor this experience as a reminder of his mother's continuing love and devotion.

Visual ADCs are extremely powerful experiences because they confirm that our loved ones have survived the transition called death and are fully alive in another dimension. They give us a vivid and lasting mental portrait of our deceased family members and friends being completely healed and whole, regardless of their age when they died or their cause of death. And, finally, they provide very convincing evidence that we too can look forward to an exciting and joyous new life following our own physical death.

What is it like to see a "picture" of a deceased loved one with your eyes open or closed? The next chapter appraises ADC visions, experiences of seeing a relative or friend who has died and resides in another dimension of life.

CHAPTER 8

A Glimpse Beyond: ADC Visions

I firmly believe that when you die you will enter immediately
into another life. They who have gone before us are
alive in one form of life and we in another.
—*Dr. Norman Vincent Peale*

Imagine seeing an image of a deceased loved one in a "picture" that is either two-dimensional and flat or three-dimensional like a hologram. This is a general description of ADC visions, which may occur externally or internally. They are a relatively less common type of after-death communication.

External ADC visions are seen with your eyes open and may be compared to looking at a projection of a 35 mm slide or a movie suspended in the air. Internal ADC visions are seen in your mind with your eyes open or closed.

These visions are usually composed of bright, vivid colors that radiate their own inner light, similar to a stained glass window that is illuminated from behind. Having an ADC vision is like looking through an opening into another dimension and intuitively knowing you are seeing beyond this world into a spiritual one.

An ADC vision may include one-way or two-way telepathic messages. Such communication is most frequently reported during internal visions, which may be experienced while in deep relaxation, meditation, or prayer.

The first eight accounts are examples of external visions that were seen by the experiencers with their eyes open. They may have observed the image of the face, a portion of the body, or the entire body of their deceased loved one. After each external vision we'll point out how it differs from visual ADCs that were described in the two previous chapters.

Patty, age 44, is an accounting clerk in Georgia. She needed to be uplifted after her 15-year-old son, Todd, died in an automobile accident:

> About a month and a half later, I recall sitting on the sofa in the den reading a book about a mother who had lost her child. She talked about going into a deep meditation. When I got to that particular part, I just laid the book down and closed my eyes. I was thinking, "Oh, God, let me know Todd's okay."
>
> I opened my eyes, and when I did, I saw Todd's face up above me. He had a beautiful smile and a glow. He was smiling down on me like "Everything is just fine. Don't worry about me anymore. I'm all right. I am in a place where I am totally happy."
>
> His face was in a circle – it looked like a slide – it wasn't three-dimensional or anything. It was there one minute, and poof! It was gone.
>
> I felt such a relief to see Todd smiling at me. My husband was on the patio, and I remember going out and telling him about my experience, and he felt relieved also.

Patty's request was quickly fulfilled when she saw her son's face in a circle, suspended in the air "like a slide" projected onto an invisible screen. Just seeing Todd's face and his expression was all it took to more than satisfy her concern that he was all right.

Rachael is an office manager for a nursing home in Minnesota. She was filled with joy and gratitude when she had this ADC vision 4 months after her 17-year-old daughter, Dawn, was murdered:

About 11:30 one night, I was listening to the Christian radio station and reading a book. A piano version of the song "El Shaddai" came on. I looked up and saw Dawn – as though I was watching her through a window.

She was barefoot and doing a liturgical dance to this song. It was like she was floating. Her hair was blowing, and she moved her arms with the music. She had on a long, white robe that came down to her ankles, with a sash of braided rope.

Everything was very bright, very light. She was very happy, with a beautiful smile like she always had. Dawn was expressing spiritual joy through dancing. At the end of the song, she vanished. I was very grateful and began to cry.

I had prayed to the Lord to know that Dawn was okay. I'm sure I saw her in heaven, and this convinced me that she is at peace.

Rachael's prayer was answered when she saw her daughter in a vision, as though looking "through a window" into the spiritual realm. In demonstrating her complete joy and freedom by dancing, Dawn gave her mother an incredibly loving gift.

To believe your deceased child has survived death is certainly very comforting. But to truly know this because you have actually seen your son or daughter alive and well in heaven is indeed a spiritual blessing to be cherished for a lifetime.

Clara works at a center for the blind in Alberta. She had this memorable experience about 3 months after her brother, Glenn, died from an outdoor accident at age 38:

I was sitting at my desk in my office, looking at the wall. Suddenly, I had a vision. I could see my brother, Glenn, running from place to place, like a child showing off. It was like I was watching him in another dimension. I wasn't part of it, but I could see it.

His health was perfect. Nothing was wrong with his

limbs, even though they had been crippled with multiple sclerosis. Now he could run! He was radiant looking and physically fit, just brimming over with health.

Glenn was happy and smiling at me. He said, "I can do all the things now that I wanted to do before and couldn't." It was like he was saying, "Look at me, Sis! This is what I can do, and I'm really happy." Then the vision faded gradually.

How lucky I was to be seeing my brother again! I was uplifted in my spirit. It was like Glenn said "I'm happy. Now you be happy for me too."

In this account, Clara was the observer, watching and hearing her brother "in another dimension." From that moment on, she was able to remember him as a man completely healed and whole, no longer handicapped by a crippling disease.

Seeing a deceased loved one who is free from the severe limitations of his earthly body is obviously a cause for celebration. It also serves as a promise that if we are ever disabled by an accident or illness, we too will be fully restored to wholeness after we die.

Allen is a massage therapist in Washington. He saw this vivid external vision of his mother, who died of lung cancer at age 53, and his paternal grandfather, who had died of a heart attack at age 76:

About 3:00 in the morning the hospital called to say my mom had passed away. I walked over to our living room window and looked toward the mountains. At that point, a hole opened up, and I saw into another dimension.

I saw my mother with my grandfather, who had passed away some ten years before. It was like I was on one side of the glass and they were on the other. They were very solid and very real.

My grandfather looked young and healthy, rejuvenated and full of strength. He just smiled and stepped aside. My mom was wearing her white temple dress that she was married in. She was vibrant, healthy, and full of life. She told me she was fine and didn't hurt anymore – that she felt wonderful. I told her that I loved her.

I started to cry and turned my head. And when I looked back, they were gone. I really kicked myself for turning away because when I did, the window to that dimension closed.

Allen was able to see and hear his mother within minutes of her death when "a hole opened up" into another dimension. It was also very reassuring for him to realize that his grandfather was immediately available to assist her when she died.

Edie is a chaplain and bereavement facilitator for a hospice in the Southeast. She gained a new understanding after her 14-year-old stepson, Michael, was killed on his bicycle by a hit-and-run driver:

We arrived for the viewing at the funeral home and stood in front of Michael's casket. I quietly said a prayer. All of a sudden, with my eyes wide open, I saw what was like a filmstrip in front of me, just slightly above my eye level.

I saw a pretty green rolling field with flowers, birds, and butterflies. It was very brightly lit, and the colors were clear and vivid. I saw Michael skipping and running along! He stopped and looked at me and had a beautiful smile.

His eyes were sparkling, and his face had the happiest grin. He was healthy, he was joyful, and he was not in pain. He was surrounded by love and didn't have any anger or bitterness.

Michael said, "I'm okay. Don't worry about me." And with his body language he said, "Don't feel sad about this. That's not me you're looking at in the casket. I am here!" I blinked, and he was still standing there. And then the vision just faded away.

When I looked at his body in the casket again, I realized it was just the empty temple – the place where he had lived for awhile – and he was no longer there.

As I turned away, I felt a lightness in my step, like a burden had been lifted off my shoulders. I knew Michael was fine – there was absolutely no question about it.

Initially, this experience cut short some of my bereavement. My pain left but not my grief, not the missing of my stepson as a person.

Seeing Michael in a "filmstrip" assured Edie her stepson had survived physical death. And as a hospice chaplain she was given a priceless spiritual gift to share with her dying patients.

What greater dramatic contrast can there be than to observe our deceased loved one during an ADC while at the same time viewing his empty, lifeless body in a casket? A number of other accounts in our files contain similar experiences that occurred during a funeral, memorial, or burial service.

Edie made a very important distinction when she stated, "My pain left but not my grief, not the missing of my stepson as a person." Having one or more ADC experiences may resolve our worry and concern about the well-being of our deceased loved one, but we will still miss his presence in our life and have an ongoing need to grieve the void no one else can ever fill.

Trish, age 55, is an executive recruiter for a corporation in Florida. She had this cheerful vision shortly after her close friend, Ginny, died:

I had a friend who was living in the Virgin Islands. The last time I saw Ginny, she was suffering from cancer. She was so very, very ill, so drawn and distraught looking.

I received a telegram from her husband saying she had died. I thought, "Oh, how awful!" I felt so depressed about her death.

Later, when I was in my car driving home from work, I was having a hard time stopping the tears from running down my face. All of a sudden, I saw this wonderful picture of Ginny out in front of me! She was smiling from ear to ear, and her face was very animated. Her eyes were shining, her skin was glowing, and her teeth were sparkling.

I felt she'd come to say "Don't cry. Look at me! I'm so happy!" Ginny made me feel everything was fine. The feeling of peace I got was wonderful.

When Trish saw a "wonderful picture" of Ginny suspended in front of her, she knew at once that she no longer needed to feel sorry for her friend. Most people feel terrible after a loved one dies and may think, "Poor soul, her life is over." If she had a long, painful illness, they may console themselves by saying, "At least she isn't hurting anymore." This ADC implies not only has Ginny's suffering ended, but she has also entered a happier, freer, more wondrous new life.

Katie is a homemaker in the Southeast. She became a widow when her 30-year-old husband, Dick, was murdered by an intruder who broke into their home:

The day after Dick's funeral, the police took me back to the station for questioning. They left me alone in a room for about fifteen minutes. I was sitting there wondering where he was and saying, "Please, Dick, let me know. Just do something to let me know that you're okay."

While looking out the window, just staring off into space and trying to piece everything together, I suddenly saw this image. It was about the size of a picture, maybe 12 inches by 12 inches. I couldn't believe what I was seeing – I saw my husband!

He was wearing exactly what he had been buried in. There were three people on one side of him and two people on the other side, all facing me. I could tell that two were male and two were female, and the fifth was indistinct.

Dick's arms were outstretched, embracing these people. The look on his face and the feeling that I got was "Katie, look, I'm whole again! I'm happy! I'm going to be fine, and you're going to be fine." I knew what he was saying, even though he didn't speak.

He was so incredibly happy, with the happiest grin I had ever seen on him. He was at his best. His emotions were so powerful that I could feel the feelings radiating from him. Then the image faded away.

Later that night, Dick's parents and I were sitting around the table talking. For some reason, we got on the topic of my experience. All of a sudden, like a light bulb, the image flashed back. I knew immediately those four people with Dick were his grandparents, and I described them to his parents. I still don't know who the fifth person was.

Now I'm no longer afraid to die. I know when my time comes, Dick will be there for me.

Though Katie was comforted when she saw the "image" of her husband, nothing can fully erase the traumatic memory of a loved one's violent death. This is especially true for the survivors of murder, who are forced to give up their privacy and endure many painful years of involvement with the judicial system and the media.

Gay is a 36-year-old college student in Louisiana. She had this magnificent vision of her 5-month-old nephew, Luke, who died of cystic fibrosis:

My sister was very distraught when her baby died. She had gone through such a rough time watching Luke suffer and blaming herself. She kept repeating, "I wonder if he's upset about everything he went through? I wonder if he knew that I was always there with him?"

Later, as I was putting on my makeup before going to the funeral home, I heard a little voice calling me, "Aunt Gay! Aunt Gay!" My eyes were wide open as I turned and saw a vision right in front of me of Luke in a heavenly environment.

He was sitting on a woman's lap. I couldn't see her face, but in my heart I felt it was Mary, the Blessed Mother. She was wearing a long, white robe that came down to Her feet, and Her small, feminine hand was around his bottom to hold him steady.

Luke was dressed in a little blue baby's suit, with a collar and buttons down the front. His hair was combed, everything was in place, and he looked perfectly healthy. His face was radiant, and he was smiling.

He was just a baby, but he spoke with an intelligence that amazed me. He said, "I want you to tell my mother that I knew she was there. I knew she did the best that she could for me. Tell her I'm fine and that I love her."

Then he said, "You have to tell my mother today because it will be the only way she can get through the funeral tomorrow. She will believe you!" He made me promise, and I said I would.

After this vision was over, I doubted myself. I told my best friend and she said, "I believe that it happened! You have to tell your sister because you promised Luke you would."

So I went to the funeral home and told my sister of my experience with Luke and Mary. And she believed me right away!

It was exactly what she needed to hear! She now knew that Luke was happy and wasn't sick anymore. She knew her baby was in heaven, and she had a little bit of peace.

This beautiful ADC vision allowed Gay to see her nephew in a "heavenly environment." And, fortunately, she had the courage to deliver Luke's urgent message promptly, which brought solace to his mother just before she had to face the stark reality of his funeral.

It may seem surprising that a 5-month-old baby could speak

as Luke did and give such an elaborate message to his aunt. While this can't be explained in earthly terms, Gay's is one of several ADCs in our files in which deceased infants or young children demonstrated awareness and abilities far beyond their chronological age.

This account is also the first of several experiences in the book that involve a well-known religious figure such as Mary. The other reports include Jesus or an angel.

The remaining accounts in this chapter are examples of internal ADC visions that appeared suddenly inside the experiencers' mind and were perceived with their eyes open or closed. Perhaps these "pictures" or "movies" are transmitted to us from our deceased loved ones by telepathy or a similar process that is still unknown.

In each of the next four accounts the experiencers had their eyes open.

Ross, a chiropractor in Virginia, had this internal vision of his mother-in-law about 6 months after she died of cancer at age 58:

> I was in my mother-in-law's house, in her kitchen, where she spent a lot of her time. My eyes were open when a very clear and unequivocal picture of her came into my mind. It was accompanied by an absolute sense of delight.
>
> She was a very dignified woman when she was alive. Now she was dressed like a cheerleader, in a plaid skirt with a white blouse, looking about thirty years younger than when she died.
>
> She had a great beaming smile, with that kind of buoyancy that people have when they are really excited and really happy about something.
>
> My mother-in-law was quite literally jumping up and down, waving and smiling. She was nodding her head, as if to reassure me that all was quite well and that she was being taken care of.

After seeing his mother-in-law in an internal "picture," Ross was able to report she looked thirty years younger than when she died. As you've probably noticed, many deceased loved ones appear years younger during an ADC than they were at the time of their death. If our earthly body ever becomes infirm or diseased, imagine the joy we'll feel after dying when we discover we have a perfect non-physical body that reflects our true spiritual identity.

Toni is employed by an economic development association in Florida. Her father died of heart disease at age 70:

> Driving home from my mother's house, my father came before me in a vision three weeks after he passed on. It was something I was seeing inside my head.
>
> At first he appeared the same age as when he died. Then he brightened up considerably and had a big grin on his face. As he began smiling, he took on a very youthful appearance. He was very healthy and very happy, glowing with peace. His whole communication seemed to be "I'm all right. This is the way you should remember me."
>
> Then I saw all my relatives that had passed over come around him, as though they were meeting him. They looked as they did when they were still alive. They were very healthy, very happy, and very loving.
>
> This experience gave me peace and made it easier to accept my father's death.

ADCs are often remarkably similar. Compare this account of Toni's inner vision of her father with the next one of Gary's internal vision of his daughter.

Gary is a purchasing assistant for a university in Washington. He had this heartening experience with his 3-month-old daughter, Lauren, who died of sudden infant death syndrome (SIDS) and with his father, who had died of a heart attack in his early 40's:

This internal vision in my mind occurred as I was driving about five days after Lauren's death. My eyes were open, and I was focused on the road.

All of a sudden, I had this image of my daughter sitting on my father's knee! He had one of his arms wrapped around her waist. Lauren was wearing a pink pinafore dress and was happy and smiling.

My grandmother was standing next to them, and my uncle was behind my father. In the background were some of my other relatives who had passed on. It was a very calm place, and everybody was happy.

I could tell from my father's expression that he was really proud of Lauren. The vision ended with my dad saying, "She's okay." I smiled, and it gradually faded out.

I felt totally relieved, as if a burden had been lifted from me. Lauren was happy and was going to be all right. I knew she was with my family, and I really felt at peace.

As Gary's and other ADCs in this book indicate, our deceased children are promptly met and lovingly cared for by a multitude of family members who welcome them with open arms and open hearts. With such nurturing and wise guidance, we can expect our children will continue to grow emotionally, mentally, and spiritually until we are united with them again.

Elaine, a homemaker in rural Canada, had this exquisite ADC vision about 10 days after her two daughters, Noelle, age 17, and Christie, age 10, were killed in a farm accident:

My husband and I were sitting on the couch in the living room opening sympathy cards. I had my eyes open, when all of a sudden, I saw the girls inside my head. It seemed like I was looking at a picture on a TV screen in color. It was very realistic but not completely three-dimensional.

Noelle and Christie were standing there, hand-in-hand, sort of looking up. They were bathed in a very bright, clear white light. The light was indescribable! It

was brighter than anything I've ever seen, and it should
have hurt my eyes, but it didn't.

The girls were surrounded by the light and looked very
clear, but everything else around them was hazy. The
look on their faces was rapturous. They were so happy
and so peaceful!

I heaved a sigh of relief that Noelle and Christie were
okay. What had been bothering me was "Were they all
right? Were they missing Mom and Dad? Were they
homesick?" And that kind of thing.

Then I knew I didn't have to worry about them anymore. All I had to do was deal with my own grief and get
my life back on track.

Before, I was pretty skeptical. I had always been
doubtful when I heard a story like this. But this experience renewed my faith. God knew what I had been feeling, and it was His way of comforting me and letting me
get on with the rest of my grieving process.

What greater comfort can a newly bereaved mother receive
than to know her two deceased children are together in the
light! This is surely the same brilliant spiritual light that so
many children and adults have seen while having a near-death
experience.

The remaining accounts in this chapter are examples of internal ADC visions that the experiencers saw with their eyes
closed.

Wendy, a nurse in Massachusetts, received this inner vision
after her 19-year-old son, Dean, died in a motorcycle accident:

Dean had been a sophomore at Harvard when he was
killed. This was three years later, and it would have been
his graduation day.

I went out of my office to have a cigarette. I was sitting in a chair in a room by myself and closed my eyes.
All of a sudden, I saw a picture of my son with a man who
appeared to be Jesus. It was an internal vision, and the

picture was so clear it was almost as if they were in front of me.

Dean had on a black graduation cap and gown, and Jesus was wearing a long white robe and had long hair and a beard. They were both smiling, and Jesus seemed pleased. Dean was very happy, and I figured he was in heaven.

The vision lasted no more than a minute, just that brief time to let me know that everything was all right. Now I know where my son is, and I am very happy for him.

Evidently, Wendy spontaneously entered a state of meditation that enabled her to see Jesus with her son. The next two ADCs also occurred during meditation.

Faith is a psychologist who works with terminally ill children in Florida. She was given an important assignment about 2 weeks after her 13-year-old patient, Suzie, died of leukemia:

I was in a meditation circle and all of a sudden, Suzie appeared to me in a vision. She said, "Call my mother and tell her not to worry about my quilt." She was very happy, very cheerful, and there was a lot of light around her face and head.

I knew if I called, I'd get caught up in a long conversation. Secondly, what was this about a quilt? So again, the child appeared to me and said, "Call my mother about the quilt."

The next day, I phoned Suzie's mother. She told me, "I'm so glad you called because yesterday was the worst day I've had since Suzie died. I was so upset that I got Suzie's quilt and went outside. I lay down under the tree and just cried and cried."

I said, "Wait, I need to tell you something! Yesterday, at a prayer group, Suzie appeared to me and asked me to tell you, 'It's okay about my quilt.' Does that mean anything to you?"

Suzie's mother burst out crying and said, "You won't

believe it, but when I was lying under the tree crying, I was upset because Suzie had had this quilt ever since she was a baby. She took it with her everywhere, every place, and was never separated from it.

"When we buried her, I couldn't bear to part with her quilt. I felt so guilty about keeping it. You don't know how good it makes me feel to hear this. I'm so glad you called!"

Fearful of appearing foolish or being rejected, we may hesitate to deliver an ADC message, especially if it has little or no meaning for us. But, as Faith's account clearly illustrates, such a message may hold great personal significance for its intended recipient.

The final account is by Claire, a psychologist in New Jersey. She had a meditative ADC after her father died of heart failure at 87:

After my father died, I felt a tremendous sense of loss. Even though I had no religious affiliation, I felt the need to pray for him. I went to a Presbyterian church and found the service very moving, and I was invited to join their Christian prayer and meditation group.

I started meditating purely for the purpose of finding faith for myself. But the first time I attempted it, I fell asleep. Nothing happened the second time. The third time, I had this experience.

I was sitting in our living room, just relaxing, and my husband was playing the piano, Pachelbel's "Canon in D." The music had a soothing, repetitive quality that seemed to facilitate the meditative state. My eyes were closed, and I was holding my hands with the palms up, symbolic of allowing something from God to come through.

All at once, I saw a vivid image of my father, but only from the waist up. He was in the prime of his life, which would have been in his fifties. He had a solid appearance and his face was relaxed–he looked restored and healthy.

I had a very intense feeling of connection – a profound feeling of my father's presence. The experience was very simple, and when I opened my eyes, it was over.

It had an intensity unlike any experience I've ever had. I felt as though I'd been in communication with my father and had made a connection to something beyond this world.

When we meditate with our eyes closed, we may see a vivid picture or movie on our inner visual screen. And sometimes it may be an image of a deceased loved one who might use this opportunity to communicate with us, just as Claire's father did.

Whether they are seen externally or internally, with our eyes open or closed, all ADC visions are basically alike and convey similar information. These vivid images invariably reveal that our deceased loved ones are filled with peace and joy in their new life.

Can you recall that warm, relaxed feeling you have when you are falling asleep or waking up? The next chapter presents reports of people who had an ADC experience in this twilight state.

CHAPTER 9

Encounters at Alpha: Twilight ADCs

Just as a little bird cracks open the shell and flies out, we
fly out of this shell, the shell of the body. We call that death,
but strictly speaking, death is nothing but a change of form.
—*Swami Satchidananda*

A number of ADCs occur just as people are falling asleep or
as they are waking up. This half-awake, half-asleep level of
awareness is usually referred to as the twilight state or the alpha state. We call these experiences twilight ADCs, which are
a fairly common type of after-death communication.

The alpha state is a level of consciousness that can be attained by various relaxation techniques, meditation exercises,
hypnosis, and deep prayer. You may enter this state of awareness spontaneously whenever you are daydreaming or feeling
creative. According to our research, you can be contacted by a
deceased loved one more easily if you are in a relaxed, open,
and receptive frame of mind.

Any combination of the following types of ADCs may occur
during the alpha state: sensing a presence, hearing a voice, feeling a touch, smelling a fragrance, partial or full appearances,
and visions. The purpose of this chapter and the next one,
which is devoted entirely to sleep-state experiences, is to
demonstrate that the ADCs people report are essentially the
same whether they are wide awake, in the twilight state, or
sound asleep.

The accounts in this chapter are presented in a progressive

sequence, ranging from sensing the presence of deceased family members or friends to seeing them in ADC visions.

Gene, age 27, works for a cemetery in Oklahoma. He received a much-needed message from his brother, Roger, who died in an Army helicopter crash in Korea at age 24:

> We were expecting Roger's phone call on Christmas Eve, but it never came. Later that night, an Army officer arrived at our house. He read from a telegram and told Mama that the Army regretted to inform her that her son had been killed while serving his country. When we got the news, we just couldn't believe it!
>
> During the afternoon on Christmas Day, I was tired and lay down. You know how you are when you're in between awake and asleep and still hear everything that's going on, but you're not really aware of it?
>
> Roger came to me. I could feel his presence there, but I couldn't see him. I felt he said, "Everything is all right. Everything is okay. Tell Mama that I'm all right and not to worry about me. Tell her that I love her." He was telling me to comfort Mama as much as I could and make sure she handled it okay.
>
> It lasted maybe three minutes. As soon as I woke up completely, I went in and told Mama, and it made us both feel better.
>
> Since Roger came, it's proven to me there must be life after death. And now I believe he's in heaven.

Gene provides a good description of what it feels like to be in the twilight state while falling asleep. At this level we are aware of, but can be detached from, our immediate surroundings.

Cora is a 31-year-old farmer and midwife in Tennessee. Her father returned to her soon after he died of a heart attack:

> I received a phone call from my mother telling me my dad had died. The whole next day I was terribly upset

and crying. In the afternoon, I lay down for a nap and fell asleep rather quickly. The next thing I remember, I awoke into a semi-consciousness.

I heard myself saying, "Hi, Dad! How are you? Are you okay? Do you like it where you are? Are you happy?" Then I heard my father say telepathically, "Yes, I'm fine. Everything's going to be okay. Don't worry. Yes, it's great here!"

A distinct feeling of peace seemed to pervade my being and the entire room. This was such a change from what I had been feeling. I suddenly felt like everything in the universe was in its proper place.

I knew I would be able to handle the whole situation – going home, Mom, and dealing with Dad's funeral. I felt so thankful to God and to my dad for this experience.

Cora passed through the twilight state as she was waking up. The peace of mind she received from this ADC gave her the strength and self-confidence she needed to face her father's funeral and the other emotionally difficult days ahead.

Jack, a retired New York City police officer, lives in Florida. His beloved wife of 49 years, Kitty, died of cancer at age 68:

I'm a realist. I've been a very realistic person all my life. I've never really gone for any of these strange experiences.

But about a month after my wife died, I was starting to fall asleep one night. I was half asleep and half awake. I was lying on the right side of our queen-size bed and had my left arm extended across what Kitty always called her "hugging pillow."

All of a sudden, I could swear that Kitty squeezed my left hand tenderly. I knew it was her! I actually felt the pressure of her soft, warm hand.

It felt like the whole room was filled with an aura of peace and love. It was like she was trying to reassure me not to worry, that everything was okay. I got the feeling

Kitty was trying to tell me, "Don't hurry. I've got a spot picked out for you, and I'll be up here waiting." And I've felt a lot better since that experience.

Both Cora and Jack reported their entire room was permeated with an all-encompassing sense of peace during their ADC. This implies our deceased loved ones radiate a spiritual energy that may remain even after their visit is over.

Lisa, who manages a recreation center in the Northwest, had this affectionate encounter 2 months after her partner, Julie, died of cancer at age 40:

I had taken my cat to be put to sleep because of feline leukemia. When I came home, I was pretty emotionally drained and exhausted. So I lay down about 4:00 in the afternoon.

Suddenly, I could smell the Shalimar perfume Julie always wore. Then I felt the bed depress as she sat down by my legs, and I felt her lean over and kiss me on the cheek. It was a real warm, loving feeling.

I was trying so hard to open my eyes to see her and touch her, but I couldn't. Then I heard her voice, and I just relaxed. Julie said, "Sweetheart, it's all going to be fine. I'm okay, and you're going to be okay." She was very consoling.

The feeling lasted several minutes, and then I felt her weight lift from the bed, and her scent went away. As the warm feeling was dissolving, I could open my eyes, and I became fully awake.

I felt very blessed. I thanked Julie and I thanked God that she got to come back. This reemphasized the love I knew we had.

Julie clearly timed her visit to console Lisa on a day she really needed comfort. Grieving the loss of the companionship of a dearly loved pet can be a very lonely process because bereaved pet owners seldom receive the emotional support they deserve.

Helga is a former secretary in Florida. She had a significant meeting with her mother, who died from a stroke at age 78:

> It was very early in the morning, three weeks after my mother's passing. I was in that state of trying to wake up – sort of half asleep and half awake. I saw my mother by my bedside, between the wall and the bed, from her waist up. She was very solid and about two or three feet away.
>
> I could see her very clearly. She looked in her fifties, when she used to wear her hair in little brown curls. She was wearing a dress that she liked very much, a brown and lilac floral print.
>
> Mother looked very concerned because she was worried about me. She said in German, "Helga, don't grieve for me anymore. I am doing just fine. I am released from everything." She spoke with her actual voice. She loved me so much that she wanted to reassure me she was all right.
>
> With that, I was up and fully awake, looking for her, but she wasn't there anymore. I was stunned by this experience. It was beautiful, but I really didn't know what to make of it at the time.

An account like Helga's may cause you to wonder about those who have been bereaved but never had an ADC experience. Are they less worthy? Have they been abandoned? Should they assume their deceased loved ones don't care about their loss and suffering? This issue will be covered fully in the final chapter of the book.

Bruce is a 43-year-old consultant to a defense contractor in Florida. He arrived at a new awareness of life shortly after his father died of heart disease:

> This was within a week after Dad died. I was half awake, half asleep when I perceived my father was at the foot of my bed. I wasn't frightened, but it invoked my cu-

riosity. He looked much younger and was very healthy, like he was about forty.

Dad was floating about three feet off the ground, wearing what looked like a bright, white jumpsuit. He wasn't totally solid, but he wasn't transparent either – I couldn't see through him. He was kind of glowing, almost radiant. He was very tranquil and purposeful.

As I became aware of him, I went from this twilight period to being fully awake. I watched him for several seconds. I clearly heard Dad say in his voice, "Don't worry about me. Everything is going to be all right." Then he began to dematerialize and faded away. That was it.

Personally, I don't care if I convince anybody else because I know it happened. I know what I saw – my father was there – there's absolutely no doubt in my mind!

After that, I began to feel that life is a continuum, and this life is but one step. Death is just going through a doorway.

As Bruce progressed from a twilight state to being fully awake, he became certain that his encounter with his father was real. His insight that "life is a continuum" is another way to express the concept of immortality. ADCs suggest that life extends beyond the doorway we call death. As we pass through this change and enter the next stage of life, we evidently retain our identity, personality, and memory. That is, we seem to bring everything with us except our physical body and our material possessions.

Sandra is a homemaker in Ohio. She was only 21 years old when she was confronted by her father, who had died of a heart attack at age 56:

Seven or eight months after my father died, I was still grieving very hard and really wasn't getting on with my life. I had a hard time accepting his loss and was drowning in my sorrow.

This experience felt like a dream, but it was more like

an alpha state. I felt my father's presence and heard him say, "I want you to knock this off! I love you and I love your mother. But it's time for you to get on with your life. I'm happy now where I am. Please stop wishing me back. I've got other things to do. You've got to let me go!"

After that, I was very alert, very awake. I saw my father standing in the corner of my room. I could see him fairly clearly, from his head down to his waist. He had a look of contentment, like he wanted to show me that he was okay. I felt love from him, and then he was gone.

This changed me almost instantly. I felt like a ten-ton weight lifted off of me. I felt such peace and acceptance about my father's death that I could then go on with my life and not continue in a downward spiral.

Sometimes our deceased loved ones exercise tough love to get our full attention, just as it took this strong reprimand from Sandra's father to move her beyond despondency. Her immediate shift in perception allowed her to finally accept his death and end her "downward spiral," which probably freed her father to move on with his life too.

Throughout our research, we found that many ADC accounts contain passionate pleas from deceased loved ones to "let me go." Apparently, our emotions of prolonged sadness and heavy grief can hold them back, almost magnetically, from progressing in their new life. Perhaps they also have a spiritual obligation to help us with our pain before they are able to continue forward.

Here's an analogy that may make this clearer. Suppose you're a college student who has won a full scholarship and gone abroad to attend a prestigious university. How would you feel if every day you received tearful phone calls and letters from your family and friends saying how much they miss you and can't live without you, wishing you would come home as soon as possible?

Imagine our freedom if we knew, beyond doubt, our deceased loved ones are enjoying a happier new life. It would be much easier to release them, to let them go, certain we will all be reunited again.

Marge is a real estate agent in Florida. She had this surprising visit from her husband's first wife, Emily, who was 38 years old when she died of cancer and left her two young children behind:

> I never was introduced to Emily – I only knew her through photographs. This occurred about three months after Stephen and I married. It was in the wee hours of the morning when I was half asleep and half awake.
>
> There was Emily standing beside our bed! She looked just like her photographs. She was in a white flowing gown and was so calm and peaceful and loving. I sat halfway up and was kind of groggy.
>
> It was like Emily was standing there in real life. She was glowing! There was a white, bright aura – a big circle of light – surrounding her. She was beautiful, absolutely beautiful!
>
> She said, "It's okay. Don't be alarmed. You're going to be good for the children and your marriage will be fine. You're going to really help my kids." And then she left.
>
> I was always nervous and tense about the situation until that night. After my experience with Emily, I was more at ease, knowing she approved of me to help raise her children.

It's likely Emily achieved exceptional clarity after dying, which enabled her to fully accept Marge and express her loving approval. If only all mothers and fathers could be as generous to the stepparents who care for their children.

Louise, age 40, is a receptionist in North Carolina. She was asked to perform a favor by Ryan, a family friend, just before his funeral. Ryan was in his 20's when he drowned:

I went to bed and Ryan appeared to me. I was sort of in between awake and asleep, but my eyes were open. I saw him standing at the foot of my bed! He looked very healthy and very strong. He was very, very calm and had a real peaceful look on his face.

He said, "Louise, I want you to do something for me. I want you to tell my mother to have an altar call at my funeral. I've got lost loved ones that I want to be saved." When I sat up in bed, Ryan disappeared.

An altar call is when they play soft music, and the preacher asks if there is anyone who has not been saved and given their heart to the Lord. He then asks them to please come to the altar and pray and turn their life over to God.

I was real hesitant to tell Ryan's mother because I knew his family didn't attend church regularly. So I didn't know how she would handle it.

But the next morning I told her what had happened. She said she believed her son came to me, and if that's what he wanted, then that's what she would do.

So there was an altar call at Ryan's funeral, and his brother, Eddie, was saved. This made quite a change in Eddie's life because he had been kind of wild – and now he's a policeman!

Fortunately, Louise had sufficient courage to take the risk of passing along Ryan's message. In turn, his mother was open enough to accept his request and act upon it. Perhaps Ryan knew in advance that having an altar call at his funeral would provide a spiritual opportunity for his brother to redirect his life.

Maria works for the federal government and lives in Maryland. She was in the alpha state when she had this poignant experience with her mother-in-law, Angelina, who died at age 80:

My mother-in-law lived in our home for about five years before she died. She was a double amputee and blind due to diabetes. We were very close, like mother and daughter.

Two days after Angelina died, my grandson, Tony, who was two years old, was lying next to me on my bed, and I was waiting for him to go to sleep. I don't know if I was in a half dream state or half awake.

All of a sudden, I looked up, and Angelina was standing next to the bed! In my mind, I said, "Oh, my God! She's got her legs back!" It just amazed me that she was standing. She didn't look old anymore — she looked twenty years younger. Her skin was perfectly smooth, like when I married her son. She had a beautiful, brilliant white dress on.

But Angelina wasn't looking at me, she was looking at Tony who was lying horizontally across the bed. He had been the joy of her life. She said, "My dearest darling," with so much love in her voice. Her face radiated a brilliant light. She had this smile, and her eyes just glowed with love.

I leaned up and said, "Oh, Angelina! You're back! You're back!" Then she turned and looked at me and said, "No, darling. I have just come to say good-bye." With that, she looked back at Tony and said, "My dearest darling, I love you so much."

She leaned her face down, almost touching my face, and said, "I love you too, Maria. Good-bye." Then she disappeared quickly, and I became totally awake.

I thought to myself, "Oh, it was a dream." But when I looked at Tony, he was lying exactly in the same position I had seen him in. So I knew at that moment it was not a dream — it was a true visitation by Angelina!

It's exciting to learn that Angelina, who had been blind, was at last able to see her precious great-grandson. Perhaps someday Maria will tell Tony about the time his great-grandmother made a very special visit to say good-bye to him after she had died.

Faye is a court reporter in the Southeast. She was overcome with grief after her 16-year-old son, Chris, died from an undetected heart ailment:

> Chris's father took his own life right after Chris died, which was a double tragedy for all of us. I was beyond consoling.
>
> My experience occurred shortly after his father's death. It was right before morning, and I was somewhere between awake and asleep. I guess you would call it twilight sleep.
>
> Chris sat on my bed! He was very solid and very real. I could feel his presence and smell him. I could look into his eyes and see his smile. I could even see the little beauty mark under his eye and the little cleft in his chin.
>
> He looked peaceful, golden, and beautiful! He appeared his exact age and in very good health. He said, "Mom, I wanted to come and tell you that I'm fine. I love you. Don't worry about me." He also said his dad was all right but was going to have to work through his problems.
>
> I just lay there for half an hour, basking in the simple bliss that you sometimes have when you're a child. All I could think was "This is a gift! Chris really came!" And I was elated.

Faye's account is unusual because it's one of only a few in our files in which the experiencer gained information about someone else who had died. The news she received regarding Chris's father implies that ending our life before it's our natural time to die may carry consequences that we will have to resolve following our death. The issue of suicide is explored more fully in later chapters.

Claude, a 60-year-old dentist in Washington, had a vision of his mother's two deceased sisters, his Aunt Pearl and Aunt Stella:

I was reclining one night in bed, not quite awake and yet not quite asleep. I had what most people would describe as a vision. I saw the faces of my Aunt Pearl and Aunt Stella.

They appeared to be very happy. They were well groomed and their hair was neatly combed. They had pleasant facial expressions – smiles, if you will. They indicated to me a state of well-being, a state of happiness and general goodness.

If I saw two people like that on the street, I would think, "By golly, they're living a pretty pleasant life. Things are well with them. They're happy and they must be doing something good, something worthwhile."

Early the next morning, I'd say about 6:00, my father, who lived in another state, telephoned me. He said my mother had died the night before. It was really shocking! I knew she wasn't feeling too well, but I didn't think she was close to death.

It was then that I understood the purpose of my two aunts appearing to me. This vision helped me to recognize that my mother was in their good hands.

Claude's aunts chose to appear to him before he learned of his mother's death, but he didn't understand the significance of their visit until his father phoned him. This experience spared him any unnecessary worry about his mother's well-being when he realized she was in the safe company of her two sisters, who would lovingly care for her.

The final account is from Mitch, an automobile mechanic in Florida. He had this life-altering ADC shortly after his 23-year-old daughter, Becky, died in an automobile accident:

I wasn't living for the Lord at the time my daughter was killed. My resistance to God was tremendous. Becky's death was such a shock that I was ready to just give up and die. My spirit was completely broken.

That night, my nephew helped me to bed, and I finally drifted off to sleep. About 2:00 I awoke into semi-consciousness and had a vision.

I saw Becky and two other young girls who had been killed in similar automobile wrecks. She knew these girls growing up in school. They were all sitting on a bench, and the background was a very bright light.

I could see a man standing there – he looked just like Jesus! He was wearing a purple robe and had His arms folded. He was looking at the three girls and was smiling like He was well pleased with them.

Becky looked at me and smiled, saying, "Dad, I'm okay. Just make sure you come to see me." She was very, very happy. She looked in very good health, exactly like she was before she was killed.

After the vision, I was fully awake. I woke my wife up and told her, "We don't have to worry about Becky anymore! I've seen her! She is with God and she is in heaven. We don't have to cry because she's okay."

Even though I was in sorrow, I was able to go through the funeral and not dread it. I had such peace in my heart and in my soul. I knew beyond a shadow of a doubt I would see Becky again one day.

I think God said, "I gave you a sign that your daughter is all right, and now you will go to work for Me." God transformed me so fast it was amazing!

Immediately, I had a completely different outlook on my life, and I knew that I was a changed person. It was just like a regeneration. I started living for the Lord and going to church and working with teenagers as best I could. And I'm still doing it today, eight years later.

This story illustrates the potential transformational power of an after-death communication experience. Despite being profoundly bereaved, Mitch underwent a spiritual rebirth and discovered a new direction and purpose for his life. As other accounts in this book demonstrate, many people achieve dramatic personal growth as a result of having an ADC.

The twilight experiences in this chapter are virtually the same as the ones people reported having when they were wide awake. The only difference is that our deceased relatives and friends can contact us more easily when we are in a relaxed, open, and receptive state of consciousness.

Is it possible to have ADC experiences while you are sleeping? The next chapter is devoted to accounts of sleep-state ADCs, and it will answer this and many other questions.

CHAPTER 10

More Than a Dream:
Sleep-State ADCs

Six weeks after his death my father appeared to me
in a dream.... It was an unforgettable experience, and
it forced me for the first time to think about life after death.
—*Carl G. Jung*

Many people reported they had been contacted by a deceased loved one while they were sound asleep. Because they didn't have any other name for their experience, they usually called it a "dream." However, most quickly added, "But it just wasn't like an ordinary dream." We call these experiences sleep-state ADCs, and they are a very common type of after-death communication.

There are many significant differences between an ordinary dream and a sleep-state ADC. A dream is generally fragmented, jumbled, filled with symbolism, and incomplete in various ways. Though some are very intense emotionally, they typically have a quality of unreality about them and are often soon forgotten.

In contrast, sleep-state ADCs feel like actual face-to-face visits with deceased loved ones. They are much more orderly, colorful, vivid, and memorable than most dreams. In fact, some may be ADC visions that occur during sleep.

As you read these accounts of sleep-state ADCs, notice they are basically very similar to ADCs that take place while people are wide awake or in the twilight state.

Of course, many sleep-state experiences that include a

deceased family member or friend are not ADCs. Most are just regular dreams based upon memories and other emotional material from the subconscious mind. For the bereaved, these dreams are a normal and beneficial part of their grief process. Those who have dreamed about their deceased loved ones and also had sleep-state ADCs with them say they can easily distinguish between these two different kinds of experiences.

A loved one who has died can contact you more easily if you are very relaxed, open, and receptive, such as when you are in the alpha state or asleep. This is the time you are most likely to set aside the distractions of the material world and attune your heart and mind to the spiritual dimension.

The first three accounts are examples of sleep-state ADCs in which a deceased loved one "broke into" an ordinary dream.

Robin is the director of a child care center in Florida. She had this timely visit from her grandfather several years after he died of a heart attack in his 70's:

> I was in my first year at college, sleeping in my dorm room. I was dreaming about something when Grandpa broke into my dream! He was right there, and I could smell his cologne and tobacco and feel his warmth.
>
> He seemed concerned and protective. He said, "Lock the windows! You're supposed to remember to take care of yourself! Lock the windows!" It was a definite warning.
>
> I woke up startled and sat up and looked around. My room had one set of windows that looked out onto a courtyard and another set over by the fire escape. So I got up and locked all the windows.
>
> About half an hour later, there was a scream from the girl in the room down the hall. A man had come up the fire escape and apparently had tried my windows, and then he had gone on to hers. Later he was caught!
>
> Grandpa appeared when support was obviously needed. He proved that he would be with me forever.

When a deceased loved one breaks into a dream, it's like those times we are watching a television show and a voice suddenly says, "We interrupt this program to bring you a special announcement!" Robin's grandfather indicated he was watching over her by voicing his urgent message "Lock the windows!" when she really needed protection.

Jay is a 45-year-old attorney in Montana. He had this lively encounter with his friend and client, Neil, who had died suddenly at age 70:

I was probating Neil's estate, which was valued at well over a million dollars. He wrote his will himself the day before he died. The will was long and contained numerous mistakes. It was quite literally a legal nightmare, the kind of mess that could end up in the courts for years.

I had gone to sleep and was dreaming something pleasant when Neil barged into my dream with the same hurried attitude he had when he was alive. He looked like he did in life – active, joyful, and bouncy.

I looked at him and said, "Wait a minute, you're dead! But here you are alive!" I was pondering how Neil could be alive and walk into my dream.

He conveyed to me, "Don't worry, everything is going to come out all right." I immediately thought, "With all the problems I see from a legal standpoint, I have some doubts." He said, "No, everything will come out all right." I wanted to talk to him some more, but he was real busy like he had been on earth, and he walked out of my dream.

Just as Neil predicted, everything has worked out real well. Considering the estate's size, the amount of work, and the possibilities of conflicts and confusion, that was an amazing prediction.

Neil broke into Jay's dream, delivered his message, and exited rapidly, all in keeping with his personality. Apparently, some people change very little after they die, at least at first, as they continue to live in character in their new life.

Gayle is an artist in North Carolina. The ordinary dream she was having was interrupted by her 21-year-old son, Alex, who had drowned in a boating accident:

I had been under a lot of distress, as any mother is with the loss of her child. Two days after his burial, I woke up around 5:00 in the morning. I couldn't sleep and went into the living room and sat down. I kept praying, "God, please! I have to know where my son is. I have to know if he's okay."

I felt impressed to go back to bed, so I lay down and fell asleep. I started dreaming that I was in the kitchen fixing breakfast for my two younger sons – and Alex walked in!

I realized he wasn't supposed to be there. So I spoke aloud and said, "Alex is here!" His brothers looked at me like "What are you talking about?" Then I realized they couldn't see him – I was the only one who could.

Alex had the most glorious smile on his face. He had a glow, a celestial radiance. His expression was one of complete peace, happiness, and contentment.

I walked up to him and said, "Alex, you are with Jesus, aren't you?" He put his hands on my shoulders, and I put my hands around his waist, and he said, "Yes, Mama."

Then I woke up with the most peaceful feeling because I knew Alex was okay. I know his spirit is with God and that he is waiting for the time the rest of us will be with him.

It's quite common to have a sleep-state ADC that involves a number of people who are physically alive as well as a deceased loved one. Interestingly, in nearly every case the experiencer is the only one able to perceive and communicate with the person who has died, while the others remain completely unaware of his presence. For instance, Gayle was having an ordinary dream that included her two younger sons when Alex suddenly appeared in answer to her prayer. However, neither of his brothers was able to see him or hear him or had any awareness that he was there.

The next four accounts are typical sleep-state ADCs that took place in a familiar setting.

Henry, a retired music arranger in Florida, had this elating ADC a month after his father died of a lingering illness at age 89:

> I refer to this experience as a dream. There was Dad in living color standing by the front door. He looked between seventy and seventy-five, and instead of being bald, he had white hair. He had on dark blue pants, a light blue shirt, and a dark blue tie.
>
> He was very enthusiastic, very happy, and said, "Come outside." I remember opening the door and going out, while squeezing his right arm. It was like touching my arm or your arm, he was that real. I said, "Is this really you, Dad?" He said, "Yes, this is really me."
>
> Then Dad stepped back and said, "Look, I can walk! I can see!" He had a great sense of humor and did a little step with a spring in it. When he was alive he could not walk without his walker, and he was totally blind when he passed on.
>
> When I woke up, I was overjoyed. This confirmed life after death for me. There is no death – there is only life.

No wonder Henry was so thrilled by his experience. Whether we are awake or asleep during an ADC, it is always a joyous occasion when we learn that the lame can walk and the blind can see in their new life.

Ethel is a kindergarten teacher in Georgia. She had this vivid reunion with her brother, Vern, who died of cancer at age 60:

My brother, Vern, was a first lieutenant in the Army. He was wounded in Vietnam. Eventually he was unable to walk and was confined to a wheelchair in his later years.

I had a hard time dealing with his death because I had tried to be so brave for him. When he died, I had held my emotions in for so long that I wasn't able to cry.

About six weeks after he died, I dreamed Vern was standing in the door of my bedroom. He was no longer crippled from the war! He was wearing his full-dress uniform, his blues, that we had buried him in. He was very snappy and spit shined, just perfectly attired.

I got out of bed and said, "Vern!" He was smiling and reached out his arms, and I ran to him. He hugged me and I could feel his arms around me. I looked up at him and it was wonderful. I said, "You're all right! You can walk!"

Vern said, "Yes, I'm fine!" Then he kissed me and told me he loved me and that he would always be with me. He consoled me as nobody else could, and I started crying tears of joy.

I put my hand on his face, and he said, "Don't cry. We'll always be together." We were hugging each other, real close, and then he started disappearing very slowly.

I woke up when he left and cried for hours that night. Before he died, we had agreed he would find a way to come back if he could. Vern definitely fulfilled his promise!

If Ethel hadn't told us she was asleep when she had this ADC with her brother, we might have assumed that he had made a full appearance to her while she was wide awake. This is another example of someone who had made a compact before he died and later kept his promise.

Ann is an art framer in Maryland. She was 21 years old when she was contacted by her 18-year-old brother, Barry, who had died in a motorcycle accident:

After Barry was killed, I was feeling so angry and bitter at the world. About a month later, I had what I call a dream, but it wasn't a dream. It was like I was talking to him face-to-face.

I was in the backyard at my parents' cottage, and Barry came walking towards me. He was wearing jeans and a flannel shirt – his usual costume. His blond, curly hair was full of light. He looked beautiful!

He seemed very happy, content, and full of love. He seemed worldly, like he knew everything – no doubts, no questions, just full of confidence. A beautiful light was behind him and around him – a gorgeous, warm light.

I said, "Barry, what are you doing here?" He looked at me and said, "I came to tell you that everything is all right." I asked, "What do you mean? Didn't it hurt when you died?"

Barry said, "It did for a minute. It felt like a squeezing sensation. Then I was riding down a dark tunnel. And all of a sudden, I came into this beautiful, brilliant white light."

He kept smiling at me, and I was feeling full of love and light myself. It was so intense! He said, "I just want to tell you that I love you, Ann." Then he turned around and walked away.

I immediately woke up, and all the anger and frustration I felt were gone. I really believe Barry came to tell me he was fine so that I would be okay. I call it a dream, for not being able to give it another name. But it really happened!

Many people are distressed by how much a loved one may have suffered while dying. This is especially true in the case of a sudden, violent death due to an accident, murder, or war. Ann asked her brother a question almost everyone wants to know about such a death, "Didn't it hurt when you died?"

Barry's response to his sister is very reassuring. It is also representative of several similar accounts in our files. Consistently, our deceased loved ones want us to know that they left their body very quickly and felt little or no physical pain at the time of their death. In fact, there is some evidence, based upon our research and from other sources, that in the case of imminent and certain death, our loved ones leave their body just before or at the moment of impact. This applies to such situations as automobile collisions, plane crashes, industrial accidents, explosions, natural disasters, fires, murders, and warfare.

Near-death experiencers assure us this is true. Although they usually felt some pain initially, most quickly rose up out of their body and floated above the scene of the accident or battlefield, or hovered near the ceiling of the hospital room, or began moving through a tunnel toward a bright light. Of course, all NDErs returned to their injured physical body and generally had to endure more suffering when their experience was over.

Barry also mentioned he had passed through a "dark tunnel" and emerged into a "beautiful, brilliant white light." Several accounts of ADCs that are very similar to descriptions of near-death experiences will be presented in the next chapter.

Greg is a 20-year-old college student in West Virginia. He had this rendezvous with his friend, Evan, who was electrocuted in an industrial accident at a construction site at age 20:

> Evan and I were best friends for nine years. We did everything together, except when we were at school or working or started going out with girls.
>
> Two nights after Evan died, I had a dream. I was where the road splits to go to my house and to his house. We were standing and facing each other, and everything was lifelike.
>
> We were really excited about seeing one another. Evan was so happy and cheerful. He appeared the same as always and in good health. He had a great big smile on his face.
>
> I asked him, "What happened?" He said, "I was up

putting a light fixture on a twenty-foot pole when I hit some electrical wires. Something happened and I started to fall." He put one hand vertically and one hand horizontally to show me how he fell.

Evan said he felt scared at that moment, and then he felt nothing else. He said, "I promise, I didn't mean for that to happen." He also wanted to assure me that he suffered none whatsoever through that experience.

He told me he didn't want any of us worrying about him or being extremely sad that he was gone because he was in a great place. He was well taken care of and very happy, waiting for us to join him someday. Then I woke up.

I never had a dream like that before. It was very special to me that I was able to communicate with Evan after he died. It was like we parted with the realization that we will be back together someday.

Evan assured Greg that he hadn't suffered when he died. Greg also found out details about his friend's death that he didn't know before and couldn't have learned from anyone but Evan. Such information is sometimes received from those who died in an accident or by accidental suicide or were murdered. But, in general, most deceased loved ones seem reluctant to supply any specifics about their death other than to say, "It wasn't painful."

The next five accounts are examples of sleep-state ADCs in which the experiencer and the deceased loved one met each other in a new and unfamiliar setting.

Dee is a 31-year-old homemaker in the Southeast. She had this hopeful experience with her 1-year-old son, Joey, who was born with Down's syndrome and died from a congenital heart defect:

Joey had been ill from the time he was born. He spent half his life in the hospital and suddenly passed away the day after Christmas. I could never imagine being happy again.

Four months later, I had what I felt was a dream. Joey was riding a carousel, the kind we see in amusement parks. He had a huge smile on his face and looked the happiest and healthiest I had ever seen him! He was full of peace and joy and love.

Joey was showing me that he was in the most wonderful place and that the pain he endured while here on earth was now gone. No more heart difficulties, no more pain from the operations he underwent, and no more medications. I felt so happy for him! And I woke up right after that.

I felt Joey had come back to visit me from heaven. It was as though he came to give me a message that he was happy and for me not to be sad or to worry about him anymore.

I felt wonderful because I got to see my baby one more time. I will remember that dream for the rest of my life!

What greater blessing could bereaved parents receive than to see their chronically ill or handicapped children completely healed and whole and free of pain? Like Dee, they now have a new, lifelong memory to sustain them until they are finally reunited with their son or daughter when it's their time to die.

Once we realize our deceased loved ones are in a happier, freer state of existence, we can truly rejoice for them. And, knowing this, we too can heal emotionally right here and right now, certain this is what they want us to do for ourselves and for them.

Maureen, age 57, is a retired office manager in Florida. She enjoyed a beautiful moment with her 33-year-old daughter, Jill, who had suffered a lifetime of chronic asthma:

A couple of months following Jill's death, I dreamt she came to visit me one night. There was a rainbow in the background and white billowy clouds.

She was dressed in a lovely, white flowing robe. It had very large sleeves at the cuff line, like a graduation gown.

Her hair was beautiful, and she radiated an aura that lit up the entire area. She looked so serene and so happy – happier than I had ever seen her in her entire life.

I said to Jill, "Why were you taken from me? I love you so much, and I don't understand." She said, "Don't cry for me anymore, Mother. I'm happy! I'm free now, and I can soar with the birds!"

As she spoke, the enthusiasm for where she was now and the happiness she was experiencing were very obvious. I felt Jill was talking to me directly from heaven.

Then she extended her arm, and her fingers touched mine. She said, "Don't mourn for me anymore. We'll be together again someday."

When I woke up, I felt relief because she had achieved the peace she was longing for. She finally was enjoying life! I'm positive that when I pass over, Jill's hands will be there for me.

Maureen could finally release her painful memories of her daughter as a chronically ill young woman. She learned that Jill had graduated from this level of existence and entered another, where she is now a free spirit who can "soar with the birds." What more can any of us truly desire for our deceased loved ones?

Janet is a nurse in North Dakota. She became a bereaved mother when her 4-year-old son, Toby, died of a brain hemorrhage:

This occurred approximately one year after my son died. I recall the dream as if I had just had it last night. I was standing on a river bank and looking over at Toby on the other side.

His side was a lush green with beautiful trees. The water was a beautiful blue, and there were birds I could hear. It was a paradise, like the Garden of Eden. Everything was so quiet and peaceful.

Toby was standing in grass and flowers up to his

waist, close to the edge of the river. He was a little boy, the same little guy that I lost. He was wearing a striped T-shirt and blue jeans and was so very real and happy.

I kept trying to get over to Toby, but I couldn't. He looked up at me and spoke with such a calmness. He said, "No, Mom, you can't come over here. I'm okay. I'm fine. But you can't come over here." He had to tell me that several times because I wanted to cross the river to be with him.

Toby was calming me like an adult would. I almost felt like a child in comparison, as if an older, wiser person was talking to me. He was telling me to settle down and realize that his life is good now. He gave me the sense that he is at peace and that he's where he belongs.

The dream seemed so real, as real as life itself. When I woke up, I felt crushed that the dream was over. And yet I felt so comforted by it.

Janet has a permanent memory of seeing her son in a celestial environment. Toby's wisdom and authority beyond his years made it possible for her to accept that "he's where he belongs."

This is one of several sleep-state ADCs in our files in which there was an obstruction between the deceased loved one and the experiencer that neither was allowed to cross. Similar barriers are also reported in some accounts of near-death experiences.

Rosemarie is an administrative assistant in North Carolina. She had this enlightening ADC experience about 4 months after her grandmother died of cancer at age 66:

One night when I was sleeping, I saw my grandmother – it was like a beautiful dream. She was right there with me. It felt like we were on another plane or in a different dimension.

I only saw her face and shoulders – she was very young and beautiful. Grandma looked like she was a girl in her early twenties. I was surprised she was so youthful, but I recognized her instantly as my grandmother. It was like she could choose to be whatever age suited her.

As she came closer, she was glowing and radiating love. I felt an energy and warmth envelop me. It felt like a very nice, tingling massage. I was overcome with this feeling of unconditional love, like nothing I had ever done was wrong.

I was telling her over and over, "I love you, I love you, I love you." She was saying, "I know you do. I'm happy and I'm fine. You don't have to worry about me anymore. I'm in heaven."

Grandma affirmed there is a heaven, and that no matter what you've ever done, in God's eyes you are forgiven. You are pure, and you are loved in the way only He could love you. It touched me so deeply that I knew it was true.

All of a sudden, I realized I was sitting up in bed and Grandma was gone. But I didn't grieve for her after that at all.

Few of us ever experience on earth the degree of unconditional love Rosemarie did. This is reminiscent of the all-embracing love so many people say they encountered when they had a near-death experience and journeyed to the higher spiritual realms.

Vickie, an administrator at a college in Utah, was 39 years old when she had this meeting with her father. He died at age 69 of a staph infection he developed in the hospital after open-heart surgery:

When my father died, I was furious! I wanted to sue the hospital! I felt if he hadn't contracted that infection, he would have been all right and we would have continued to be a family.

My dream occurred the night of my birthday, almost three weeks after my father died. The background was kind of a gray mist, in a completely different space and time. Dad and I were facing each other, and he appeared healthy. It was as if we were standing together in the flesh!

He was holding my arm as I was telling him, "Dad, it wasn't right that you should go." He replied very intently, "You shouldn't be angry. I was ready to go. It was my time." He pulled me towards him and held me in his arms.

At that point, I knew Dad was right. He had come to tell me that and to comfort me. It was wonderful to see him again, and I felt very grateful. I kept saying over and over, "Thank you, Dad!"

When I woke up, I had an intense feeling of joy – joy in the midst of sorrow. I realized Dad came to me because I had misdirected anger that would keep me from resolving my grief. In spite of any errors that had been made in his medical care, he had lived a full life. He had prepared for death and was ready to go – it really was his time.

I feel Dad gave me the greatest gift of his life. It was a real comfort to know that I hadn't been abandoned, that spiritually we were still close. The bonds we have as father and daughter and the love we share will go on forever.

Today we have such high expectations of medical technology it is almost unthinkable that a loved one could die in a hospital of a common infection, especially after having successful open-heart surgery. When this happened for Vickie, her shock, outrage, and confusion were understandably overwhelming.

The healing power of an ADC is illustrated once again by the dramatic shift Vickie underwent when her deceased father contacted her on her birthday. His explanation, "I was ready to go. It was my time," and his warm hug said so much with so few words. As a result, Vickie was able to release her anger and accept his death, knowing their loving relationship is eternal.

The next two accounts are examples of sleep-state ADCs in which a deceased loved one returned to provide comfort and support to the experiencer during a period of uncertainty.

Jean, age 32, works in reservations at a family theme park in Florida. She welcomed emotional support from her godmother, Miriam, who had died of cancer:

> Five years later, I needed a hysterectomy. This was the first surgery I had ever gone through. About a week before the operation, I was getting concerned because I had never been under anesthesia.
>
> One night, I was especially upset before I went to bed. Then I had a dream that Miriam came to me. It felt different than a regular dream – it felt real. We were standing together in a nice, calm space. She was very serene and in good health.
>
> Miriam said everything would be okay and that she would be with me during my operation. I would not be alone. Then she gave me a hug. When I woke up, it felt like she was still hugging me.
>
> I had never awakened like that before – I was perfectly relaxed and peaceful. The feeling of nervousness and worry wasn't there anymore. It was like somebody had waved a magic wand and it was gone.
>
> I was calm when I went under the anesthesia because I knew Miriam would be there, and I didn't have to go through it alone. I even got out of the hospital two days early!

Facing an operation that requires general anesthesia can reveal the hidden fears we have about dying. At such times, we may become frightened and feel very vulnerable, very alone. Miriam's promise to attend the operation provided great comfort for Jean. Furthermore, rather than pacing the floor and drinking black coffee in the hospital's waiting room, her deceased godmother could hold Jean's hand in the operating room without being seen by the doctors and nurses.

Kaye, a bereaved mother in Indiana, was given inspiration by her 12-year-old son, Bryan, who died of cystic fibrosis:

I've had five children – three sons and two daughters. My sons had cystic fibrosis, and we lost all three of them within a fifteen-year period.

As a result of being at the hospital with my boys all those years, I became interested in helping dying children and their families. I wanted to do for others what had been done for me.

So a year after my last son, Bryan, died, I took my entrance exam for nursing school. But it had been twenty-five years since I had been in school, and I began to waver about my decision. And then I became worried when I hadn't received my letter of acceptance.

One night, I had this dream. I was in a restaurant that was being set up for a big party. I walked over to the buffet table, and Bryan was standing there!

He was no longer my thin, pale, twelve-year-old boy. He was over six feet tall and appeared to be about twenty-five years old! He looked healthy and robust! He looked very happy and peaceful and secure in himself.

Bryan was smiling at me and held his hands out and gave me a big hug. I could feel him – he was totally real! I grabbed ahold of him, and he let me cry all over his jacket.

I said, "Bryan, what are you doing here? You look so good!" He said, "I'm fine, Mother. I had to come back to remind you of the things you taught me."

I asked, "What's that, Bryan?" He replied, "Mother, you need to follow your dreams. Do what you think you should do, and accomplish what you feel you need to accomplish. Many times this is what God wants us to do." That's how the dream ended, and I woke up crying because it was such a vivid conversation.

The mail came at noon the next day, and I received my

acceptance to nursing school! At that point, I knew becoming a nurse was something I should definitely do.

Now I am a registered nurse and work in pediatrics and with the parents of children with cystic fibrosis. I really feel it's where I am meant to be.

It's deeply moving to learn that a mother who has lost three children to the same disease would choose to become a nurse, specifically to help others who are facing similar trials. Who could better minister to such patients and their families than someone who had been there herself so many times? This is the philosophy of all successful support groups, including those for the bereaved.

Only a year after Kaye's son, Bryan, died at age twelve, he came back to her as a young man in his mid-twenties. This ADC is one of several accounts in our files in which a baby or a young child appeared markedly older than when he passed on. At first, it may seem like a startling idea that a child could advance in age so rapidly. But just as elderly people may choose to return to the prime of their life after they die, apparently deceased children can move forward to an age that feels appropriate to them.

The following two accounts are examples of sleep-state ADCs during which the experiencers encountered two deceased loved ones who returned together for a very special purpose.

Margo is a homemaker in Florida. She had this compassionate visit with her stillborn baby, Ann Marie, and her mother-in-law, Nadine, who had died of cancer at age 45:

When I was six months pregnant, my baby died. She was stillborn because the umbilical cord had a defect where it was attached to her. I only saw Ann Marie once, when they delivered her.

A month later, my mother-in-law, Nadine, came to me in a dream. I had never met her because she had died about ten years before I met my husband. But I recognized her from pictures I had seen. She looked like she was about my age, wearing a dark skirt and a white blouse.

It was daylight – a real bright morning – and there was a large, old-fashioned baby carriage in the background. Nadine was smiling and holding our baby. Ann Marie appeared to be alive, but was real tiny, like a doll. She was wearing a pink knitted blanket and a little pink hat.

My mother-in-law said, "Everything is okay now. I have your baby. I'm going to watch over her until you come here to join us."

When I woke up, I felt relieved because I knew Ann Marie's short life wasn't over. I knew my baby was with her grandmother and still alive up there in heaven.

A bereaved parent of a miscarried or stillborn baby knows only too well what Elisabeth Kübler-Ross describes as "the grief of the loss of something we never had." Margo's pain and suffering are just as real and equally deserving of support as that of any bereaved mother or father who has loved and nurtured a child who was born alive and healthy but died later on.

Alana is a business owner in Ohio. Her first husband, Craig, died in an accident at age 21, and her 18-month-old daughter by her second marriage, Amber, died as a result of having aspirated:

Approximately six months after Amber died, I had a dream. It was the most vivid, most colorful, most peace-giving dream I've ever had in my entire life!

It was a bright, sunny, summer day, and I was looking down a country lane. There were big maple trees lined up on each side of the road. I could see the sun filtering through the leaves, and I could hear birds singing.

Directly in front of me, walking away from me down this lane, was my first husband, Craig. He was holding hands with Amber, my little girl.

They slowly turned towards each other, and then they made a 90-degree turn towards me. Amber was smiling, looking at Craig, and then she looked at me. Craig said, "Alana, don't worry. Amber will be all right. I'm going to keep an eye on her."

Craig was smiling and happy that Amber was walking down this lane with him, like they had known each other forever. Then Amber smiled again, and they turned around and continued walking away.

At that point I woke up, but I knew it wasn't a dream. I knew it was real! The peacefulness that came over me was unbelievable.

I feel Craig intended to give me a little peace because I was in such turmoil after Amber died. He wanted to let me know that my little girl was all right. Then I knew she wasn't somewhere all by herself with nobody to watch over her.

Many bereaved parents anxiously wonder "Who will take care of my child in heaven since nobody in my immediate family has died?" The two previous accounts suggest there will always be loving caregivers to greet our deceased children. In fact, it appears everyone can be assured there are innumerable spiritual helpers to welcome and assist all our loved ones when they die.

Some people have more than one sleep-state ADC with the same person. Lynette is the director of the state chapter of a national charitable organization in the Southeast. Her brother, Jerry, died at age 36 of pneumocystis pneumonia as a result of having AIDS:

Jerry was 6'1" and had gone from over 200 pounds down to 117 before he died. His gauntness made him look older than he was. After he died, I was so distraught about my brother, so sad, that I ached all the time for him and my loss.

About eight weeks later, I found myself talking to him in a dream. It felt like we were sitting in my living room, and Jerry was in a rocking chair across from me. I had my hand on his knee, which felt extremely real and tangible.

I said, "I'm so hurt, and I miss you so much." Then it hit me! "But I can't be talking to you. You died!" Jerry was smiling as he said, "I know. I wanted to come back to let you know I'm okay. Everything's fine, and I want you to be okay too."

He was healthy looking. He appeared to be about 180 pounds and seemed a little younger. He was wearing his usual clothes – a flannel shirt and cords. Jerry was well again! He was fun-loving and full of life!

This wasn't something I dreamed about – it was totally different. I believe Jerry really came to me! It was such a peaceful thing, and I felt so good about it. It resolved for me that my brother was okay.

About a month later, I was feeling real down and real low because I still missed my brother. Again I was dreaming, and this time I was looking out a window at the sky and saw a rainbow. To me, rainbows are a sign of something wonderful and good.

I felt somebody come up behind me, and I knew it was Jerry. He put his arms around me very firmly and gave me a bear hug. I felt his presence and the warmth of his body – he was very tangible.

Jerry knew that I needed him then. It was like he was saying, "I'm with you, and you are going to be okay." His hug was so real that it woke me up! I knew he had been there – it wasn't just a dream.

These two experiences have remained very comforting to me over the span of time. They have not diminished in any way after nearly six years.

It is fairly common to have two or more ADCs with a deceased loved one. They may be the same type, such as the two sleep-state experiences Lynette had with her brother, or they may be different types. Multiple contacts assure us that we are receiving ongoing love and assistance in our life and need not feel alone.

•   •   •

The final account is from Julia, a 31-year-old homemaker in Georgia. She surely never expected to hear from Patrick, the 6-year-old son of her neighbors, Debra and Jim. Patrick was killed by an automobile while he was riding his bicycle:

> The night after Patrick was buried, I went to sleep and was dreaming like I normally do. All of a sudden, I heard the voice of a little child – he just broke into my dream. I definitely heard an audible voice calling, "Mama." It seemed to be coming from a distance.
>
> Then I realized it was Patrick! It was like he was really there, although I didn't see him. I got the impression he was saying, "I'm giving you a message. Tell my mom and dad that I'm okay. I want them to know that I'm safe. I know they're hurting, but please tell them not to cry for me." It was like the whole thought was implanted in my head.
>
> I awoke and bolted straight up in bed! My heart was beating a mile a minute! It was so real that I can still hear the sound of Patrick's voice.
>
> Shortly after this, I went out of town for a few weeks, but the dream never went away. It was still as vivid six weeks later as it was that night.
>
> Then his mother, Debra, came over to my house one day. I told her about Patrick coming to me, and she was totally receptive. She said she needed to hear that, even though it didn't make the pain go away or the grieving stop. But it was something to hold on to, and it continues to provide comfort to Patrick's parents.
>
> Though we were just acquaintances before, Debra and I have become the best of friends since then. We will always have a common bond through Patrick.

This is an excellent example of receiving a message from someone who has died, knowing who to give it to, and having the courage to deliver it. Little did Julia realize at the time how important it would be for Patrick's parents to hear his words of comfort and reassurance.

We also interviewed Patrick's mother and father. Here is what Debra, Patrick's mother, told us:

> I got chills when Julia told me. I believed her right away. It made me feel so good that Patrick went to Julia, for he knew I would believe her. It helped us to know that he's okay. I wish every bereaved parent could have a Julia!

And Jim, Patrick's father, stated:

> I didn't know Julia very well at that time, but when she told us, I sat there in total belief. I didn't doubt her at all. I felt a burden was lifted and had a sense of relief. I was so happy that Patrick came to her. Since that time, our life has taken a very positive spiritual turn.

Julia's experience produced very positive results. Everyone benefits when we overcome our fear of being labeled "strange" or "weird" or "nuts" and take the risk to share an ADC message. Until we do, we'll never know how much good can come from it or how many people may eventually be helped.

If you have an ADC and receive a message for another person, write down your experience word for word promptly so you won't forget it. Details that may seem insignificant to you may have great meaning to someone else. If you feel uncomfortable delivering the message, you can always start off by telling the intended recipient something like "I had the most unusual dream last night...."

The accounts in this chapter have demonstrated that sleep-state ADCs are substantially different from ordinary dreams. They can provide as much information and comfort as the experiences people have when they are awake or in the alpha state.

Are you familiar with out-of-body experiences? Have you heard reports of encountering a deceased loved one during an OBE? This is the fascinating subject of the next chapter.

CHAPTER 11

Homeward Bound:
Out-of-Body ADCs

I experienced the reality of the spiritual body and learned that
it has every faculty of the physical body, though with
greater sensitivity and some dimensions added....
There will be nothing shocking in the transition,
only a continuation of who I am now.
—*Catherine Marshall*

This chapter contains accounts from people who stated they had contact with a deceased relative or friend during an out-of-body experience. We call these remarkable encounters out-of-body ADCs or OBE ADCs for short. They are a relatively less common type of after-death communication.

Out-of-body experiences are not a new phenomenon. They have been consistently reported throughout history, and accounts of them have been researched and written about for more than a century. A number of books supply detailed instructions for achieving OBEs.

The basic premise is that you are a spiritual being who is wearing or inhabiting a physical body during your lifetime on earth. You can temporarily leave your body and travel a short distance or journey to the stars. Some people claim they are able to visit other dimensions, including the spiritual realms.

Spontaneous out-of-body ADCs can occur while you are awake, in the alpha state, or when you are asleep. They are extremely vivid, intense, colorful, and vibrant experiences that people often say are "more real than life itself."

Many who have had an out-of-body experience or studied them assert there is ample evidence to believe they are genuine.

Millions of people who have left their physical body and seen it below them during a near-death experience are certain they have had an OBE.

It is not within the scope of our research to explain or defend the reality of out-of-body experiences. Instead, we'll present accounts from people who believe they have had an ADC during an OBE and invite you to form your own opinion about this subject.

The first two accounts are examples of OBE ADCs in which the experiencers traveled within their own home.

Shirley, a nurse in Wisconsin, had this mystical encounter with her 5-month-old daughter, Amanda, who died of a congenital heart defect:

> About three or four weeks after Amanda died, I was lying in bed, but I wasn't asleep. All of a sudden, I felt myself being pulled out of my body. I felt I was higher up in the bedroom, near the ceiling, looking out the window.
>
> The entire window became filled with the brightest golden light that I could ever imagine! It was like someone coming at you in a car with their high beams on. I felt absorbed by the light, and I felt the presence of my daughter.
>
> Then I saw Amanda! I saw her spirit in that light! And I heard her – it was a telepathic communication. She said, "Thank you very much for all that you gave me. I love you very much."
>
> Suddenly, I felt a very, very powerful presence – the presence of God. I felt the most incredible sense of love and understanding that I've ever experienced in my life. And at that moment, I understood everything!
>
> I remember being so overwhelmed by the whole thing. It was like being in a state of wonder. It was a feeling of total acceptance and total love for who I am. It was a spiritual love with no strings attached. And after that, I fell into a deep sleep.

This was a lot more than just a dream. I really feel it was a communication with my daughter. And I feel it was a gift that was given to me.

Shirley's incredibly beautiful and transformative out-of-body ADC became a sacred experience for her. Once again, a very young child communicated a mature, loving message that was well beyond her chronological age.

Peter, a salesman in Florida, had this meeting about 6 months after his daughter, April, died of a brain hemorrhage following an automobile accident at age 20. A series of olfactory ADCs he and his wife had with April was presented in Chapter 5:

One night while I was sitting up in bed, I had this out-of-body experience. Suddenly, I found myself in the hallway of our home. My daughter, April, was standing there!

She was in a white robe. I could see her hands and forearms, her neck and shoulders, and her face. Her skin tone was just perfect, and her hair was gorgeous. April was absolutely flawless!

I kept saying to her, "April, I love you! I love you!" over and over and over again. And she said, "Dad, I know that. It's all right." I wanted to touch her, to hug her and kiss her. But as I went forward, she backed away and said, "Dad, you can't touch me yet." And I became understanding of that.

Then I asked, "April, are you in heaven?" She said, "Yes!" I asked her, "What is heaven like?" My daughter, who had a tremendous sense of humor, said, "You know what those lifestyles of the rich and famous are like? Well, that's like living in poverty compared to heaven!"

Then she said, "I have to go now." I kept repeating, "I love you, April, I love you." She said, "Yes, I know, Dad," as she went backwards through the door and out of the house. And I went back to bed and got a good night's sleep.

The following morning, I told my wife of this experience, and she thought I was a little bit nuts.

While earlier accounts in this book have included hugging and kissing a deceased relative, Peter was not yet allowed to touch his daughter. Similar statements are reported in some visual, sleep-state, and out-of-body ADCs as well.

In each of the next four ADC accounts the experiencer made a considerably longer out-of-body journey while having contact with a deceased family member.

Nora is a 44-year-old homemaker who lives near Orlando, Florida. She had this OBE ADC with her mother, who died of heart disease at age 72:

My mother died in June, and I went on vacation to Sanibel Island in August. I was lying in bed, when all of a sudden I felt something come over me.

I rose up out of my body! It was a very, very strange feeling. I could see my body lying on the bed, and then, just as quickly, I was standing in the kitchen back in my house.

I was thinking, "What am I doing here?" when I heard a voice say, "Hello, Nora." I turned around, and there stood my mother! I couldn't believe it! I was so shocked when I saw her, I just said, "Mom!"

She looked so beautiful. Her face was glowing and there was light around her. She appeared to be fifty years old and was the happiest I'd ever seen anybody look.

My mother took my hand, and we walked out of the kitchen. When we got to the front door, she patted my hand and said, "I came to say good-bye. I love you, and I will always watch over you and your children." Mom radiated the most wonderful, angelic smile as she said this. Then she was gone.

I was standing there alone, but within seconds I felt myself lowering down into my body, back on the bed at

Sanibel Island. I lay there wide awake and felt so secure and protected, like when I was a child.

There is no doubt in my mind this really happened to me. It proved to me there is life after death, and it showed me that I don't need to fear death.

It's easy to recognize a classic description of an out-of-body experience while reading an account like Nora's. As she rose up into the air, she was able to look down and see her physical body sleeping on the bed. And when Nora came back, she reentered her body, which was safely awaiting her return.

Each leg of Nora's 300-mile round-trip, from Sanibel Island on the Gulf of Mexico to her home in central Florida, occurred almost instantaneously. It seems time and distance are not limiting factors during out-of-body experiences because travel is evidently achieved at enormous speeds.

Jonathan is a 20-year-old college student in Massachusetts. His sister, Erica, died in an automobile accident when she was 17:

A few months after Erica died, I was sleeping in my room – I was sound asleep. The next thing I knew I was floating above the center of Stockbridge, my home town, about a mile and a half away from my house. I felt very much alive and very real.

I looked over and saw my sister! Erica was right next to me, holding my hand. I could feel her hand in my hand very, very clearly.

We were floating high above the rooftops. I could see the colors of the buildings just as plain as day, and I could even see the traffic lights.

Erica was all in white – she was wearing a bright white robe that was illuminated and glowing. It looked very soft, like an angel's robe. The bottom of it was flapping in the wind.

She had her typical smile – a bright, brilliant, happy

smile. She appeared as she did the last day I saw her, in perfect health.

Erica was telling me everything was okay and not to worry. Then she rose up slowly into the light and waved good-bye.

When I woke up, I was very happy. It was like, "Wow! Erica is my angel and she's watching over me!"

Although many people clearly remember leaving their body and returning to it during an OBE, some, like Jonathan, simply don't recall this part of their adventure. Spontaneous out-of-body ADCs can be highly unpredictable, especially for a novice. While it's not uncommon for someone to find himself traveling through a nearby and known area as Jonathan did, others are just as likely to arrive at a totally unfamiliar destination that is possibly thousands of miles from their original starting point.

Ron is a 46-year-old real estate broker in California. He had this cosmic experience a year after his sister, Bobbie, died at age 53 of complications that occurred during a hospitalization:

Prior to my bedding down for the night, I was in a prone position and was resting in a semi-meditational state. Suddenly, I felt the presence of my sister, Bobbie.

She flew down to my being and grabbed my right hand. I could feel her touch – she was real! Bobbie was wearing a white gown made of a light, flowing, gossamer material. She was much younger and physically in perfect condition.

My sister was the happiest I had ever seen her, smiling and laughing the entire time. She had real bright, sparkly eyes and was very content. Bobbie said to me telepathically, "Let's go and have some fun, Ron!" And I said, "Okay."

So my sister and I suddenly burst out into space. It was quite an exhilarating experience! I could see stars and planets and all kinds of stellar constellations going by. Everything was very vivid, very intense, and very bright.

I didn't look back, although I felt a bright light surrounding and trailing behind us like a jet stream. As we went faster and faster, Bobbie turned around and said, "Isn't this a wonderful experience!" I said, "Yes, let's do some more!" We both laughed and continued our ascent straight up. I'm sure we were traveling at light speed or even faster.

Then I began thinking, "Now, hold it! Where are you taking me? How far am I going? How am I going to get back to planet Earth?" Bobbie felt my fear and resistance, and within moments I was back on earth and in the same prone position on my bed.

I was still tingling, and my whole being was totally energized. I opened my eyes and said, "Wow!"

A few people reported being invited by a deceased loved one to "Come with me" and then had a delightful OBE ADC. Others received the same invitation but feared it and turned it down. This was probably because they were not familiar with out-of-body experiences, or they mistakenly assumed that such a request meant they were being asked to die and join their loved one permanently.

Maryann, a homemaker in Florida, took an extended journey about a year after her 18-year-old son, Shawn, was hit and killed by an automobile:

I was sound asleep, and it was like there were two of me. One of me was lying in bed. The other one, the real me, was being drawn up and up. I could look down and see my body was sleeping.

I was being drawn higher – I was above the house looking down on the trees – I went higher and higher – way up – and all of a sudden Shawn was there! I was so surprised to see him! It was very bright, but there were no earthly surroundings. I had a floating feeling like we were suspended in space.

My son and I hugged each other – it was so intensely joyful, it was just overwhelming! There were no words, just this great joy and the fact that Shawn was really still alive. There was this understanding like a communion, a knowing, an accepting.

I knew my son was all right and that he still cared about me. He was aware of my life, but he also had a life of his own. His was an unrestricted life with unrestricted freedom and knowledge far beyond what we have here on earth.

Then I was back down in my body on my bed, and I was awake. I thought to myself, "This existence seems more like a dream. That existence seems more real than life!" It was the most comforting and the most real experience I've ever had.

I know that I will see Shawn again someday and that he will be waiting for me – I just know these things.

I still cry because I miss my son. But I no longer cry because I don't think he's alive. I no longer cry because I don't think I'll ever see him again.

Having left her physical body, Maryann traveled in her spiritual body an unknown distance to visit her deceased son. Apparently, in that existence, which "seems more real than life" we can meet as eternal beings and achieve a state of communion with our deceased loved ones that may be more intimate, more complete, and more fulfilling than the reunions we have here on earth.

The next two out-of-body ADCs were experienced in another dimension of existence.

Betsy is the manager of a retail store in the Southeast. She was at the wheel of her car when she and her sons, Nathan, age 6, and Travis, age 4, were in an accident. Though Betsy was not seriously injured, her two boys were killed instantly:

While I was in the hospital, I didn't want to live. Nothing made sense, and I just wanted to give up and die. I didn't want to live without my sons.

An angel came to me and took me firmly by the hand. I felt a love that I had never felt before. He took me to this beautiful meadow. It was the prettiest emerald green with the most vibrant clear blue sky. The colors are hard to describe because they are not like the colors we see here.

There was a bright white and lavender light around this meadow, but it didn't hurt my eyes. It was a very soothing, loving atmosphere.

As the angel and I were hovering above the meadow, I heard a lot of laughter. I heard my sons – Nathan and Travis! I looked down to see what they were doing. My vision was really, really good – I could zoom in on them with my eyes.

Nathan and Travis were with a bunch of other boys and girls. They were very vibrant and healthy – all happy and running and playing. There was so much beauty, so much love, that it filled the air.

The angel told me, "Your sons are fine, and you will see them again. Do not worry." As I went to reach for Nathan and Travis, I was suddenly thrust back into my bed in the hospital. And that was the end of my experience.

The angel knew I had to see that my boys were okay. I have never known a greater love than this.

Angels are occasional participants in ADC experiences. They often serve as compassionate escorts who can lead us directly to our deceased loved ones. Whether they act upon their own or are sent as divine messengers, presumably they are able to assist us in a multitude of ways.

Like Betsy, experiencers may gain some expanded abilities while visiting the spiritual dimension. If people or objects appear far away, we can easily adjust our sight to perceive them more clearly. This is called "telescopic vision." Another reported benefit of this realm is that the majority of communication is accomplished by telepathy. Even people who spoke vastly different languages on earth can seemingly understand and converse with each other. And while the inhabitants can walk from place to place, evidently there is a more efficient method of transportation, especially over longer distances. They merely have to visualize the person or place they wish to visit, and almost instantly they will be there.

Ginger is a 41-year-old nurse in New Jersey. She had this celestial reunion with a former patient about 6 months after he died:

> Corey was a little baby under my care in the neonatal intensive care unit. He had very severe birth defects, including a cleft pallet, a cleft lip, facial deformities, and major heart problems.
>
> I had become quite close to his mother, and right from his birth, we knew he would die. Corey lived approximately five months and died on Christmas Day.
>
> Soon after, I started a support group for parents who had experienced the death of their baby. One evening, Corey's mother stayed on and met with me one-on-one because she was having a very rough time with his death.
>
> Later that night, I had an out-of-body experience and went to another plane, another dimension of reality. This is a spirit plane where children gather – groups of highly evolved little beings.
>
> There were lots of flowers around and many gorgeous colors. Everything was very crisp and clear, brighter than usual and more alive than in our dimension.
>
> Corey came to me from a group of little babies he was playing with. He was absolutely gorgeous and radiant. He was no longer handicapped or malformed – he was healed and whole, without any defects at all! He was a very beautiful baby!

He communicated with me by telepathy, saying, "Thank you for taking care of my mother. You're really helping her. I want you to let her know that I am all right and that everything is fine. I am happy now."

I don't recall traveling back to my body, but this experience was very, very clear when I woke up.

I shared my story with Corey's mother, and it gave her great comfort and peace. She was especially relieved to hear that her baby was healed.

A nurse like Ginger, with her well-deserved credibility, was the perfect intermediary to convey Corey's message to his mother with both humility and conviction. Based upon our research, nurses have more ADC experiences than members of any other profession. This isn't surprising because they develop so much emotional and spiritual sensitivity through caring for their patients, especially the terminally ill.

The remaining five reports of out-of-body ADCs sound very much like near-death experiences, but there is one extremely important difference. All the people who had these OBE ADCs were in good health and were not in any kind of physical danger or close to dying when they made their trip. As you read these NDE-like accounts, notice the experiencers traveled in their spiritual body through a tunnel towards a bright light and met with one or more deceased relatives and friends. When the visit was completed, they returned through the tunnel and reentered their physical body.

Pauline, age 55, is a disabled homemaker in Georgia. She had this exhilarating round-trip excursion with her husband, Art, after he was murdered:

I had a dream several months after my husband died. Art came and took my hand, and we went through a tunnel. It was like going through a spiral, and there was white light at the end.

Art was perfectly healthy and was dressed as normal.

He showed me a little two-room house he was staying in. He said he was going to a halfway house to help him get over the shock of crossing over so suddenly when he was killed.

He showed me what he was doing – he was working with flowers. I've never seen such beautiful flowers in my life. I can't begin to describe their colors. There were roses that were the size of dinner plates! And there were butterflies too. It was all so pretty!

Then Art brought me back through the tunnel. When I woke up, I was crying – tears were running down my face. My experience was really beautiful!

Some people who had an OBE ADC called it a "dream" because they were not knowledgeable about out-of-body experiences. While most had heard the term, few had ever read any accounts of them.

Based upon our research and other sources, one of the purposes of a "halfway house" is to assist people who have undergone a very sudden and violent death due to an accident, murder, or warfare. These rehabilitation centers seem to provide orientation, education, and emotional and spiritual healing for those who have been traumatized by such an event. They apparently ease the transition of people who need to rest for a while after suffering a long-term, spiritually debilitating illness. And these facilities also reportedly serve as welcoming centers for those who had denied the possibility of life after death and must undergo a period of adjustment to their new and unexpected state of existence.

Ellie is a data processor in Michigan. She attained a new understanding of life 4 months after her son, Don, was killed in an automobile accident at age 26:

I had gone to bed and had my eyes closed, but I know I wasn't asleep. Then I noticed I was moving towards a tiny pinpoint of light. I was in a tunnel and the light was getting bigger and brighter, but it didn't hurt my eyes. I knew this wasn't a near-death experience because I wasn't even sick!

This intensely bright light was peaceful and comforting – I couldn't take my eyes off of it. It seemed to pull me towards it, and I could see the outline of a figure in a flowing robe with his hands outstretched like he was welcoming me. As I came closer, I could tell it was my son, Don! He was in this light.

I heard Don's voice in my head very firmly say, "Stop! It's not your time yet, Mom. Go back! I'm all right and you have much to do."

I don't remember going back down the tunnel. The light just pulled away from me and disappeared, and then I was fully awake.

I had never thought about my own mortality before, but now I'm not afraid of death. I know that someday, when my work is done here, I'll be with Don again.

This certainly sounds like a typical account of a near-death experience, and just like many NDErs, Ellie was emphatically told "It's not your time yet." This supports the theory that physical life on earth is a school, and we are not ready for graduation until we have completed all our courses. Our primary spiritual lessons seem to be learning how to love and serve one another.

Rosalind, a homemaker in Missouri, had an exceptional visit with her 19-year-old son, Charlie, about 3 years after he died in a motorcycle accident in 1985:

It was a regular evening and I had done what I do every night – took a shower and got into bed about 10:00. I don't know when the dream started, but I was walking through this very bright tunnel. There was a sweet, fresh smell like flowers. The tunnel was really, really long, and I didn't think I'd ever get to the end.

When I did, Charlie was standing there! He was

dressed in a pair of blue jeans, a rock group T-shirt he always wore, and tennis shoes. He was happy like when he was alive, just laughing and joking. He appeared the same age and in very good health.

Then I saw my mom and dad! Dad died in 1966 and Mom died in 1980 – they looked just the same. I felt like I had died and gone to heaven!

Charlie grabbed me and said, "Mother! What are you doing here?" I said, "I've come to be with you and your grandparents." He said, "It's not time for you to come here yet."

I went over to Mom and Dad and said, "I've come to be with you." They said, "No, you've got two kids at home. You've got a husband and a granddaughter and you need to be there. You're not ready to come here yet."

I kept saying, "I want to be with you." My parents kept saying, "No! No, you can't. You have to go back. We're taking care of Charlie and he's in good hands." I didn't want to leave, but all of a sudden I was going back through the tunnel and I woke up. It was a wonderful experience!

It wasn't my time to be with them yet, but someday I will. It made me happy that I could see them and talk to them again. I know that Charlie is in a good place and that my parents are taking care of him.

When it's not yet our rightful time to be in heaven, it seems the issue is nonnegotiable. Despite Rosalind's desire to remain with her deceased parents and son, like many near-death experiencers she was forcefully reminded that she must return to fulfill her responsibilities to her family on earth.

Dottie, a 44-year-old homemaker in Michigan, was given a glorious tour of a spiritual realm:

In a dream, I went floating through the middle of a long, dark tunnel that seemed to go on endlessly. It appeared to be made of stone or dark brick.

There was a very bright, warm, white light at the end of the tunnel with a hint of gold streaming out of it. Something kept pulling me forward – I had to go to that light! I felt a very loving presence, and I knew this light wouldn't hurt me. Then I merged into the light like walking into a fog.

I was greeted by a lady who had both hands outstretched towards me. I felt she was Mary, the Blessed Mother. She never said who She was, but I knew Her and I loved Her. She took my hand very gently, and I could feel Her warmth and Her love.

I was relieved and felt very peaceful being with Her. She was wearing a white cloth robe, so bright that it glowed. I knew She cared for me and loved me.

The Blessed Mother was my guide to a beautiful garden with a clear, pure stream running through it. I touched the water, and it was real. The grass and trees were bright green, and there were flowers of all kinds.

I was in a park-like setting and could see big crystal buildings off in the distance. There was a bright light from somewhere, and all the colors were very vivid.

I saw my father, my stepfather, and my father-in-law all sitting on the bank of a river. They were waving to me and saying, "Hi, Dottie!" They were fishing with rod and reel – they had all been fishermen in life. But they had never known each other when they were alive here on earth.

It was a very relaxed atmosphere. I felt very happy, very peaceful, very restful. Once there, I didn't want to leave. Everybody was happy, and I didn't see anyone working. I met a friend who had died a long time ago, and she said, "Don't worry. I'm really happy now." And I saw my young cousin too.

The Blessed Mother said, "It's time to go," and She led me back to the tunnel entrance. I sensed She stayed until She knew I was through that light. But I don't remember coming back through the tunnel.

I feel I've been entrusted with knowledge that most

people don't have. I was always a very religious person, but I feel much closer to God now.

Graciously accompanied by the Blessed Mother, Dottie must indeed have visited heaven! The radiant light, the all-encompassing love, the ineffable beauty, and the sparkling sense of aliveness that were present there are frequently reported in accounts of prolonged near-death experiences. It's also quite interesting that three men who had been members of the same family, but never knew each other on earth, met and formed friendships after their death. Perhaps one day all of us will discover we belong to a far larger spiritual family.

The final account is from Michelle, who is a receptionist for a chiropractor in California. She had this joyful ADC 2 years after her 11-year-old daughter, Angela, died in an automobile accident:

Shortly after I fell asleep one night, I felt a pulling sensation, and then I felt myself going really fast through a tunnel. I saw light up ahead, and I was frightened.

A voice came to me and said, "Don't worry. Don't be alarmed. You won't be harmed. You're not going to die. If you want to go back, you can. If you want to go forward, you can." I decided to go forward and kept going fast. I felt the wind on my cheeks and my hair blowing. I had a real euphoric feeling.

I looked around and saw beautiful trees, a blue sky, beautiful flowers, and green grass. The colors were so vibrant and everything was very vivid. I could even hear birds singing. I thought, "Well, wherever I am, it's wonderful!"

I walked along and saw some children. Four little girls were sitting on a blanket, playing and having a tea party. I walked over and asked, "Do you know my daughter, Angela?" We communicated telepathically. One of the girls told me that she was in the playhouse and pointed it out to me.

I walked over to the playhouse and looked in the window. I saw Angela at a table playing cards. I was so happy! As I knocked on the window pane, I could hear the sound and I could feel it.

Angela looked up and saw me, and then she came out. We hugged and I just started babbling, saying, "I'm so sorry it happened to you." The thought of my daughter dying in a car accident had been a hard thing for me to deal with, so I was just crying and crying.

Angela was real loving and calm and serene. She said, "You know, Mom, it's okay. It's all right. I'm not hurt. I'm fine. You have to stop worrying about me. I'm okay and I'm happy here."

I calmed down and really looked at her. She looked beautiful! There were no scars on her. She was wearing a white dress, kind of shimmery, with gold in it. And when she moved, her clothes seemed to shine.

I totally relaxed, and then I felt my energy fading. She said, "Mom, I know you can't stay. But it won't be that long, and we'll be together. You'll see!"

We hugged each other and Angela said, "You have to go back now, Mom." I went the same way I came, backwards through that tunnel. By the time I returned, I was wide awake.

I can remember everything in detail from that experience. It was wonderful! Even though I wrote it down, I don't have to read it – it's printed in my mind forever.

Like Michelle, countless near-death experiencers have made an out-of-body journey through a tunnel, seen a very brilliant light, and visited a heavenly realm. They too have frequently met deceased loved ones or celestial beings, and their extraordinary testimony has comforted and inspired millions of people who have responded to the ring of spiritual truth in their NDE accounts.

As you've read in this chapter, our research revealed it isn't necessary for someone to be close to death to have an out-of-body experience that involves traveling through a tunnel and meeting deceased relatives and friends in the light. The last five OBE ADC accounts demonstrate that anybody can have a "tunnel experience" while in very good health.

There is still another kind of NDE-like experience that does not include contact with anyone. One woman we interviewed was in fine health and wide awake while she was standing at her kitchen sink. She spontaneously left her body, traveled through a tunnel, and encountered a very bright light that transformed her life. Our files contain several similar experiences that occurred when the participants were in the alpha state or asleep.

During our ADC research we learned there is a wide spectrum of "tunnel experiences" people may have while they are in good health. These usually involve seeing a brilliant light and may also include meeting deceased loved ones or religious figures and touring a spiritual plane. Future studies of these NDE-like experiences could provide additional evidence of life after death.

Have you ever had a telephone ring and, when you picked it up, heard the voice of a deceased loved one speaking to you? This can occur while someone is asleep or awake, and telephone ADCs will be discussed fully in the next chapter.

CHAPTER 12

Person-to-Person: Telephone ADCs

You live on earth only for a few short years which you call
an incarnation, and then you leave your body as an outworn
dress and go for refreshment to your true home in the spirit.
—*White Eagle*

Imagine you hear a telephone ringing. When you answer it,
you hear the voice of a deceased loved one and receive a brief
message. Or you may have a two-way conversation. We call
these experiences telephone ADCs or ADC phone calls, which
may take place while you are sound asleep or wide awake.
They are the least common of the twelve major types of after-
death communication.

Receiving a telephone call and having a conversation with a
deceased relative or friend while you are sleeping is like any
other sleep-state ADC. The only difference is you are speaking
to each other on a phone rather than meeting face-to-face.

An awake telephone ADC has some interesting characteristics. Your phone actually rings. When you pick it up and say
"Hello," you hear a deceased loved one on the line. His or her
voice may sound strong and clear, or it may seem to be coming from far away. After the call is completed, you won't hear
the receiver at the other end being hung up. For that matter,
there won't be any kind of disconnect sound or even a dial
tone. Instead, the phone will be silent as though the line had
been cut.

• • •

The first four accounts are examples of telephone ADCs that occurred while the experiencers were asleep. Since they didn't have any other language to describe these unusual events, they usually said their experience took place in a "dream."

Alice is an accounts payable manager in Massachusetts. She received this ADC phone call after her 16-year-old son, Trey, died by drowning:

> Trey was the kid who was always getting the stitches and whatever. When he drowned, I didn't go to see him in the emergency room. To go in there and not be able to fix it – I just couldn't do that. I felt so badly afterwards and kept saying, "I couldn't even go and say good-bye to my own son."
>
> Shortly after he died, the phone was ringing in my dream. I picked it up and it was Trey's voice. He just said, "Ma," real quickly like something had happened. That's the way he always talked.
>
> I said, "Trey, is that you? Where are you?" He said, "I just called to say I'm okay and I love you." He spoke slower and more peacefully than usual, but it was definitely his voice. He was calm like he didn't want to worry me. It all seemed very real. Then the phone went dead.
>
> Trey had to tell me he was all right because he knew how I worried about him. This dream also convinced me it was okay that I hadn't said good-bye.

Nearly all people feel regret afterwards if they didn't have a chance to say good-bye to a loved one who was dying. Like Alice, others may also have feelings of guilt if they had the opportunity to be present but were emotionally unable to do so.

Our deceased loved ones seem to easily understand and accept our human limitations. Evidently, they want us to release ourselves from needless self-blame and guilt so we can be free to move forward in our lives. This again affirms the healing message of love contained within so many ADC experiences.

Carole, a 43-year-old hypnotherapist in Michigan, had this telephone conversation about 12 weeks after her mother died:

My mother was killed in a gas explosion. It was very sudden, and there was no physical body to be viewed. So I was having a difficult time about how she died. I would find myself thinking her death wasn't real. I just wasn't accepting the fact that she was gone – I was totally in denial.

While I was sleeping, a telephone rang in my dream. I answered the phone, and I heard my mother say, "Carole, this is Mom." An energy shot right through me when she said that. And I knew it was her!

I began crying uncontrollably, saying, "Mom! Mom! Mom!" I don't remember our conversation clearly, but I believe she said, "Carole, I am on the other side. I am no longer on the earth plane. I'm not coming back."

When I woke up, my pillow was soaking wet, my face was wet, and my nightgown was wet. I felt emotionally drained, but I was finally at peace.

This phone call pushed me over the hump. I finally moved out of denial and could go on with my grieving for my mother.

When a loved one dies suddenly and viewing the body is not possible, we often have difficulty accepting the reality of the death and can be left in an emotional limbo. This particularly applies when someone is lost at sea, dies in a mass accident like the crash of an airliner, or is killed during a war.

Having an ADC experience after such a death is especially valuable, since it often moves the experiencers past the denial stage of grief and allows them to progress towards full acceptance. This is also true for those who are in the anger stage of their grief for a prolonged time, which often happens when their loved one has been murdered, committed suicide, or killed by a drunk driver.

Sheila, age 46, is a nurse in Iowa. She benefited from a supportive message 7 months after her father died of emphysema:

My husband and I were having many problems and I was very distraught. I had gone through a lot of mental abuse and I wanted to get out of the marriage. But I couldn't do it yet – I had been putting this decision off for about three or four years.

When my father died, I felt like the only important man in my life was gone. My husband didn't even give me a hug to say that he was sorry my dad had died. There was no emotional support, and I was in a really depressed state.

In a dream, shortly before I woke up in the morning, I got a telephone call. When I held the phone up to my ear, my dad was on the line – it was definitely his voice! He told me, "Don't worry! I will be with you as long as you need me. Whatever you decide, I'm here for you."

I needed to know that my father did love me and was going to stand by me no matter what. This was an affirmation that I didn't get from him when he was alive.

The next morning, I felt the most wonderful peace, more peace than I felt in years and years. The turmoil wasn't there anymore. It was a turning point, and suddenly I knew I could do what I had to do.

About five months later, I finally got things going and filed for divorce. I don't think I would have been able to do it then if it hadn't been for that telephone call from my dad.

Notice that Sheila's father didn't give her any specific advice but assured her of his continued support regardless of what she decided to do. This is truly an example of unconditional love. If only more of us could express such "love without strings" or "love without hooks," as Elisabeth Kübler-Ross calls it, the world would be a much happier and emotionally healthier place.

Terry is a travel agent in Florida. She had a series of telephone ADCs with her mother, who died of cancer at age 76:

> Mother had bought two new pairs of shoes, but she had not been able to wear them when she got really sick. She was a very thrifty, very frugal person, and before she died, she asked me to take them back and get the money out of them for myself. But I had not done it.
>
> Within a period of six weeks after she died, I had three phone calls while I was asleep. Each time, a phone rang in my sleep, and when I answered it, it was Mother!
>
> The first time she talked to me, I asked her how she was. She said everything was fine, and I told her that I missed her. She asked, "Have you taken the shoes back yet?" That seemed to be worrying her. I said, "No" and started to cry. Then the call was terminated when she said, "I have to go now. Good-bye."
>
> About a week later, the second call was basically the same. Again, she asked me if I had taken the shoes back. And I said, "No, not yet. But I'm going to."
>
> The third time she called and asked about the shoes again, I started crying. Then she said, "Terry, if you don't quit crying, I won't call you anymore." And I never received another phone call from her.
>
> A couple of weeks after the third phone call, I finally took the shoes back and got a refund. I knew she wanted me to do it, and so I did.

Some people apparently have a need to "tie up loose ends" after they die. In other ADC accounts in our files, deceased loved ones have asked their relatives to return library books, scientific research papers, or sums of money they had borrowed.

Many experiencers reported that a deceased loved one had told them the exact location where money, securities, important business papers, and similar items of value had been hidden. Accounts like these will be covered in a later chapter.

Beverly, a 45-year-old waitress in Louisiana, was asked to fulfill a request after her boyfriend's mother, Jane, died from a massive coronary. But Beverly doesn't know whether she was awake or asleep at the time she had this ADC:

> This was about a month after her death. My boyfriend, Roy, and I were living together. We didn't have a telephone in the bedroom – only in the living room.
>
> I was asleep when the phone rang and woke me up. I got up, went to the living room, and answered it. Roy's mother, Jane, was on the phone! She asked, "Will you please take care of my son for me?" It was a tender request, and when she asked for this commitment, I told her that I would.
>
> Then I woke up in bed. But I wasn't sure if I had actually gotten out of bed and answered the phone in the living room or whether the whole thing had been a dream.
>
> I knew Roy's mother very well. We were close confidants and friends before she died. Roy was a dependent man in a lot of ways, and Jane was asking me to be the emotional support for her son in her absence.
>
> I stayed with Roy for three more years, and then I left that relationship. There was some guilt involved for me because I hadn't kept my promise to Jane. Though I had made a commitment to her, I had an overriding commitment to myself.

After their death, it seems that most people are very concerned about the welfare of their surviving loved ones. Occasionally, as Jane did, they may return to ask someone to take care of a particular family member on their behalf.

All the remaining accounts in this chapter are examples of telephone ADCs that occurred while the experiencers were awake.

Ramona, a homemaker in California, was astonished by a call from her husband, Stanley, who was 43 years old when he died of an aneurysm:

This was within weeks after Stanley's death. It was morning and I was cleaning up after breakfast. The phone rang and I picked it up. My husband said, "Hi, honey!" It was Stanley – the voice was his!

He sounded as clear as could be, just as though he had called me from work. That was all he said and the phone went dead – there was no disconnect.

For a minute, I thought I was going batty. But I know the phone rang. I was holding it in my hand, and I know I heard my husband's voice!

If a telephone rings while you are performing a routine activity and when you pick it up you hear a deceased loved one speaking, you may be greatly surprised or even shocked. It's likely you might question your sanity, just as Ramona did. Yet what could be more tangible than holding the receiver in your hand after the call is over?

Monica is a 52-year-old bookstore owner in Missouri. She heard from her father in an unusual way 3 months after he died of a heart attack:

My father died in June, and this was in September. I was at home one day and called a company about something very routine. The operator came on the line and told me to wait, and then the elevator music began.

Suddenly, the music cut off, and I heard my father say, "Hello, Dolly!" That's what he always called me. Then he said, "You know who this is!" I knew his voice, but I didn't say anything because I was so stunned!

A few seconds went by and then he said, "This is your daddy." His voice was very gentle and sounded exactly the same as ever. It was like a long-distance connection, but there was no static and the line was perfectly clear.

Then the operator came back on the line to tell me the person I was calling wasn't there, and I hung up. Naturally, I tried calling that number again to see if anything would happen, but it didn't.

This unique experience was so real that I cannot question it. It shattered my skepticism about such communications. Perhaps my father chose this method so that I could in no way doubt the reality of it.

As these first two awake telephone ADCs illustrate, sometimes the message from our deceased loved one is simply a big "Hello!" that affirms he or she is still alive and well and cares about us. This seems to be the primary intention of nearly all ADCs, though most contain additional sentiments or have a more specific purpose.

Because communication by telephone is such a routine activity, we no longer question hearing someone's voice without also seeing the person who is speaking to us. Many people contend that hearing a deceased loved one's voice on a phone is far more concrete than receiving a message by telepathy. The added feature of a physical telephone often provides a greater degree of certainty about the reality of their experience. Perhaps this is why our deceased family members and friends may choose to contact us in this manner.

Ellyn, a human resources manager in Nevada, had this phone ADC after her 12-year-old daughter, Ashley, died of leukemia:

> This was more than three years after Ashley died. I was going through a real bad health problem. I had been diagnosed with a lung disease, and I was afraid I was going to die too.
>
> That night, I was making spaghetti on the stove and the phone rang. I picked it up and I heard this little voice say, "Mommy!" I thought, "What? Who is playing this terrible joke?" So I asked, "Please, who is this?"
>
> She said, "This is Ashley. What are you doing, Mommy?" I said, "Ashley? I'm cooking." And she said, "You're making my favorite meal. You're making spaghetti!"
>
> It was Ashley's voice – she sounded strong and healthy – and nobody could imitate her voice. At that

point I thought I was crazy, but no one knew what I was cooking for dinner because it was a spur-of-the-moment thing to make spaghetti.

Then I asked her, "Ashley, are you okay?" And she said, "Mommy, I'm okay. I just called to tell you that you're going to be okay too." Then the phone went dead. There was no dial tone. No noise. Nothing. I just sat there with the phone in my hand for the longest time.

I had lung surgery six months later. A month ago I went to the doctor. My blood count was normal for the first time in three years, and next month he'll start weaning me off my medication. Ashley was right – she told me I was going to be okay!

No wonder Ellyn was stunned! Not only did she hear Ashley's voice on the telephone three years after her death, but she couldn't begin to find a rational explanation for how anyone could possibly know she was cooking spaghetti at that very moment.

Sylvia is a retired dental hygienist in Indiana. She received two messages from her 36-year-old son, Joe, after he was murdered:

It was four or five weeks after Joe's death. Sometime during the night, when I was fast asleep, I heard the phone ring. I picked up the receiver, which is on the night table next to my bed, and I found myself sitting up.

I said, "Hello?" And the answer came, "Hello, Mom. This is me." This is the way Joe always started his conversations when he called us. He said, "Please stop grieving for me. Please stop crying. I want you to know that I'm happy and I'm at peace."

Before I could say anything, he was gone – just like the phone went dead. It was like a regular telephone conversation, but I didn't hear him put down the receiver. I was wide awake at the time, and I know that I heard Joe's voice. But for a while I couldn't believe it.

Finally, I woke my husband up and told him and he

said, "You must have been dreaming." I didn't want to tell anyone else about it because I thought they would laugh at me and say, "Oh, that couldn't have happened!"

About three weeks after the first call, it happened again! During the night the phone rang. I picked it up and I sat up in bed.

This time Joe didn't even identify himself but said, "Mom, you're not letting me go. You're still crying and grieving. Please stop. I can't be at peace." I could hear him just as plain as could be. I opened my mouth to say something, but my son was gone, and that was it.

I've wanted to hear from Joe again. I've waited for something, and yet there hasn't been any communication in all this time, which is over ten years. But I know you cannot wish it and make it happen.

Assume you are the one who has died. What would you want your surviving loved ones to know? How would you feel if they were very unhappy and grieving deeply for you? What would you say if you could communicate to them?

Once we realize we have survived the change called death, we will know that life is continuous and that separation from our loved ones is only temporary. We will have an overview of life and death that those still on earth can only imagine. From this higher vantage point we might be compelled to say to them, "Don't grieve for me. Please let me go on with my new life," certain that we will all be reunited in the future.

Penny is a former loan officer for a bank in Florida. When she was only 16 years old, her 35-year-old mother died in the recovery room following an emergency operation. As a result, Penny and her two sisters never had a chance to say good-bye:

A few months later, I was in bed one evening, not really asleep – just lying there thinking. I heard the phone ring two or three times at about 11:30. I jumped out of bed and answered it. On the other end was my mother!

She said, "How are you girls doing? I'm sorry I didn't

get a chance to say good-bye. You girls behave yourself and take care of each other. I love you and I'll be watching over you."

It was like she was happy and wanted us to go on with our lives. I was so happy to be hearing from her. Yet I kept thinking, "This can't be happening. I know my mother is dead."

About that time, my father came around the door and asked, "Who were you talking to?" I said, "I know you aren't going to believe this, Dad, but I was talking to Mom."

Then he said, "Penny, you know Mom passed away. You must be upset or you must have been dreaming." I said, "No, Dad, I'm wide awake!"

He came over and took the phone from me. On the other end there was a dead silence as if someone was listening. We looked at each other and I said, "I don't understand how this happened, but I know why it did. Mom wanted to say good-bye."

Later my father and I sat down and discussed everything. He said he knew I was upset about my mother passing away. He felt it was hard for me to accept her death and thought that maybe I needed some professional help.

So I spoke to the pastor of our church and told him of my experience. After this conversation, he told Dad he believed this really did happen to me because I was so sincere, mentally and emotionally. After that, Dad just dropped the subject.

No one will ever convince me that it wasn't my mother on the telephone that night. I always knew I had to listen to my heart and my own conscience and say, "Yes, this really did happen to me."

Penny was fortunate that the pastor of her church was willing to listen to her with an open mind and to accept her telephone ADC. But, more importantly, she trusted herself and never doubted that the conversation she had with her mother was real. One of the most empowering lessons we can learn in life is to trust the validity of our intuitive experiences and, when appropriate, to act upon them.

The final account in this chapter is from Hilda, who was contacted by her 82-year-old father about 2 weeks after he died from cancer. Coincidentally, she is currently employed in Florida as a telephone operator:

> We didn't have telephone service for two days because they were widening a two-lane street into a four-lane highway behind our house. We had a crew of telephone people in our backyard, and all the wires were disconnected and lying on the ground.
>
> My seventeen-year-old daughter, Greta, and I were at home watching TV when the telephone rang. I have three extension phones in my house, and Greta answered the kitchen phone – the only one that rang.
>
> She kept saying, "Hello? Hello?" But all she could hear was a sound like the ocean – like when you hold a large seashell up to your ear. So my daughter hung up.
>
> Approximately ten minutes later, the telephone rang again – only that one phone. Greta picked it up and said, "Hello?" and heard the same noise.
>
> Ten minutes after that, the phone in the kitchen rang a third time, and this time I picked it up. At first I heard the same sound, like ocean waves, but then I could hear a voice coming closer and closer.
>
> I heard my father saying, "Hilda, Hilda, I love you." He only spoke Polish, and he told me how much he loved me.
>
> I kept calling, "Daddy! Daddy! Daddy! I love you too!" But as soon as he spoke, his voice began fading away and was gone. Just the sound of the ocean remained, and then the line was dead.
>
> I looked at Greta and she asked me, "Mother, what's wrong? You look as white as a sheet!" I said, "I just heard Grandpa talking to me!"

I ran outside and spoke to the engineer in charge of the phone crew and asked him, "Are we having telephone service again?" He said, "No, ma'am. The wires are still lying here, and you won't have any service until tomorrow."

I said, "Are you sure? I just received a telephone call. Is it possible that they may have done something from the main office?" He said, "No, ma'am. There's no possibility of that whatsoever." He looked at me kind of strangely, and I felt I had better go back in the house before he thought I was crazy.

My daughter was right there with me when the phone rang three times. So I have a witness that I received a phone call from my father – when there was no telephone service whatsoever. I don't know what to think of all this, but I know it wasn't something imaginary.

What could cause a telephone to ring three times when all the wires were down and the phones were supposedly out of service? This isn't the only account of an ADC phone call that is baffling. A woman in Michigan reported she clearly heard the voice of her deceased mother on a telephone she had unplugged while her little boy was playing with it!

These have been a few of the nearly fifty telephone ADCs we collected during our research. Since telephones are simple electrical devices, some of our deceased loved ones can seemingly manipulate electrical energy to achieve this type of communication. Other people described receiving ADC messages on their telephone answering machines, pagers, tape recorders, radios, televisions, or computers. Those accounts didn't qualify to be included in this book, however, because we didn't have enough of them in our files.

Have you ever noticed any unusual physical events that occurred after a loved one died? The next chapter explores different forms of ADCs involving physical phenomena that the experiencers believe were messages from their deceased family members and friends.

CHAPTER 13

Material Matters:
ADCs of Physical Phenomena

Death is not the end, it is simply walking out
of the physical form and into the spirit realm,
which is our true home. It's going back home.
—Stephen Christopher

Many people who were interviewed reported experiencing an unusual physical occurrence following the death of a relative or friend. They regard these events as messages from their deceased loved ones. We call them ADCs of physical phenomena, which are a rather common type of after-death communication.

Examples of physical phenomena include lights being turned on and off; radios, stereos, televisions, and other electrical devices being turned on; mechanical objects being activated; pictures and other items being moved; and a long list of similar happenings.

At first we were very skeptical about these accounts. It seemed that whenever a door opened or closed by itself or a window shade rolled up without being touched, somebody would invariably say, "Grandma died a couple of months ago. This must be her way of letting us know she's still around."

However, the quality of the reports we continued to receive made it impossible to dismiss them all as mere coincidences or figments of overactive imaginations. Eventually we became convinced that some physical phenomena are authentic after-death contacts.

All the ADCs of physical phenomena reported in this chapter occurred while the experiencers were fully awake. The first seven accounts involve lights and other electrical devices being turned on and off.

Gloria, age 45, is the director of a hospice in Maine. She had this completely unexpected visitation the same evening her patient, Duane, died of complications related to AIDS:

> I turned off the light to get into bed and started to feel that somebody was there. I knew instantly that it was Duane! It was a total experience of recognition.
>
> In that moment of shock, I had an intake of breath. Just when I did that, the light went on, then off – then on and off again! It wasn't just a flicker – it was like somebody had turned the switch. Then I picked up a sense of elation from Duane and the message that he was all right.
>
> It happened! What I experienced was as real to me as going out and getting in my car.

Not only did Gloria experience her light being switched on and off twice, but she also sensed Duane's presence and felt his mood. Lights and other electrical devices can stop operating at any moment due to a power failure, a faulty circuit breaker, or a burned-out fuse. But there is no reason they should turn on by themselves when the switch is in the "off" position.

Dorothy is a 37-year-old medical secretary in Virginia. She had a series of playful ADCs shortly after her father died of cancer:

> One night, I was lying in bed and reading a book. I said, "Well, Dad, if there really is an afterlife, let me know." And my bedroom light went off!
>
> I thought, "All right, I asked for this." So I said, "Okay, Dad, if you're still there, let me know it," and the light came back on.
>
> A few nights later, I was lying there thinking about Dad again. And the light went off again! It did that two or three

different nights when I would be thinking about him. The light would either go off if it was on, or it would come on if it was off. I knew then that Dad was really there!

Dorothy and her father presumably achieved ongoing two-way communication when he responded to her thoughts by turning her bedroom light on and off several times. A few people told us of ADCs involving their touch lamps. They mentally established a code with a deceased loved one who answered their questions by blinking the touch lamp once to answer "yes" and twice to signify "no," or vice versa.

Carole, age 43, is a hypnotherapist in the Midwest. She had this timely response from her father 13 years after he died of cancer. A telephone ADC with her mother is described in Chapter 12:

My brother, Kenny, was living in Las Vegas by himself. He was critically ill, and they didn't expect him to survive beyond that night. Not knowing if he was going to be alive when I got there, I was struggling with whether or not I should go. I had to make an immediate decision.

As I was sitting in a chair and crying, I asked God, "Please, please help me with this decision. Should I stay or go?" All of a sudden, I could see my deceased father. He just appeared briefly, and as fast as he appeared, he was gone.

Then the lamp on the table blinked on and off three times. And I heard my father say, by mental telepathy, "You need to go and send your brother to the light. He's very afraid of dying."

I said, "I guess that answers that! I'm going!" I immediately got into gear, threw my stuff in a bag, and was out the door heading for the airport.

Since Carole's father wanted her to assist her dying brother in going "to the light," he evidently caused the table lamp to blink on and off three times to punctuate his request. Carole trusted his guidance completely and was at her brother's bed-side when he died.

Rebecca, a 48-year-old mental health counselor in Alberta, had this contact 6 months after her grandmother died of heart failure:

It was quite late, and my husband and I had done our usual routine. We had checked the kids, locked the front and back doors, and turned off all the lights. Then we turned in.

Something awakened me from a very sound, dream-less sleep. I sat up and realized Granny was sitting on the foot of my bed! I sensed her presence more strongly than I could actually see her. But I could see she was smiling at me.

I woke up my husband and said, "Granny is here! Look, she's sitting down by my feet!" He couldn't see anything and said I was crazy.

Then we heard something from the living room. We looked at each other, got up, and headed that way. The stereo and every light in the room were on! The dining room was lit up too. Even the kitchen light was on and the oven light. We were really freaking out!

As we passed the back door, it was unlocked and the outdoor light was on. Then we decided to go down to the family room in the basement. There the television was going, and all the lights were blazing too!

My husband went around the outside of the house and found the front door light on as well. There was noth-ing that could be on that wasn't on. Everything was go-ing – everything!

From that point on, I felt a sense of peace about Granny. Deep in my heart I knew she had come back to say good-bye to us. I know she is never far away – she is just in another realm.

There was nothing subtle about this extravagant display of physical phenomena! Apparently, when Granny realized Rebecca's husband was an ardent disbeliever, she instantly staged a spectacular electrical demonstration that even he couldn't possibly deny.

Katherine is a 47-year-old nurse in New Jersey. She had cause to rejoice long after her husband, Steve, died of a massive coronary aboard his sailboat:

> About five years after my husband's death, I was still missing him very much. I lay down in my bedroom with a little light on and was playing some soft music.
>
> I said, "Steve, I would really like to know if you're all right. But don't scare me or do anything crazy. I just need to know that you're okay wherever you are."
>
> There was a weather radio that he once kept on his sailboat. It had been in my bedroom for almost a year. You have to push down a button for it to play.
>
> Suddenly, it came on all by itself! It played and played until I shut it off. And then I knew Steve was telling me that he was okay.

Some people want to have an ADC but are fearful of actually seeing or hearing a deceased loved one while they are awake. So they will often ask for an indirect form of contact, as Katherine did, and are frequently rewarded in a nonthreatening way.

Alexis is a systems analyst in Washington. Her husband and she experienced these physical phenomena approximately 3 weeks after their daughter, Jeanne, died of cancer at age 31:

> It was about 11:30 at night and my husband, Rick, and I were in bed. He was sleeping and I was looking through a magazine. All of a sudden, the halogen lamp beside the bed flickered. Then, a second time, it almost went out and came back on. Halogen lamps never flicker – never!

I stopped reading and heard music playing. The music even woke Rick up, and he said, "Is there a car outside with its radio on or something?" I kind of smiled, thinking, "No, that's not it." I got out of bed and went downstairs to the living room.

Our stereo was playing the song "How Do You Talk to an Angel?" There is no way that stereo could have come on by itself! My husband is very fussy and goes around at night and checks everything. I knew then that all this had something to do with Jeanne. It was soothing to know she was communicating to us in these ways.

Later I asked Rick, "Would you have believed me if you hadn't heard the song on the stereo too?" He said, "Yes, I would, but probably nobody else will believe us!"

Experiencing unusual physical phenomena definitely stretches our mind because these occurrences seemingly defy the known laws of physics. But what is unknown today may be understood and commonplace tomorrow, as science is continuously proving.

Until that time, it will always be reassuring to have a witness present during an ADC, one who is sharing the same experience and can validate its reality for us. Then we'll be less likely to question ourselves if we encounter any skepticism from others.

Laurie is a massage therapist in Virginia. Bert, the father of one of her closest friends, kept his word soon after he died of a stroke at age 67:

Before he died, Bert indicated he was very fearful to pass over. So we talked about it in depth, and he gradually released his fear.

Then I asked him to let me know after he passed over if everything was as we had discussed. I asked this not only for myself but for my mother, who was also very fearful about death.

For some time I had been playing a music tape for Bert from the movie *Out of Africa*, and it became his favorite. He promised this music would come back to me in such a way that I would know it was not my imagination.

About two weeks after Bert died, my mother was visiting me. All of a sudden, in the early hours of the morning, I found myself standing in the upstairs hallway. Mother had come out of her bedroom too.

We were staring at each other wondering, "What on earth is happening?" We suddenly realized that the stereo downstairs was turned on as loud as it could go! And the music from *Out of Africa* was playing! There was nobody else in the house who could have turned it on. And Mother had double-checked everything before bedtime.

Bert had waited until Mother and I were together, and from then on her fears of death were gone.

We continue to marvel at the creativity demonstrated in so many after-death communications. Bert clearly designed an original way to fulfill his compact. The well-timed delivery of his musical selection not only provided a convincing physical signal for Laurie, but also gave her mother just the evidence she needed to overcome her fear of death.

The next five accounts are examples of ADCs that involve mechanical devices and other physical objects.

Esther is a nurse in Florida. She had this delightful experience about 3 months after her husband, Victor, died at age 66 of cancer:

I have to tell you about this music box. My oldest daughter gave it to me years ago after one of her trips to Europe. It was supposed to play "Lara's Theme" from the movie *Doctor Zhivago*, but it had not worked in a long, long time. It had been wound up, but it wouldn't play when I opened the lid.

One day I was resting in the afternoon. I woke up about thirty minutes after I had gone to sleep because I heard the music box playing – and the lid was still closed! I felt very peaceful and thought, "Honey, if you're around, that's a nice way to tell me." It played until it unwound completely.

I looked up the words of the song, and the last part speaks of meeting again someday. I thought, "That's really neat. I like that!"

We talked a lot during Victor's final illness, and I said, "If there is any way you can let me know there is something beyond this life, I'd like to hear about it." He was definitely a nonbeliever of this type of thing.

So I feel very comfortable with this communication. You could look at it as a fulfillment of a contract.

Several people reported hearing a music box suddenly begin to play, including some that had previously been inoperable. Each time this happened, they intuitively sensed it had been activated by a particular deceased loved one.

Maryellen is a victims' advocate in the Midwest. She and her husband shared this meaningful occasion with four others following the death of their 26-year-old daughter, Bonnie:

On our thirtieth anniversary, my husband, Rob, and I renewed our marriage vows with a beautiful wedding at our church. When we came back to the house, Rob and our daughter, Bonnie, threw a big surprise party for me. How they pulled it off, I'll never know!

Five months later, Bonnie was murdered in Florida.

On our next anniversary, my sister and her husband and my best friend and her husband took Rob and me out to dinner. Everyone was very conscious that this had been a special time for us only a year earlier.

There was a little clock on our wall that Bonnie had left with us when she moved to Florida. When we walked into the house at about a quarter to twelve, that clock on the wall was ticking away like crazy!

Everybody just stood there and stared at Bonnie's clock. We were all flabbergasted because it had not been running – it had never been wound or even touched!

A common feature in ADCs of physical phenomena is perfect timing, and many involve clocks and watches. Evidently, deceased loved ones intentionally create events at a specific time that will be noted by the experiencers and have personal significance for them.

Cecilia is a 44-year-old homemaker in Newfoundland. She had this touching communication after her 8-year-old daughter, Holly, died of leukemia:

Holly was sick for nineteen months, and I was with her day and night. Every night she would wake me up for a midnight snack.

One evening about two weeks before her passing, she said, "Mommy, instead of having a midnight snack, why don't we have a drink tonight? Can I have some Baby Duck?"

So I said, "Yes." And every night after that, Holly woke me up for her midnight drink of Baby Duck, which is a sparkling beverage.

After that bottle was empty, a friend brought her a new one. Holly was fiddling with the foil and the wire, but she was too weak to open it. I asked her, "Do you want Mommy to open it for you?" And she said, "No. I will open it myself when I'm strong enough."

The next day Holly passed away, and the unopened bottle was put on our china cabinet in the living room.

Three days later, at exactly midnight, there was a noise. When we looked at the bottle of Baby Duck, the cork had popped out and hit the ceiling and had come down beside it. The bottle hadn't been tampered with,

and there was no excessive heat in the house to cause
that to happen.

Then I felt Holly's presence and knew she was here
with us. And I realized she was telling me, "Yes, now I'm
strong enough. I opened the bottle of Baby Duck myself!"

Baby Duck is a light, sparkling wine produced in Canada.
Like some American champagnes, the bottle is sealed with a
plastic cork, held in place with wire, and covered with foil. It
would be virtually impossible for one of these bottles to open
on its own. Since Holly wanted her family to know her health
and strength were fully restored after she died, she apparently
found a way to open the bottle, just as she had promised her
mother.

James is a professor of music at a university in Missouri. He
had this endearing moment with his wife, Christina, who died
of cancer when she was 43:

The night after Christina's funeral, I woke up about
4:00 in the morning and went to the kitchen to make
some coffee. There were some glasses on the counter
close to the coffeemaker.

All of a sudden, one of those glasses rang out three
times, very loud and regular – loud enough to be startling.
I stood still and then shifted my weight from side to side,
to see if I could cause anything in the kitchen to move, to
ring, or to make a noise. But I couldn't do so.

Simultaneously, I had a feeling of great warmth and
got a communication from Christina, "Thanks, with love.
I'm okay now." Then I knew she was all right and released from a lot of pain and sorrow.

I think Christina wanted to show appreciation for
some really loving care I had given her for several years.
It showed me that her mind was still working well. She
could think, she could cause things to happen, and she
still had her sense of humor.

I like the fact that this experience dealt with sound –

because I'm a musician and so was Christina. I am absolutely sure it was not a hallucination and that it happened. It gave me a sense of great peace and wonderment and delight.

Christina's familiar personality and sense of humor came shining through to James when she created a musical sound or "love note" to gain his attention. Her short verbal message became the crowning touch that assured him of her complete well-being.

Madeline is a homemaker in Delaware. Her husband, Alec, her friend, Lilly, and she observed a gratifying physical display 2 years after her daughter, Sue, died of pancreatitis at age 36:

When Sue died I went to my minister and asked, "Why did God take my daughter away from me?" And he said, "Madeline, God didn't take Sue. He received her."

A couple of years later, I was in the kitchen getting coffee for my girlfriend, Lilly. In our living room we have a 5″ by 7″ black and white photograph of Sue and her older sister from when they were children.

As I was walking into the living room, I looked over at the picture and saw it was aglow! There was a yellowish light just around Sue's face, like the halo you see in paintings around the heads of saints. It was beautiful!

I was so taken aback, I hollered, "Oh, my God!" Lilly turned around and saw it too! My husband, Alec, came running in from the hallway, and he also saw the picture glowing. All three of us saw it!

It was a gray day, and the sun wasn't shining. So Alec went looking around to see if something else could have caused this, but he didn't find anything. The glow lasted three or four minutes.

I think the light came from God and Sue letting me know that she is fine. It was like Sue was saying, "Don't worry about me anymore. Now I'm watching over you."

When I saw my minister again, he said, "If you feel you want to tell this story, tell it. Because you saw a miracle!"

Light plays a dramatic role in several types of ADCs. Just as radiant light is often seen surrounding our deceased loved ones, it may sometimes be noticed emanating from physical objects as well.

The remaining five accounts in this chapter include a variety of items that were either moved or appeared spontaneously.

Iris is a retired hospital dietitian in New York. After being married 38 years, she was given some assistance by her husband, Jacob, who had died from cancer at age 76:

After my husband passed away, one of my neighbors called to tell me that the local tax bill was due in December. Jacob had always taken care of paying the taxes. He had been an attorney and had an office in our home where he kept all of his papers and legal files. He kept very accurate records and would not let anyone touch them.

So I had no idea where to look for the tax bill or even what it looked like. I spent all day looking and couldn't find it. I was so frustrated and angry! Here I was, left with the responsibility of taking care of something that I knew nothing about!

I stood in the middle of his office and started to cry. I screamed, "How could you do this to me, Jacob? How could you leave? How could you leave me with all this to do?"

Suddenly, as I was standing there, Jacob's appointment book opened! It's a fairly thick book with a hard cover. The book had been closed on his desk and I saw it open! I couldn't believe what I had just seen!

So I walked over and looked. The book was opened to a page in December, and there was the tax bill! And I just said, "Thank you, Jacob."

Because many husbands are in complete charge of the family finances, their widows are often overwhelmed when they must assume this responsibility. Jacob not only showed Iris where he had filed the tax bill, but he also revealed his system for paying future bills.

Joan is a homemaker in Florida. She was widowed when her husband, Frank, died of kidney failure at age 56:

> My husband, Frank, was always in the kitchen because he loved to cook. Before he died, he told me, "If I ever come back, you'll find me in the kitchen."
>
> Just before my husband's funeral, my son and I were in the kitchen talking. I have a tin measuring cup that Frank liked to drink out of because the water would stay cold in it.
>
> Suddenly that cup came right off the hook! It flew between us and landed on the floor! My son and I looked at each other, and I said, "Dad's here!" I know it was Frank because that cup couldn't come off the hook by itself!

An ADC may be so dramatic that our mind can't believe what our eyes have seen. If Joan's son hadn't witnessed this startling event, she might have doubted her senses and questioned her sanity.

Patti, a postal clerk in Kansas, had this provocative ADC after her mother died of adult respiratory distress syndrome at age 46:

> My sister, Rachel, and I went out to Mom's house to get clothing for her funeral. Our husbands came with us and stayed downstairs in the kitchen.
>
> We were upstairs in Mom's bedroom, and all of a sudden, we both felt her presence, like a feeling of electrical energy. At that precise moment, her heavy framed mirror, which was about four feet tall and two feet wide, came flying off the wall! It just came straight out over the top of

the chest of drawers and fell down flat onto the carpeted floor.

Rachel and I ran downstairs to our husbands and said, "Mom is in the bedroom!" When we told them what had happened, they tried to calm us down, saying there was a logical explanation for this.

So we all went upstairs, and my husband, Len, who was a carpenter, checked the mirror. The wire on the back was very sturdy and still intact. Then he checked the nail – it was not only still in the wall, it was very solidly in a stud!

Len was very puzzled and said there was absolutely no logical explanation for what had happened. But my sister and I just knew it was Mom trying to communicate!

We can't explain how a deceased loved one can cause a tin cup to fly through the air in a kitchen or a heavy mirror to do the same in a bedroom. But one thing we can say for certain is that those who have been present when ADCs of physical phenomena have taken place are not likely to forget them for a long time!

Glenda is a homemaker in Ohio. She was uplifted by a series of occurrences 4 months after her son, Randy, drowned at age 19:

It was a rainy day, and I was ironing in one of my upstairs rooms. As I was doing one of Randy's shirts, I started crying.

There was a small basket with a lid sitting on a desk nearby. When I looked over, a picture of my son was lying on that basket! I don't know how the picture got there. I know it wasn't there before because I had just moved the basket, and there was nothing on it.

It was a picture of Randy when he was about nine years old. He wasn't one to laugh in his pictures – he would only smile a little bit. But in this one he was laughing. In fact, it's the only picture I have of him laughing.

At first, it startled me because I hadn't seen that picture for so long. Then it calmed me down because I felt Randy was trying to tell me that he was happy. So I put this picture of him on the table by my bed.

A few days later, as I was getting some money out, this picture was in my billfold! The same picture! This time I left it in my billfold.

And then, a few weeks later, the picture was lying on my dressing table! Again, it was the same picture! And when I checked, it was not in my billfold anymore.

This seemed to happen when I was really, really depressed, when I was having a really bad time. I feel Randy was trying to tell me he was okay.

At first, a series of ADCs may seem like unrelated, random events. But upon reflection, we can usually determine a pattern and realize they occurred exactly when we most needed the emotional support they supplied.

The final account in this chapter is from Mildred, a retired real estate agent in Florida. She reported these affectionate incidents after her husband, Albert, died from cancer at age 70:

One time when Albert was still living, we were cutting up, just kidding each other. I said, "If you die before I do, come back and do something so I will know that it's you."

We had two little ceramic dogs. We kept them sitting on the windowsill in the kitchen. Everybody that knew us knew that when we were upset with each other, we would move the dogs apart, separating them. And whenever we were happy, they were kissing each other, snuggled up. Even the kids, when they came home, would go to the kitchen window to see how these little dogs were getting along.

A few days after Albert died, I was standing at the sink in the kitchen looking at the windowsill. His little dog was knocked over. Since I live alone, I thought, "I wonder how it got knocked down?" So I picked his dog up and put it back with the faces snuggled together. Then I didn't think anymore about it.

About three days later, his little dog was turned backwards, walking away from my little dog. They were about six inches apart! Then I understood that Albert wanted me to know that he had to leave me.

This really happened! But sometimes you are scared to tell people things like this for fear they will think you are nuts!

Albert chose a very familiar and trusted method to convey his message. Their long-standing form of nonverbal communication allowed Mildred to easily comprehend his intended meaning, "Now it's time for me to say good-bye."

These have been a few of the best ADC accounts of physical phenomena we've heard. They depict some of the many imaginative ways our loved ones can use to communicate with us after they die.

Have you ever wanted to receive a sign to assure you that a deceased loved one continues to exist? The next chapter contains a variety of symbolic ADCs that people experienced spontaneously or in answer to their prayers.

CHAPTER 14

Butterflies and Rainbows:
Symbolic ADCs

Ask, and it shall be given you;
seek, and ye shall find;
knock, and it shall be opened unto you.
—*Jesus of Nazareth*

Many people reported receiving a sign which affirmed that their deceased family member or friend had survived physical death and continues to live in another dimension of existence. We call these symbolic ADCs or ADC signs. They are a relatively common type of after-death communication.

Some people are sent a sign spontaneously as a gift, while others ask or pray to receive one. Depending on their belief system, they may ask their deceased loved one to give them a sign, or they may pray to God or the "universe" for one.

Typical symbolic ADCs include butterflies, rainbows, flowers, many different species of birds and other animals, and any number of inanimate objects. Whether a sign comes immediately or takes days or weeks to arrive, most people intuitively recognize their sign right away and feel it was intended just for them.

ADC signs provide much hope to those who are grieving deeply, especially bereaved parents and the widowed. But because they are a symbolic form of communication, the receiver must interpret his or her own experience and assign personal meaning to it.

• • •

In the first four accounts of symbolic ADCs the experiencers received a butterfly as their personal sign.

Caroline is a secretary in Illinois. She had this informative experience after her 24-year-old daughter, Lindsey, was killed by a drunk driver while riding her bicycle:

> After my daughter's Catholic funeral service, we went out to the cemetery. While Father was saying the final prayers, a big white butterfly landed on Lindsey's white casket and stayed there the whole time.
>
> When the service was over, Sister Therese hugged me and said, "Oh, Caroline, did you see the white butterfly too? A butterfly is a symbol for the Resurrection!" I never knew that meaning before, and this put me at peace.

The butterfly is the most frequently mentioned ADC sign. It is a spiritual symbol for life after death because of its metamorphosis, or transformation, from a caterpillar that crawls on the ground to a beautiful, almost ethereal creature that flies through the air. It has also become a symbol for personal growth and spiritual rebirth.

Margot, age 31, is a clerk for an antique store in Washington. She had this lovely ADC after her uncle died of cancer:

> We were at my Uncle Teddy's funeral in our Catholic church. I was praying during Mass and thinking of him. All of a sudden, this butterfly came fluttering down the aisle and stopped right by us. It was a real pretty orange and brown one.
>
> It fluttered around us, then turned and went up to where my sister was playing the piano. It did a twirl, then went over by the casket and up by the altar. Then the butterfly just flew off.
>
> It was wonderful! It was a miracle! As long as I have gone to that church, that is the only time I've ever seen a butterfly inside. Of all the churches in the world, how many do you think had butterflies in them at that moment in time?

Elisabeth Kübler-Ross often speaks of the numerous drawings of butterflies she saw in the barracks at concentration camps in Europe. These lasting symbols of hope had been scratched into the wooden walls by courageous children and adults during the Holocaust.

Today, pictures of butterflies can be found throughout almost every hospice. This symbol is also used extensively by many grief counselors, spiritual centers, and support groups for the bereaved.

Fran is a retired bookkeeper in Ohio. She was elated by this encounter 5 months after her 17-year-old grandson, Johnny, died from complications of spina bifida:

> I was sitting at my kitchen table looking out the glass storm door. A large monarch butterfly flew to the center of the glass. As it stayed there fluttering, a strange sensation came over me.
>
> I called my husband and we went to the door. The butterfly turned and flew to a large flower box at the far end of our deck. It fluttered around the flowers as we stood and watched for several minutes.
>
> I felt my grandson was here. Mentally, I said, "Johnny, if you really are here, please send the butterfly to the door one more time."
>
> Immediately, the butterfly flew to the center of the glass, right to my face. It fluttered there a few more seconds. Then I received a telepathic message from Johnny saying, "I'm alive and I'm okay." The words were very clear.
>
> This experience left me with the feeling that I'll see my grandson again – that there is life after death and that love is eternal.

A symbolic ADC can be distinguished from an everyday event by a combination of the timing, the setting, and the uncharacteristic behavior of a butterfly. But usually experiencers must rely upon intuition to identify the significance of such subjective experiences.

Al is a retired New York police officer now living in Florida. He had this unforgettable contact 10 months after his daughter, Diana, died in an automobile accident when she was 17 years old:

> On the Fourth of July, we were up at our summer home in Pennsylvania. I was there with my wife and her aunt, her uncle, and her cousin. We were sitting out on the lounge chairs, and I was having a cigar.
>
> This butterfly just happened to be flying around. I looked at it and right away thought of my daughter, Diana. I thought, "If it's you, Diana, come down and tell me." And it did!
>
> Immediately, the butterfly landed on my finger! It walked up and down on my finger, then onto my hand, back and forth. I could even see its little feelers moving. I couldn't believe it! My wife sort of looked at me – I think she knew what I was thinking.
>
> I finished my cigar and got up. The butterfly stayed right on my hand. I walked all the way to the house, went to the kitchen sink, and drank a glass of water. The butterfly was still with me – I couldn't believe this!
>
> I said, "Well, I gotta go take a shower. You gotta go outside." I opened the door and went out on the deck. I sort of pushed the butterfly with my finger and it flew off. I watched it fly away, down the yard.
>
> It was just unbelievable! Never had a butterfly landed on me before. Then I went in to take a shower and cried.
>
> I really didn't know that the butterfly had any significance to The Compassionate Friends until I went to their annual conference a few days later. During the opening ceremony, I realized, "Oh, my God! Their symbol is the butterfly!"

Founded in 1969, The Compassionate Friends has more than 650 local chapters throughout the United States and Canada. It is the largest self-help organization for bereaved parents, siblings, and grandparents in the world. For further information about

TCF and other organizations that serve the terminally ill and the bereaved, see the *Resources* section at the end of the book.

June teaches science at a junior high school in Illinois. She and her husband, Lyle, interacted with a close relative of the butterfly soon after their son, Chad, died of a heart attack at age 16:

> June: About two weeks after Chad died, I was in the kitchen, and my husband called and said, "June, come out here!" I went outside, and there, in the middle of the day, was this large moth. It was a chartreuse color and about five inches across. I had never seen such a gorgeous moth!
>
> Lyle: I found the moth out in the backyard. I picked it up and put it in my hand, and it didn't fly away. I've never seen a moth act like that before. Then I placed it on a branch of a bush.
>
> June: We called our sons, Cory and Clay, to come look at it too. We all watched it quite awhile, and finally it fluttered away.
>
> Later, I looked it up in a book on butterflies and moths and was dumbfounded! It was a luna moth, and luna means moon in Latin. Chad's hobby was astronomy, and he wanted to be an astrophysicist. The family the luna moth belongs to is *saturniidae*, and above Chad's desk is a picture of Saturn!
>
> Therefore, we all think Chad sent us this sign to let us know he is in a new life.

ADC signs often contain multiple levels of meaning. June's curiosity caused her to delve deeper and learn a great deal more about her son's message than was apparent at first glance.

The next three accounts contain rainbows, the second most common form of ADC signs.

Ellie is a data processor in Michigan. She received a splendid gift 5 months after her 26-year-old son, Don, died in an automobile accident. Her account of an earlier ADC with him is in Chapter 11:

> On my birthday in December, I was driving home from work. It was a cold, gray day, and I was feeling kind of blue because Don wasn't there.
>
> As I was driving down the street, I happened to look up. There in the sky the gray clouds had separated a little bit and made a perfect circle. Within the circle I saw the bands of the colors of a rainbow.
>
> It certainly is uncommon to see a rainbow in December in Michigan. I sensed immediately that Don sent me this rainbow for my birthday. It was my son's gift to me! I said out loud, "Thanks, Don! I got your message!"

As we're all aware, even on the most overcast day, the sun is still shining brightly behind the dark clouds. But when we're feeling sadness, it's important to remember that a sparkling rainbow may be up there too, perhaps right above our head!

Mindy is a postal clerk in Wisconsin. Her daughter, Kimberly, died of sudden infant death syndrome when she was 7 months old:

> Before Kimberly was born, we painted a huge mural of a rainbow and sunshine on her wall. Her whole bedroom was decorated with rainbows. And a lot of the gifts she received had rainbows on them. Kimberly was our rainbow kid!
>
> Ever since she died, on her death date and on her birth date, there are rainbows here. It's sunny, it rains, the sun comes back out, and then there's a big rainbow in the sky! That's Kimberly's way of coming to us and reassuring us that there's life after death.
>
> Last year on her death date, we went to her grave. As we were leaving the cemetery, a big rainbow appeared in

the sky in the east. It gave us shivers and chills and brought tears to our eyes – and smiles too!

The rainbow is one of mankind's oldest symbols of hope and eternal life. It's no surprise, therefore, that many bereaved people report seeing a magnificent rainbow on various anniversary dates following their loved one's death.

Belinda is a banker in the Yukon Territory, Canada. She had this symbolic ADC after her husband, Lou, died of cancer at age 65:

> I had three children who were all married, and I had eight grandchildren. Lou had always wanted to have a little, blue-eyed, redheaded granddaughter because my three children and I all had red hair, but none of the grandchildren did.
>
> A week before Lou died, my younger daughter, Shelley, phoned and told him that her pregnancy was confirmed, and she would name the baby after him. He was so excited he gave me some money right away to buy a present for the baby, knowing he might not be alive when the child was born. Within a few days, Lou went into a coma and died.
>
> Eight months later, a little granddaughter was born with blue eyes and red hair just like her mother. When I got the call, I drove to the hospital, but I was upset and crying because Lou wasn't there to see this baby.
>
> As I approached the hospital, a rainbow appeared over it! I felt the rainbow was a sign from God that Lou knew this was the little, blue-eyed, redheaded granddaughter that he had wanted so badly. It was a miracle!

Even eight months later, Belinda intuitively recognized the rainbow connection between her beloved husband and her newborn grandchild. While most people believe their ADC sign is a direct communication from their deceased loved one, others regard it as a gift from God on behalf of the one who has died.

Walter, a 58-year-old real estate broker in Arizona, had this transcendent moment after his wife, Arlene, died of cancer:

> It was a misty, rainy, totally overcast day. There was no sky visible anywhere. I spread Arlene's ashes around a tall ponderosa pine tree up in the White Mountains and said a prayer. Then I walked back to my car about forty feet away and said another prayer.
>
> As I stood up, a shaft of bright, golden light came through the clouds and shone around the base of the tree. It only lit up that particular spot where Arlene's ashes were. The light did not illuminate anything else.
>
> It was an amazing experience – it was just incredible! I thanked the good Lord. I knew it was God letting me know that Arlene was with Him again.

Several people reported seeing a beam of bright light suddenly shining on a particular object or place as Walter did. Some of these accounts describe a ray of golden light illuminating a casket during a funeral service or highlighting a memorial stone at a cemetery.

Flowers frequently play a significant role in symbolic ADCs too, as the next three accounts reflect.

Joanne is a secretary in Missouri. She was given a consoling sign after her 28-year-old son, Matthew, died by suicide:

> Right after Matthew's funeral, I removed a gorgeous mum from his coffin. Mums last a very long time, so I took it home and put it in some water and placed it on my kitchen windowsill.
>
> A couple of weeks later, the mum was totally dead. I remember thinking, "I can't bear to part with this." And I chastised myself because I couldn't even throw away a flower. But I put the mum in some fresh water anyway.

The next day the mum was totally alive again! I took that very definitely as a sign that Matthew was trying to tell me he was okay.

Flowers are very popular not only for their natural beauty, but for their powerful emotional and spiritual healing properties as well. In this instance, the revitalized chrysanthemum became a symbol of life after death for Joanne.

Raymond is a 59-year-old industrial designer in Illinois. He became a widower when his wife, Cynthia, died of cancer:

Cynthia and I had a Christmas cactus that was a little forlorn thing. It had never bloomed or shown any particular life. We kind of jokingly called it "Cynthia's plant."

After my wife died, I went on a trip and came home on her birthday. When I opened up the house and went around to look at the plants, here was this Christmas cactus bursting with a profusion of flowers!

Usually a Christmas cactus blooms around the holiday season. But Cynthia's birthday is on June 14th!

Symbolic ADCs can be viewed as nonverbal greetings from our deceased loved ones. It's as if they are saying, "Hello from heaven! I'm all right, I love you, and I'm watching over you and your life."

Darlene is a special education teacher in Massachusetts. She was thrilled by a life-affirming sign from her husband, Martin, who died of a heart attack at age 40:

Martin was a person who knew nothing about outdoor work or gardening. He managed to mow the lawn, although once he sliced through the cord of the electric mower.

One afternoon about six years before he died, he came home with a stick in his hand. He said, "Darlene, this is going to be a flowering plum tree." I said, "You've got to be kidding!"

He planted that stick right outside the kitchen window. Sometimes he talked to it, and lo and behold, it began growing. It grew into a beautiful, large plum tree, but never once were there any buds or flowers on it.

Martin died on Thanksgiving Day. The following Easter morning, I got up and went into the kitchen and looked out the window. I was totally set aback! There were millions of bright pink blossoms on Martin's tree! It looked magnificent!

My husband never believed in life after death or in God. So I found it interesting that this happened on Easter Sunday. There's no question the flowering plum tree symbolizes his new birth.

Experiencers regard these events as signs that their deceased loved ones are all right, while skeptics believe they are just coincidences. If reality is in the eye of the beholder, perhaps both views are valid.

The next three accounts demonstrate how various species of birds and mammals can also play an important role as ADC signs.

Pamela, age 43, is a librarian in Virginia. She experienced this stirring good-bye from her father after he died of a stroke:

After my father died, we took his ashes up to the Red River Gorge in Kentucky. It's full of holly, evergreens, and mountain laurel. We played one of his favorite songs and threw his ashes off the top of the mountain.

Right at that time, three red-tailed hawks came up from the very bottom of the gorge. They flew straight up, side by side, almost like an airplane formation. When they got just above us, they separated like a trinity. One bird flew to the left, one bird flew to the right, and one kept going straight up. It was astonishing!

I've hiked that gorge for years, and I've never seen three red-tailed hawks together. To me, this was my sign from my father. It was a final salute, the final "So long! Wish you well!"

We heard many accounts of symbolic ADCs that involved birds. Other species included blue jays, Canadian geese, cardinals, crows, doves, eagles, hummingbirds, ospreys, owls, pigeons, and robins.

Mary Kate is a bookkeeper for a business in Washington. Her husband, Stewart, died of leukemia at age 48:

Stewart's dream from childhood was to have his own airplane, and after we found he had leukemia, we bought one. Those five years we had with that plane were the happiest he had ever been. Stewart loved flying and the freedom he had in the air, and he loved the book *Jonathan Livingston Seagull*.

Around three weeks after his death, I was planning to go back to work for the first time – and I was dreading it! I was sitting at my dining room table just crying and crying.

Then I looked out at our deck. The biggest seagull I have ever seen in my life was perched right on the corner of the railing, looking in at me as if to say, "You can make it!"

I live about 350 miles inland from the coast, and I had never seen a seagull in my yard or on my deck – ever! So I got in the car, and the seagull followed me all the way to work!

Time and time after that, while going to work, I would look up and see this seagull following me. It was so clear to me that this bird was sent from heaven to uplift my spirits and give me the courage to go on.

I feel Stewart was there with me at that time looking over me. It made me realize that he is okay, that he's not suffering anymore, and that he's free to fly through the heavens like he did when he was here.

Richard Bach's *Jonathan Livingston Seagull* has inspired millions of readers to consider the possibility that life is eternal. After Jonathan dies and enters a new world, he encounters a teacher who encourages him to work on his lessons of kindness and love.

Phillip is a retired hotel pool and cabana manager who lives in Florida. He had these two outstanding symbolic experiences after his son, Gregory, died of leukemia at age 27:

When Gregory and his sister were very young, we took them on a vacation to Key West, Florida. During this trip, Gregory was able to swim with a porpoise at a recreation area. That was the biggest thrill he ever had as a child.

Through the years, Gregory loved the environment, loved the water, and of course, he loved porpoises. In fact, he loved everything in life. Before he died, he requested his ashes be placed in the Gulf Stream at sunrise so his ashes could travel all across the world.

After Gregory's death, a friend of ours picked me and my wife up very early in the morning in his boat. Our daughter came with us, and a friend of ours who would recite the Kaddish, which is a Jewish prayer for the dead.

We started out from Miami Beach, and it took about an hour and a half to get to the Gulf Stream. Exactly at sunrise, my friend said the Kaddish, and my wife placed Gregory's ashes in the water.

No sooner were the prayers finished than a school of at least six to eight porpoises came alongside the boat. The porpoises stayed with us, swimming on both sides, as they escorted us practically all the way back to the beach. But that's not the end of the story.

A few years later, my wife and I went to a regional Compassionate Friends conference in Clearwater, Florida. At the end of the conference, everyone tied a message of love for their child to a helium-filled balloon.

We all faced the Gulf of Mexico and released the balloons at 3:00. I asked Gregory if there was some way he could send us a message that he loves us, to please do so.

No sooner did we release our balloon than a single porpoise came swimming toward us, to within forty to fifty feet of the shore. It disappeared a moment, came back up again, and then just glided away.

These two experiences have given me delicious moments to think about and to keep inside my heart forever.

It's the extraordinary behavior of many kinds of animals that is so highly noticeable in these beautiful symbolic ADC accounts. Such signs are unmistakable to the experiencers because they often dramatically reflect the deceased loved one's long-term affinity for a particular bird or mammal.

With the exception of the last account, each of the ADC signs appeared to the experiencer spontaneously, and none of them had been requested beforehand. Significantly, they all involved forms of nature, and their symbolic meaning was immediately understood.

Many people reported they instinctively knew to ask for a sign to assure them that their deceased loved one continues to exist. Subsequently, most had a symbolic ADC experience very similar to the examples that have already been presented. The remaining accounts in this chapter are from people who specifically requested a sign from God or their deceased loved one.

Lucy, a bookkeeper in New Jersey, became a bereaved mother when her 9-year-old son, Steven, died in an automobile accident:

The night before the one-month anniversary of Steven's death, I was carrying on in his room, saying, "Give Mommy a sign! Give Mommy a sign!"

The next day I was in his room again. I had gotten Steven a kitten three weeks before he was killed, and the kitten was on his desk. But I didn't want anything touched on his desk because I wanted to leave Steven's room exactly the way he had left it.

Then the kitten knocked over a painted bottle that Steven had decorated! I quickly shooed the cat off the desk and picked up the bottle with my index finger in the neck. I felt some paper inside, so I pulled it out and opened it up. Steven had written in marking pen, "I love you, Mom!!!!"

I was so happy that I had gotten my sign! It made me feel so ecstatic that I was laughing and crying at the same time.

The kitten's actions at that very moment were essential for Lucy to find the written message from her deceased son. Was this purely "coincidental," or could it be that the kitten was prompted to play its part in a larger plan?

Claudia is a high-school teacher in Kentucky. She immediately recognized this sign was from her 12-year-old daughter, Jodi, who had been killed by a car while riding her bicycle:

This was about two weeks before the first anniversary of my daughter's death. I called out, "God, please let Jodi give me a sign! You have zillions of people up there with you. All I'm asking is that one little girl send her mother a sign that she is okay." I said this over and over all day long, and nothing happened.

That night I had to go to a meeting at my church. As I was backing out of the driveway, I happened to glance down. There was a pencil on the side of the road, and something told me to pick it up. So I stopped the car, got the pencil, and looked at it. On the pencil it said, "I'm OK."

There's no doubt in my mind that Jodi did this – that it was a message from her. Jodi was constantly drawing pictures, and I think the pencil was something she knew I could identify with her.

It really helped me through the first year's anniversary. For days I was just bubbling up!

Asking is a form of prayer that opens the door to receiving. Whether or not we're aware of it, this spiritual principle applies equally not only to ADC signs but to all other aspects of life too.

Peg is a daycare worker in Pennsylvania. Her prayers were answered by her 17-year-old son, Skip, after he was killed in an automobile crash caused by a drunk driver:

Skip always gave people roses. If anything special ever occurred, he gave a rose. He gave his girlfriend roses every Monday from the time he met her because he had met her on a Monday. If it was my birthday or if he wanted to get on the good side of me, he would bring me a rose.

A month after he died, I was talking to him, saying, "Please, Skip, give me a sign that you're okay."

Later, my three sisters were with me when I stopped at the cemetery. I said, "I wish Skip would just let us know that he's okay." One of my sisters said, "In time, he will." Afterwards, we went on to church, and all during the service I was praying that I'd get a sign.

When we came out and got in the car, I saw there was a rose stuck under the windshield wiper! It was a long-stemmed red rose. I knew immediately that it was from Skip. I just knew it! My sisters all started crying because they also knew that the rose was from my son.

I still have this rose, and it's still as red as the day it was put there for me!

The power of heartfelt prayer is truly remarkable. When we sincerely pray, we actively demonstrate our openness, willingness, and readiness to receive ADCs and other gifts of the spiritual realm.

•   —   •   •

Andrea is a supervisor for a water treatment facility in Florida. Her son, Douglas, was killed in a motorcycle accident when he was 25 years old:

> Douglas loved deer. He wore a beautiful deer pin on his hat. And a few days prior to his accident, I bought him a gold deer head for his birthday to wear on his gold neck chain.
>
> Eight days after his accident, I tried returning to work, thinking maybe it would help. As I was driving, I began to cry real hard. I pulled off the road and said, "God, please give me a sign that my son, my baby, did not suffer that night, that he knew no pain."
>
> As I looked up, within fifty feet stood the most beautiful deer and her tiny baby fawn. They were standing there looking straight at me. As I watched them, they didn't run. They just walked away until they were completely out of sight. I said, "Thank you, God, for letting me know that Douglas is all right."
>
> Many times this has happened to me. I will start crying really hard and breaking down, and when I look up, there's a deer. And I always feel peace and comfort afterwards.
>
> Hardly a week goes by that I don't see one. In fact, I saw three deer today!

Many people had a series of symbolic ADCs involving a sign from nature, as Andrea did. Others reported finding a number of inanimate objects. In each case, their particular sign had a personal association with their deceased loved one.

Sunny is a homemaker in Texas. An amazing series of events began 3 weeks after her 9-year-old son, Sean, died in an accident at his school:

> I was crying one day and talking to Sean, begging him to please send me a sign that he was still with us. After sitting for a little while, I had a feeling to get up and go into his room.
>
> I just wanted to open a drawer and touch his clothes,

to hopefully feel a little bit better. But I felt compelled to pull the drawer all the way out and to look underneath it. There was a dime! Then it hit me, "This is a message from you, Sean! This is you coming through!"

When I saw that dime, I thought back to a little joke that we had between us. I used to give Sean $2.00 a week allowance if he kept his room clean and did what he was told. As I gave him the $2.00, I would say, "This is for being a good son."

Then Sean would go to the little frozen juice can he had decorated where he used to put all of his change. He would get a dime and give it to me, saying, "This is for you, Mom. This is your allowance for being a good mother!" So when I saw that dime, I felt very good because I realized this was Sean's message to me.

I had never found a dime in my life before. As it happened, I started finding a lot of dimes after that, mostly at work. Then I started finding them on special days – on Valentine's Day and Mother's Day.

I would find dimes when I really needed them – at a restaurant, in a parking lot, in front of a pet store, walking our dogs in the evening, in a hospital when my husband had surgery, at a museum, in a pizza restaurant, and getting off a train. One day I even found two dimes!

My family wanted to know that Sean was with them too, so I asked him to please give them a sign. And soon they also started finding dimes!

Ever since Sunny received her first ADC sign nine years ago, she and her husband have continued to find "dimes from Sean" everywhere. Their current total is 640 dimes!

The final account in this chapter is narrated by Kathleen, who is a preschool teacher in Illinois. She asked for a sign 8 years after her 7-year-old son, Marc, died of leukemia:

My best friend saw rainbows a lot after her son died, and she always felt they had a special meaning. I would feel good for her but also a little envious. I recall thinking, "Everybody else gets these signs. Why doesn't this ever happen to me?"

Then I decided to attend a national conference of The Compassionate Friends. One of the members had made a gorgeous stained-glass window for a fund-raising raffle. It had two butterflies in it and was very colorful. I passed it several times during the conference and thought that we had a perfect spot to hang it in our house.

When I bought my raffle tickets, I said to Marc in my head, "For all these years I've heard stories of people who have had signs or messages from their child. If you are ever going to give me a sign, this would be a really good time to do it!"

I don't recall ever asking Marc before – it just came out very spontaneously. So I bought 10 tickets, and something like 800 tickets were sold.

The raffle was held Saturday night. As the winning number was being read, I thought, "My God, I'm going to win! Marc really did this!" I did have the winning ticket. It was overwhelming!

At home we refer to our stained glass window with the butterflies as "Our gift from Marc."

Kathleen's symbolic ADC proves it's never too late to ask for a sign, just as she did eight years after the death of her son. Regardless of the time that has elapsed since they died, our loved ones continue to assure us that dying is merely a transition to another state of being or level of consciousness.

This completes our presentation of the twelve major types of after-death communication experiences. All the remaining accounts in this book consist of various combinations of them.

The next chapter covers three topics: "fearful" ADC accounts, the issue of suicide, and lower levels of life after death.

CHAPTER 15

Exceptions to the Rule:
"Fearful" and Other ADCs

There are many rooms in the Father's House just as
there are many grades in school. The period of time we
spend on earth is but one grade of life. It is but a beginning.
—*Robert A. Russell*

This chapter explores three subjects that we were frequently
questioned about during our workshops: "fearful" ADC accounts, the issue of suicide, and lower levels of life after death.

"Fearful" ADC Accounts

Almost all ADCs are positive, joyful, and uplifting events,
and they generally accelerate spiritual growth. But for a variety
of reasons, some people may experience fear when one occurs.

Many have never heard of ADCs, so if they have one, they
may think they are going crazy or losing their mind. This is especially true if they are bereaved and don't have a support system that accepts the possibility of after-death communications.

Others, who are familiar with ADCs, may have irrational
fears or superstitious beliefs about such experiences that may
cause them to be frightened when one occurs. Their emotional
reaction can usually be attributed to cultural folklore and the
negative way these events are typically portrayed in movies,
television, and books.

Adults who have had an ADC may have difficulty reconciling
it with their own personal philosophy or religious beliefs. And

young children may become confused when they attempt to relate such experiences to their parents, who don't believe them.

Based upon our research, it is not the content of an after-death communication that is fearful but rather the experiencer's reaction to it. As the following examples clearly illustrate, the intentions of the deceased loved ones seem as positive in these accounts as they are in the other ADCs throughout this book.

Suzanne is an office manager in Florida. She was 18 years old and unprepared for this encounter 10 months after her grandmother died of diabetes at age 64:

> I was getting married, and everybody was preparing the house for my wedding reception. I was really tired, and they suggested that I run upstairs and lie down for awhile.
>
> I was just lying there staring into space and thinking how I was going to miss my grandmother at my wedding. I had always counted on her being there, and she had said she would be.
>
> All of a sudden, over to my left my grandmother's face and shoulders appeared! She looked as solid and real as anybody. She smiled with a little glint in her eye and said, in a perky sort of way, "Don't you worry, honey. I'll be there."
>
> It was like a bolt out of the blue! Unfortunately, this startled me so badly, I was terrified! I was scared out of my gourd! I screamed and started crying uncontrollably and ran out of the room and down the stairs. I was in a blind panic! My mother heard all this commotion and met me at the foot of the stairs, but I couldn't even talk.
>
> Later, when I told her about my experience, she just patted me on the arm and hugged me close, saying, "I think that's so sweet, dear."

No doubt a case of "bride's jitters" caused Suzanne to be more excitable than usual during this unexpected visit. Her grandmother's immediate response to her wish certainly gives validity to the adage "Be careful what you ask for because you just might get it!"

Charlotte is a 43-year-old nurse in New Jersey. She became a widow when her husband, Glen, died of cancer:

> The night Glen died, I needed to talk to someone. So I sat down in the living room and called my girlfriend, Joni, who lived next door.
>
> As I was talking with her on the phone, I saw Glen standing right in front of me, just inches away! He was as solid as a rock, and I couldn't see through him. But he didn't look the way he did when he was sick – he looked absolutely healthy!
>
> Glen leaned down and put his hand on my knee and said, "Charlotte, it's me. I'm okay. Everything's all right. I don't have any more pain. I feel great!"
>
> Well, all I did was scream! He scared the daylights out of me! And the more I screamed, the more he said, "It's okay, Charlotte. It's okay. It's okay. You don't have to worry about me. I'm okay!" That was it, and then Glen just kind of evaporated.
>
> I sat there frozen in my chair – spellbound with disbelief! Joni wondered what on earth had happened, so she came over and we talked, and gradually I calmed down.

Though Charlotte was shocked when she saw Glen and felt his touch, he was probably equally unprepared for her hysterical reaction. While we may feel wonder, or even amazement, during an ADC, especially by the suddenness of a partial or full appearance, it's not the intention of our deceased loved ones to frighten us.

Melissa is a certified medical assistant in Maryland. Dustin, her 6-year-old son, was hit by an automobile while riding his bicycle and died later from severe head injuries:

About a month after my son's death, I was lying on my bed. All of a sudden, before my eyes, I saw Dustin sitting on a hillside. The colors were so very vivid. The sky was a color blue I had never seen before in this world. I knew the wind was blowing because the tall grass was waving.

I saw Dustin's whole body – it was my son! His little legs were drawn up with his arms to the side. He had blue shorts on and a little top, and he appeared to be in good health.

But I only saw the side of Dustin's face. He was looking down at something, but I couldn't see what it was. He had a curious look like he was trying to figure something out.

This vision lasted about ten minutes. I remember opening and shutting my eyes, but it never wavered – it just stayed there.

Then I became afraid! I remember my heart was racing, pounding a mile a minute. I was afraid Dustin would turn toward me, and I would see him as he looked after his accident. So I prayed for the vision to go away, and it faded out slowly.

What might have happened didn't happen because my fear drove the vision away.

Melissa's anxiety during her ADC vision is understandable. If only she had been better informed, she would have known that all deceased children are healed and whole in their new life.

Hope, a 35-year-old nurse in New Jersey, panicked when her father came back to her 6 years after he died of a heart attack:

As I was waking up from a nap, I looked towards the doorway. My father was standing there with one hand on his hip and the other on the door frame! He had on his black suit with a white shirt and a black tie.

I was so scared because I knew he was dead! I just

kept shaking! I was trying to scream, but nothing would come out.

Then my father said out loud in his normal voice, "Don't be afraid. I'm not here to hurt you. I've never seen my son-in-law or my grandkids before. I just wanted to see them and to see you." He was smiling and studying my face with a loving look.

But I guess he saw that I was scared, because when I looked up again, he faded away right in front of my eyes.

I know now that my father didn't come back to hurt me. But every time I think about it, I get nervous. That's how real it was!

Several people we interviewed had superstitious beliefs that ruined their ADCs. For instance, a few believed if they ever saw someone who was deceased, they or another family member would die very soon. And others automatically assumed that a loved one had come back to harm them in some way.

Robert is an educator in Florida. His 12-year-old son, Robbie, died from injuries he sustained during a fall:

This was more than a year after my son died – it was about 10:00 in the evening. I had just finished cleaning the house and was preparing to move the next day. I was in the kitchen area when I heard a noise in the back of the house.

I walked into the hallway and saw Robbie sitting on top of a metal trunk! The top would clank if you sat on it – and that's the sound I had heard.

Robbie was wearing a red pair of jeans and a checkered shirt. He had very long, blond hair that glistened. He looked great – he really did!

He waved at me and said, "Hi, Dad! Don't worry. Everything is all right." He was speaking with an audible voice and was very upbeat. It was as if Robbie had not died – he was really there! I was taken aback.

I don't know if I turned away, but at my next glance,

Robbie wasn't there anymore. Then I was really frightened because I knew my son was dead and couldn't be there. My rational senses told me there was something wrong with me.

I walked outside and thought, "This can't be! I know my son is dead! He's been dead for better than a year now." But Robbie was so lifelike! He looked just as he did the day before he died.

On the one hand, I really felt good – on the other hand, I was afraid. So I went back into the house and walked to the trunk, but there was nothing there. I thought, "This is crazy! If I tell people this happened, they will think I'm strange."

Months went by before I mentioned this experience to anyone, including my wife. But I mulled it over in my mind constantly. I kept telling myself that I made this all up from the emotions stored inside me – and that it really didn't happen.

I've lived with this experience for a long time. Now I'm convinced it was a real happening and was not just a figment of my imagination. I've come to realize it was a very wonderful moment for me. It was only a few seconds, but it was one of the most significant few seconds of my life.

Many men question their sanity after an ADC experience and are reluctant to share it with anyone. In fact, they often dismiss it entirely, simply because it doesn't fit their concept of reality. On the other hand, women are usually more open and receptive to spiritual experiences. They are generally more willing to trust their intuition and not require scientific proof for what they know is true.

Fortunately, the majority of people we interviewed who initially had a "fearful" ADC went on to have positive ones in the future after they learned more about them and overcame their anxieties.

The Issue of Suicide

We are deeply concerned that some people who are reading this book may be feeling suicidal. And they might conclude from all the glowing accounts of ADC experiences they've already read that they can escape from their emotional problems by taking their own life. If you are one of these people, please contemplate the remainder of this chapter very carefully and then read Chapter 20, *Saving Grace*.

Based upon our research, if you commit suicide to avoid your earthly problems and emotional pain, you can expect to experience different consequences after your death than people who die from other causes. Not only will you bring all your incomplete lessons with you, but your premature death will create additional suffering for yourself and your survivors.

Marlene, age 38, is a network news technician in Maryland. Her boyfriend, Wes, had a rude awakening after he impulsively committed suicide:

> About a month later, Wes came to me in a dream that was totally vivid. But it wasn't just a dream – it was a real experience.
>
> He was surrounded by a fog in a desert wasteland. It was a lonely place that was mostly dark and bleak. He was wearing a tattered T-shirt and shorts.
>
> Wes was despondent and resigned. He was definitely not at peace. He said, "I've been sentenced." I asked, "To what?" He said, "I've been sentenced to eternal life!"
>
> Wes was a lost person, and I understood. He didn't find the peace he was looking for, and I felt immense sadness and pain. I told him I would pray for him.
>
> I woke up realizing it doesn't do any good to commit suicide because you're still going to be alive. You can't escape. It's not going to be any better after death. You have to live through this life and take responsibility for it.
>
> You are always responsible for your actions, whether

you're here or there. If you abdicate your lessons by taking your own life, you can't expect that death is going to take away the pain or change the lessons you have to learn.

It's impossible to end your own life. Suicide is not a doorway to nothingness. It does not lead to a state of oblivion or a void that will end all your emotional pain. The only thing you will succeed in destroying is your physical body. You'll bring all your problems, your sense of failure, and your uncompleted lessons to your new life. In short, wherever you go, you always take yourself with you.

Leeanne, a banking executive in Georgia, had a sleep-state communication with her 30-year-old brother, Chet, who took his own life after the sudden loss of his business:

> Chet had not been a chronically depressed person. He loved the work he was doing, and the success of his business meant everything to him.
>
> His suicide was so sudden! It was awful! My parents just couldn't bear it. I was the oldest child and had to handle his funeral and everything.
>
> Maybe six months later, he came to me in a dream and we talked face to face. He was extremely sad because of what he had done to his family.
>
> I remember Chet had a melancholy and confused look on his face. He was very sorry because we were all hurting – because we were all going through this pain. He didn't want to put us through that. He seemed remorseful and bewildered. He hung his head and shook it, like he just couldn't believe what he had done.
>
> This was more than a dream, and after I woke up, I was shaking. I felt sadness for my brother because I realized this was not what he really wanted.

If you commit suicide, you will create suffering for yourself and others. Like Chet, you will be acutely aware of and possibly even feel all the pain, all the grief, all the guilt, and all the anger of the people you left behind. No amount of remorse or number of apologies will be able to make up for the legacy of sorrow you will have inflicted upon your relatives, friends, coworkers, and, most especially, your children. Saying "I'm sorry" will not make up for what you have done.

Derrick is a news photographer in Texas. His brother, Kirk, was 21 years old when he died by suicide:

> This was the first Christmas Eve after my brother killed himself. I had gone to bed and had been asleep maybe three or four hours. I remember being awakened, and I knew Kirk was in the room – I could physically feel it.
>
> I was really scared for a couple of seconds, and then I could see Kirk, peripherally, off to my left. I knew it was him! His face was dark and shadowed, but he looked as solid and real as could be.
>
> I said I was glad to see him and wanted to talk to him. But all Kirk said was, "I'm sorry. I'm sorry I did that. I didn't want to hurt anybody. I'm sorry." I started to get panicky because I didn't want him to leave me again after such a short, quick visit. Then he was gone.
>
> Afterward, I walked around the house with no feelings and a million feelings at the same time. Kirk could apologize a thousand times for putting us through hell, and it still wouldn't make it any better.

The survivors of suicide endure an enormous amount of pain. They feel all the normal grief people experience following the death of a loved one, along with feelings of rejection and abandonment. And they must deal with such additional issues as guilt, blame, and the endless question "Why?"

However, there are many motivations for committing suicide. For example, some people decide to take their own life when they are suffering unrelenting pain from a terminal disease. Others with mental illness or long-term clinical depression or chronic physical pain may also choose to end their life prematurely. According to our ADC research, it appears these people are very likely spared the negative spiritual consequences that await those who are in good physical health but commit suicide as an attempt to escape from their emotional problems.

Rhonda is a medical transcriptionist in Nevada. She was only 21 years old when she had a sleep-state ADC with Hank, a family friend who was 45 when he died:

> The night before Hank died, he got his family and my family together. I was the only one who wasn't there. He told them about his terminal cancer – no one knew of this before. He told them he planned to take his own life, and the next day he committed suicide.
>
> Four days later, Hank came to me in a dream. There was a knock on the door, and when I opened it, he was standing there. He was very healthy, not sick at all. He looked completely normal, wearing a white shirt, a tie, and black pants.
>
> Hank had a happy expression on his face and said, "It's okay. I did this because I was dying and couldn't live with the pain anymore. You and your family will be fine. Everything will be okay for all of you. Go on with your life. I love you." That was the end of the dream, and I woke up.

Did you notice that Hank's mood and appearance were very different than those who died by suicide in the earlier accounts? His motivation for taking his life was also different, since he was terminally ill with a very painful form of cancer and was not merely seeking to escape from a temporary emotional problem. A few similar ADC experiences are contained in later chapters of this book.

Because everyone's life has great spiritual significance, we personally discourage suicide under all circumstances. Please obtain professional counseling immediately if you are feeling suicidal.

Lower Levels of Life After Death

"Does everybody go to heaven when they die?" This question was sometimes asked during our workshops. The answer seems to be "No, not everyone, and certainly not right away. Some may take a very long time, by earthly standards, to arrive there."

Most people lead pretty decent lives. They are willing to face their lessons in life, make mistakes, learn from them, and commit to doing better in the future. Evidently, they are promptly welcomed into heaven after they die, as the accounts in this book attest.

To our knowledge, no one who was interviewed was contacted by anybody who had committed malicious crimes or atrocities, so our ADC research didn't reveal anything new about their state of existence. However, some near-death experiencers and out-of-body travelers have reportedly visited hell-like regions of life after death where they saw countless human souls.

Between these two extremes, there are many who fail to make amends before they die for the suffering they have caused others. Following their death, it seems they are temporarily restricted to lower levels of existence, not for punishment but for their spiritual healing and growth. Apparently, they receive ongoing opportunities to advance to the higher levels of the spiritual dimension as they experience deep remorse, sincere repentance, and true rehabilitation.

Joel is a 43-year-old sales representative in Florida. He had a series of encounters with his father, who died of cancer:

> During the last few years of my father's life, he became an active alcoholic again. He caused a lot of destruction in the family, and frankly, it was kind of a relief when he died.
>
> After his death, I often felt his presence around me. I couldn't see him or communicate with him, but I could feel the agony he was in.

Eight years later, I started meditating, and my father started coming to me again. He wanted forgiveness. He couldn't move on to whatever he was supposed to be doing because of the horror he had created before he left.

He pleaded with me to ask everybody in the family to forgive him. Apparently, I was the only one who knew what he was going through.

So I began to tell different members of my family – my mother, my sister, his wife – of his pleading for forgiveness. It was amazing to me how well everyone accepted what I was talking about and that they started forgiving him. And when I too was able to forgive my father, it took a burden off my mind.

Then all of a sudden, it was like he was relieved, and he just wasn't there anymore. I felt so happy for my dad.

We become the primary beneficiary when we forgive another. By forgiving, we release ourselves from the bondage of resentment, anger, bitterness, hate, and the desire for revenge. This will allow us to receive the ultimate spiritual blessing, the gift of inner peace.

Wanda, age 37, works in the real estate industry in Florida. She had this ADC with her husband, Norm, who died by suicide:

A year after my husband passed away, I had a very vivid dream. Norm was in a place with other people. It was not a very cheery place – it was kind of dark and a little bit depressing. I remember feeling uncomfortable there, and I didn't have a very good feeling when I saw him.

I approached him and asked, "Where are you? What are you doing here?" He told me he was in a holding place. That he had to be there until his life would have been over on earth.

After this happened, I felt a lot better because I knew

Norm was okay. He wasn't happy and he wasn't sad, but at least he was in a safe place.

It's likely Wanda had an out-of-body ADC during which she experienced the emotional atmosphere of a "holding place" on a lower level of life after death. These seem to be centers for spiritual healing that assist people in working through the lessons that were left incomplete when they prematurely ended their life on earth.

Catherine, age 35, is a homemaker in Pennsylvania. She was asked for help by her father-in-law after he died of cancer:

I had this dream about four months after Pop passed away. His whole person was very clear, even though there was no light at all. There was pitch darkness around him – like if you cut out a picture and placed it on black construction paper.

Pop was pacing back and forth in an agitated manner. He looked very distraught and was very upset. He didn't even acknowledge my presence at first. He just walked with his hands behind him, looking down.

Finally I said, "What's the matter, Pop?" He turned and looked directly at my face with a dead-on stare. He said, "I don't like where I am. I don't like it at all. I did what I did because I had to. I had children to support. But I didn't mean for this to happen."

I said, "There is nothing I can do for you." He said, "Oh, yes, there is! You can pray for me!" I said, "All right, I'll pray for you." Then he said, "Tell everybody to pray for me!" As he disappeared, he looked relieved and repeated, "Don't forget. Tell everyone to pray for me!"

I woke up immediately and told my husband. I asked what Pop had done that would cause him to have so much regret. My husband told me when Pop was a young man and trying to support his children, he did some things that were illegal. I didn't know anything about that.

When my husband told his brothers and sisters, they all prayed for their father. And I felt compelled to pray for him too.

Occasionally our deceased loved ones will ask us to pray for them. This affirms that our prayers contribute markedly to their spiritual well-being and accelerate their advancement into the higher levels of life after death, just as many of the world's religions assert.

All the accounts in this chapter have been representative of similar ones in our files.

Have you been contacted by a deceased loved one before you learned of his or her death? The next chapter provides reports of people who had an ADC experience first and then were notified at a later time that their loved one had died.

CHAPTER 16

Timing Is Everything:
ADCs Before the News

Life is eternal.... Death is but an inevitable transition
that each soul makes when it leaves the physical body. It is
a freer state which does not limit the soul to time and place.
—Betty Bethards

This is the first of six chapters that will present persuasive evidence that after-death communication experiences are genuine. By the time you have finished reading all these accounts, you may agree that ADCs are definitely not hallucinations, fantasies, or memories caused by grief. Nor are they projections of the subconscious mind or products of an overactive imagination.

Perhaps you will be convinced that the people in this book, along with many millions of others, have had direct communication with a deceased family member or friend, just as they have stated. And that there is a new life after death that awaits everyone.

This chapter contains firsthand accounts from people who were contacted by a deceased loved one before they learned of his or her death. That is, they had an ADC experience first and were informed at a later time that their relative or friend had died.

In the case of a sudden and unexpected death, you would not feel bereaved until you received the news that a loved one had died. Therefore, why would you have a grief-induced hallucination before you were aware that a death had occurred?

In these first five accounts the deceased loved ones made contact very shortly after their death.

Melinda, who is now a homemaker in Washington, had this totally unexpected meeting with her friend, Tom:

> Tom and I grew up together. We were next-door neighbors, but I hadn't seen him since he entered the priesthood. I lost complete contact with him and his family after I moved to Texas.
>
> One night over ten years later, I woke up out of a sound sleep. I saw Tom standing at the bottom of my bed in a Navy uniform! When I saw his uniform, I couldn't believe it because I thought he was a Catholic priest! He said, "Good-bye, Melinda. I'm leaving now." And he disappeared.
>
> My husband woke up, and I told him what had happened. But he said I was just dreaming.
>
> Three days later, I got a letter from my mother stating that Tom had just been killed in action. I also found out he had been a chaplain in the Navy!

This is an excellent example of an ADC before the news, and it is also a strong evidential account. Since Melinda hadn't heard from Tom in over ten years, she didn't know he had become a naval officer. So there was certainly no reason for her to hallucinate Tom's appearance in his chaplain's uniform three days before she learned of his death.

Debi is a schoolteacher in Virginia. She was only 19 years old when she had this encounter with her friend, Gary:

> Gary and I were very close platonic friends. I was in college and had not seen him for a while, and he was a graduate student living in another city 250 miles away. When we were together, we talked a lot about religion because we were both wrestling with how we were raised versus how we felt inside.
>
> One night, I had a very vivid dream in which Gary

came and sat on the edge of my bed. He was extremely happy and at peace. He was in the best health ever, looking very radiant – a glow of white light surrounded him.

Gary seemed to know my thoughts. He talked to me about how much he loved me and how much he understood my love for him. Then he told me, "No matter what happens, you have to go on because you're on the right path." I felt like we were together, and then Gary was gone.

I woke up the next morning very troubled because I didn't understand what that dream was all about. But I went to my classes anyway.

When I got home that evening, I started making supper and turned on the TV. I heard on the 6:00 news that Gary had been killed the night before in a terrible car accident!

Like Debi, many people still aren't familiar with ADCs and may not recognize one when it occurs. This is especially true if they're not bereaved at the time. Even though she didn't realize Gary was saying good-bye to her, Debi's experience served the valuable purpose of preparing her to receive the news of his sudden death.

Francine, a 42-year-old nurse in Florida, was baffled by a visit from her patient, Roland:

I was working in an extended care facility. Some of the patients were up and about, and Roland was one of those. We developed a special rapport. I realized he needed to feel needed, so I gave him little jobs to do, and he always seemed thrilled to do them.

One morning between 6:00 and 6:15, I was getting ready to go to work. I sat on the edge of my bed to put my shoes on. I turned my head and saw a faint vision of Roland standing at the foot of the bed, smiling! I recognized his face instantly. He looked happy and relaxed.

I thought I was going off the deep end! I smiled back

at him, and then he was gone. I sort of laughed and said to my husband, "I'm really cracking up now. I'm not even at work yet, but I saw one of my patients standing here!"

I went on to work, and when I walked in, they told me that Roland had died of a heart attack during the night. I had the feeling he had come to let me know that he was all right.

Francine also wasn't familiar with ADC experiences and didn't know she was having one when Roland suddenly appeared to her. Therefore, it was only natural she might doubt her senses when he showed up in her bedroom. It's very likely Roland thought as highly of Francine as she regarded him, so he probably came to thank her for their special friendship and to say good-bye.

Sue Ellen is a homemaker in Florida. Her father delivered a personal message when she was 24 years old:

I was lying on the sofa. Suddenly, I saw my father very clearly! He was definitely there with me – I could see his smiling face.

I heard him say, "It's all right, honey. It's beautiful over here! I'm really happy, so don't you worry." Then he laughed and added, "Now I don't have to pay for all that furniture your mom and sister bought." Of course, I didn't know what he meant.

Almost simultaneously, the phone was ringing. I could hear my husband in the background saying, "Oh, my gosh!" He learned my father had just died from a heart attack. My father was only fifty-three and had been in excellent health!

After that, we got a letter saying my mother and sister had gone out and bought a house full of furniture just before my father died. But my father's insurance paid for all of it! That was verification for me that my experience was real.

I believe my father came to me because he wanted to be the first one to tell me he had died.

For Sue Ellen, her father's sense of timing was perfect, as so many ADCs are. He arrived just in time to cushion the shock his daughter would have felt when she learned of his unexpected death. Her father also provided a subtle piece of information about the new furniture, perhaps anticipating that Sue Ellen would ask her family for more details. And when she did, they confirmed everything he had told her, thereby validating the reality of her experience.

Clare is a certified public accountant in Oregon. She had this thought-provoking experience with her 56-year-old friend, Hugh:

Hugh and I had known and worked with each other for fifteen years. He was somebody who was very special to me in understanding and friendship.

While I was waking up early on a Monday morning, Hugh came to me. He pinched me to get my attention! I saw him! He stood there by my bed, wearing a white shirt with his sleeves rolled up. His mood and expression were really sad, as though he'd lost it all.

Hugh said, "I'm sorry, Clare. I didn't make it." He added, "Good-bye," as if forever. Then he just vanished. I sat on the edge of the bed contemplating his message. I was wondering, "What on earth?"

Then my clock radio switched on with the early morning news. They announced that Hugh's seaplane had gone down in the Columbia River the day before. He didn't make it ashore and had drowned.

Hugh had the foresight to visit Clare before she learned of his death from an impersonal source. His consideration for her feelings is reflected by his impeccable timing.

This ADC also demonstrates that not all people are completely happy after they die. Some who have died suddenly may initially feel bewildered, angry, sad, or cheated when their physical life is over. And confusion is often the dominant state of mind for those who are utterly convinced there is no form of life after this one. Such people may become disoriented after dying and assume they are merely having a very peculiar dream from which they will awaken shortly, safe and sound in their own bed at home.

In the next four accounts the time of the ADC contact is virtually simultaneous with the death of the loved one.

Lillian is a 57-year-old homemaker in British Columbia. She received some well-timed news from her husband, Arthur:

> My husband had suffered a massive heart attack and was in the hospital. After I returned home, I was sitting alone in our living room at 1:56 in the morning. All at once, I could hear Arthur's voice inside my head just as clear as anything!
>
> He said, "I must go on. I have other things to accomplish. My job here on earth is finished. Your job is not completed yet." Then I knew that the hospital would be phoning me soon to tell me Arthur had passed on.
>
> Approximately fifteen minutes later, the phone rang. It was the nurse at the Intensive Care Unit informing me that my husband's condition had worsened, which is what they usually say when someone has died.
>
> The children were home so I woke them up, and we all went to the hospital. The nurse met me outside the ICU door, and I said, "Yes, dear, I know my husband has died." She was shocked when I quoted the exact time to her that was on his death certificate – 1:56 a.m.

The timing of an ADC before the news may coincide exactly with the death of a loved one. This will add another element of credibility to the experience that others cannot readily deny or dismiss.

•   •   •

Vicky is a 53-year-old office manager in Ohio. She certainly never expected to be contacted by her grandfather:

> I remember waking up, and almost instantaneously, this amazingly bright blue-white light was hovering near the ceiling. It was a large oval shape, about four feet tall and three feet wide.
>
> As I was looking at it, I was told telepathically that it was my maternal grandfather, who had just passed on to the next world. I remember thinking this was really strange because I had no idea he had been ill. In fact, I didn't have any close association with this man. He was a little ornery and had a poor relationship with other members of the family.
>
> The light lingered for a while, and after it left I looked at the clock and discovered it was 2:17 a.m. Then I went back to sleep.
>
> The following morning my sister knocked on my front door. I knew why she had come and said, "You came to tell me that Grandpa died, didn't you?" She looked puzzled and said, "Mom called to tell us that he died of a heart attack at about 2:30 a.m." I said, "No, it was 2:17 a.m.," and I told her what had happened.

Clearly, Vicky was not in a state of anticipatory or preparatory grief when she was visited by her emotionally distant grandfather. In fact, there was nothing about their relationship that would cause her to hallucinate or fantasize such an experience. However, it's not at all unusual for some people to "make the rounds" after they die, in their attempt to say good-bye to several relatives and friends.

Loretta, age 38, owns a veterinary hospital in Arizona. She was very grateful for the kindness of her mother-in-law, Yvonne:

> Yvonne needed around-the-clock medical assistance. So I quit my job to take care of her. While I was there for

three months, she came to love me as a daughter, and I came to love her as a mother. Then we had to check her into a hospice facility.

The next day, I was lying in my bed around 8:00 in the morning. All at once, I heard Yvonne calling my name! I just couldn't believe it! I heard her a second time, louder and more distinctly, say, "Loretta!"

I sat up and very clearly saw my mother-in-law standing at the foot of my bed! The first thing to hit me was that she had her own blond hair. With the radiation and chemo, she had become 100% bald and wore wigs. I was so shocked! She had on a pure white gown with very simple lines, like a choir robe.

Yvonne said my name a third time, and I said, "Yes?" She said, "I want to say good-bye now. I love you." Then there was nothing but a wisp of white smoke where she had been standing. I knew in that second she had died.

Several weeks later, we obtained Yvonne's official death certificate. The time of her death was recorded as 8:02 a.m. – the exact time and day she had come to me!

What greater honor can our loved ones bestow upon us than to personally deliver a loving message as soon as they die? To hear from them directly, before the news arrives, satisfies many of our emotional needs. In addition, this assures us they have survived physical death and are healed and whole as they enter their new life, which may spare us any concern we might otherwise have for them.

Dominic is a 38-year-old physician in Florida. He gained an important awareness while he and a classmate isolated themselves in a country cottage to study for their medical school examinations:

While my friend and I were studying, I experienced the extremely strong and distinctive smell of a medication that my mother used on Grandmother – camphor and alcohol. This home remedy was used as a cold compress that was applied to her forehead when she was feeling weak.

There was definitely no alcohol or camphor in the cottage. Yet the odor was so strong that I told my friend I believed my grandmother had just died. He sort of brushed it off, but I noted the time when it happened, 10:10 a.m.

Shortly after that, I felt the very peaceful presence of my grandmother. I realized that something extraordinary was happening! The whole feeling was that she was saying, "Good-bye. Don't worry. Everything is fine."

Grandmother had Alzheimer's disease. In the last months of her life, she was incoherent. But when I felt her presence, she was the person I had known before she became ill. She left me with a sense of relief and serenity and peace.

When I went home that day, my mother was waiting for me. She said, "Your grandmother has taken a turn for the worse." I told her, "Don't worry. I know what happened. She died at 10:10 this morning." Then my mother confirmed that my grandmother had died at exactly that time.

When Dominic's grandmother visited him, he was given an invaluable lesson that is rarely taught in most Western medical schools. He learned that his grandmother is an eternal being who merely discarded her earthly body like an old, worn-out garment. Imagine a world in which all medical caregivers have such knowledge.

This ADC also illustrates that when someone is afflicted with Alzheimer's or another debilitating disease, only the physical body is impaired, while the spiritual body is not affected. This explains how Dominic's grandmother could be healed and whole immediately after dying, despite the fact she had been severely incapacitated before she made her transition.

The next four accounts are examples of having an ADC before receiving the news, even when great distances are involved.

Brian, a chiropractor in Washington, was paid an impromptu visit by his grandfather, who was 74 and lived in New York:

> I was in California staying at a friend's house. It was evening, and I was lying on the couch in a darkened living room watching television.
>
> Between 10:00 and 11:00, I felt my grandfather's presence. Then the image of his face appeared before me – he was there in the room! I knew right away that he had come to tell me he had passed over.
>
> He communicated telepathically that he was saddened because he never had his 75th birthday party. This was something he had been trying to arrange and had been very preoccupied with. After he communicated this to me, the image of him left.
>
> The next morning I received a phone call from my father. My grandfather had passed away from heart failure between 1:00 and 2:00 in the morning in New York. That was Eastern time, the same as 10:00 to 11:00 p.m. Pacific time in California.

Contrary to some people's beliefs, evidently neither time nor space are barriers or limitations for our deceased loved ones, just as Brian's communication from his grandfather illustrates. Regardless of the distance involved, when different time zones are accounted for, the instant a loved one died and the time an ADC occurred will often be the same.

Fay, a 57-year-old psychotherapist in New Mexico, received validation from her Aunt Marion, who lived in Missouri:

> Aunt Marion and I always had a real connection with one another even though she lived in Missouri and I lived in California. When she was diagnosed with cancer, I flew to Missouri and spent a lot of time with her.

We often talked about what I had learned about death and dying, and I told her how important it was to go towards the light when we die.

One morning, in California, I woke up and was in that halfway state. I heard Aunt Marion's voice just as clearly as if I were in her hospital room. She said, "I just want you to know that you were right. I see the light! It makes me feel warm all over. I'm going now, and I want you to know that I love you."

I opened my eyes and looked around and thought, "What an incredible thing! Was this a dream, or was I imagining it?" I was puzzled and told my husband about it when he woke up.

Later that day, I received a phone call saying that my aunt had died that morning. I'm sure if I got a copy of her death certificate, it would verify that she died the same moment that I heard her voice.

I knew she had been ill, but I had no idea she was going to die so soon. At least I know Aunt Marion went to the light!

Almost universally, spiritual teachers instruct their students to "go towards the light" when they die. They tell us that at the moment of death we will see a brilliant clear or golden-white celestial light. By moving towards this totally loving and compassionate light, we can expect to be guided to our true heavenly home.

Kris, age 29, is a college student in Florida. He was surprised to see his grandfather, who was 73 and lived in Germany:

My grandfather raised me until I came to the United States. When I had to leave Germany, I sat next to him on the couch and held his hand. I knew he had cancer and wasn't going to be with us much longer.

Two months later in Florida, on the night of February 5th, I was sleeping and woke up at exactly 3:00 a.m. It was the strangest thing in the world! My grandfather was sitting on the right side of my bed, looking down at me, smiling. I got goose bumps, of course, though I wasn't scared. In fact, I was very relaxed and calm.

He was wearing a light blue, short-sleeved shirt, his silver watch, and his glasses. He looked just like he did when he was sixty. He was very clear and solid. He looked happy and healthy, as if he had just come from the doctor with an A-1 report card.

Grandpa always was a very firm man, a disciplinarian. But for that moment, he was happy to see me, and I could do no wrong. It seemed like he was approving of me, like he was proud of me, and everything was all right. I experienced his peace.

I closed my eyes for a moment, and when I looked again, there was nothing there. Everything was fine, so I fell back to sleep.

Later I called my mother in Germany. She told me Grandpa had died at 9:00 a.m., which is the exact time that he came to me! The time in Germany is six hours ahead of the United States.

This is another example of someone not only being healed and whole following his death, but appearing much younger, happier, and freer too. And his nonverbal communication to his grandson conveyed more love and approval than he had expressed before.

Sherry, a 52-year-old medical claims examiner in Washington, had this reunion with her grandfather, who lived in Massachusetts:

Our family planned to move from California to Minnesota to get out of the rat race. My two daughters and I went ahead of my husband and son. We were at a campground in Minnesota. I hadn't told any of my family, so nobody knew where we were.

That night a storm arose, so we couldn't sleep in our tent – we had to stay in the station wagon. I wasn't sleeping because it was one of those horrendous Minnesota storms with thunder, lightning, and pouring rain.

I happened to look out the front window, and I saw my grandfather there! I could see him very clearly, wearing a plaid shirt and suspenders. There was a whitish light around him, almost as if a spotlight was shining on him. His eyes were twinkling like there was a joke between the two of us.

I said, "What are you doing here? Get in out of the rain!" Grandpa smiled and said, "No, I'm fine. I just wanted to see you and say good-bye." I could hear him as if he was inside the car with me. And then he disappeared.

A month later, we settled in a house and got a phone. I called my mother in Massachusetts and told her where we were. She said, "I'm afraid I have some bad news for you. Grandpa died." I said, "I know that," and told her the date and the time that he had died. She said, "You're right! How did you know that?" I said, "Well, he came and said good-bye to me."

I still can't figure out how Grandpa found me in the woods in Minnesota within seconds after he died – it's beyond my comprehension!

Perhaps our deceased loved ones are able to locate us anytime and anywhere simply by applying their intuition, and if appropriate, they can travel instantly in their spiritual body to be with us. These are reportedly two of the many expanded abilities all of us will have when we enter the higher levels of life after death.

An ADC before the news can sometimes prepare us for an unforeseen event. Marilyn, a nurse's aide in Florida, was only 17 when she was bewildered by this experience with her grandmother:

When my mother remarried, my stepfather adopted me. His mother and I became very close. She always wanted to make me feel like I wasn't an outsider. Sadly, she had cancer of the spine that was very, very painful, and it caused her to be bent over.

One night, I went to bed early and drifted off to sleep. All of a sudden, the whole room lit up and Grandma was standing there! She was standing upright!

She was under a trellis with beautiful roses around her. There was a mist at her feet and a very vivid blue sky with white cushiony clouds behind her.

Grandma said, "Marilyn, tell your mom that I'm at peace now. Tell her that she has to understand how I died. I'm with our loved ones here. Someday you will share this love and joy with us."

I said, "Grandma, what are you doing there?" She said, "I'm at peace, Marilyn. Just tell your mom. Ask her to understand my messages." But I didn't know what she meant!

I started crying, and Mom came running in and said, "What's the matter?" I said, "You gotta call Grandma!" She asked, "Why? It's quarter after ten. She's already gone to bed!" I said, "You gotta call her. Something's the matter!"

Mom called Grandma's house. The phone was answered by another granddaughter, Lucy, who was sobbing. Ten minutes before, Lucy had seen the lights on at Grandma's and stopped by. She found Grandma dead in the bedroom!

The sad thing is that Grandma had committed suicide. She was in such pain from her cancer that she just couldn't take it anymore. She had laid out her clothes for her funeral – her dress, her shoes, everything. And she had left written messages asking everybody to forgive her.

Marilyn's grandmother took her life because she couldn't bear the pain of spinal cancer. But it seems she didn't suffer any negative consequences from committing suicide under these circumstances.

Understandably, most people with a terminal disease fear the physical pain that may accompany it. Receiving hospice care can be of great assistance to them because the personnel are trained experts in all aspects of pain management. If you or someone you know has a terminal illness, we urge you to contact a local hospice to learn about the outstanding physical, emotional, and spiritual support its programs provide to patients and their families.

The final account is from Christine, a 37-year-old real estate manager in Florida. The blessing of compassion was bestowed upon her at the precise instant she truly required it:

Our fourteen-year-old daughter, Heather, was spending the night at her girlfriend's house. My husband and I had gone to bed at 11:00.

I was asleep when the telephone rang and woke me up about 1:00. A dispatcher on the other end said, "Mrs. Baker, the police are at your front door. Would you please answer it?" I said, "Okay," and hung up the phone and kind of just sat there on the side of the bed. I was thinking, "Did I leave the light on in the car or what?"

I put my robe on and was zipping it up as I got to the door of our bedroom. In the hallway, I could see Heather and her grandfather, whom she had been very close to. But he had been dead for six years!

They were standing in the air, and he had his arm around her. They were very solid, and I could see them just as clear as day. It stunned me! I kind of shook my head and thought, "Why am I seeing Dad with Heather?"

Then Dad said, "She's okay, Baby. I have her. She's fine!" He was my father-in-law and he always called me "Baby." It was his voice – I could hear him. Dad was smiling at me and was very peaceful. They were both very happy. I shook my head again in amazement.

The minute I opened the front door, the police were standing there, and they asked me to sit down. I said,

"Tell me what's wrong. Please, just tell me!" They told me Heather had been killed in a tragic car accident.

I realized later that Dad was trying to lessen the blow for me, and I knew Heather must be with him. This experience has helped me in accepting the loss of my only child.

The timing of Christine's experience was absolutely perfect. It assured her that her beloved daughter was healed and whole and had been greeted immediately and safely by the welcoming arms of her loving grandfather.

These have been a few of the numerous accounts in our files of ADCs before the news. They offer persuasive evidence for disproving the common psychological assumption that after-death communications are merely bereavement fantasies caused by grief. Since none of the experiencers in this chapter were aware that a loved one had died before they were contacted, they wouldn't have been grieving when they had their ADC. Therefore, they had no reason whatsoever to hallucinate such an experience.

Do ADCs only occur shortly after a loved one has died? The next chapter examines after-death communications that took place five or more years later.

CHAPTER 17

Expect the Unexpected: ADCs Years Later

My mother and sister must be very happy to be home with
God, and I am sure their love and prayers are always with me.
When I go home to God, for death is nothing else but going
home to God, the bond of love will be unbroken for all eternity.
—*Mother Teresa*

Most after-death communications are experienced during
the first year following the death of a loved one. Many others
take place, with decreasing frequency, within the second to
fifth year.

This chapter contains accounts of ADCs that occurred five
or more years after the death of a family member or friend.
Though they are moderately common experiences, few people
are aware of them yet because so little in-depth research has
ever been conducted in this field.

Any of the twelve types of ADCs may be experienced five,
ten, twenty, thirty, or more years following a death. The motivations behind them and their messages generally have a more
specific purpose than earlier contacts.

This chapter offers evidence that your deceased loved ones
still feel a sense of connection with you, even many years after
their death. Evidently, they are aware of your daily life and are
watching over you with love and compassion. And they may attempt to communicate with you for a variety of reasons, especially to provide guidance or protection against harm.

The ADC accounts in this chapter are arranged according to
the length of time they occurred after the death of a loved one.

Donna is a chemical dependency counselor in Maine. She was contacted 5 years after her father died of chronic alcoholism at 42:

> I sat up one night, wide awake, and my father was standing at the foot of my bed! He was a glowing, iridescent figure about six feet tall. He was semi-solid and in good health. I recognized his facial features – his high cheekbones and his fairly large nose with a little mustache underneath.
>
> His expression was one of sadness and repentance. I heard an external voice as he said, "Donna, I'm so sorry. I'm just so sorry." Then he stood there for a brief moment and was gone.
>
> I knew my father was apologizing for all the abuse and the incest he had inflicted on me. When he said those words, all my rage and hate left, and this wonderful feeling of joy washed over me. I was at peace for the first time in a lot of years – I had a total sense of peace.
>
> My father's apology changed my whole life – it really did! That was a time when people were not talking about incest because it was still a taboo subject. But from that point on, I began to talk about it and began my own healing process. You have to talk to become a survivor!
>
> Twenty years have passed, and I have become a totally different person than I would have been if I hadn't had that experience. Today I'm able to look at my father with love and compassion and understanding. Now I am a survivor of incest!

Understandably, a woman who has been a victim of sexual abuse might not welcome a visit from the one who betrayed her and inflicted so much horror upon her life. But in this case, Donna was receptive to her father's apology, and their brief meeting proved to be a turning point in her eventually becoming a survivor of incest.

This account also indicates that someone who caused so

much suffering while on earth can still grow spiritually after his death. Her father's willingness to accept responsibility for what he had done and his sincere remorse and repentance were the necessary first steps in his own long-term rehabilitation process.

Jim is a publisher in Florida. He was 21 years old when he had this heartfelt reunion with his father, who had died 6 years earlier from a heart attack:

My family had a log cabin in Michigan on a river. I always loved that place and trout fished there. It was the best place of my childhood.

Shortly after my discharge from the Army, I went up to the cabin alone in the middle of February. They had plowed the road, but the snow was four feet deep across the fields and woods. The cabin is about a mile from the road.

I got out of the car at 1:00 in the morning and began to cross the field. I could see our cabin on the river bank in the moonlight. I would take three or four steps and then break through the crust of the snow, dropping in past my knees. I had to struggle to get back up on the snow to keep going.

I felt there was a presence with me. One of the times I fell, I distinctly heard a voice say, "Welcome home." I had a sense of my father, a visual sense, just as though the image of him was between me and the cabin. He had a happy look, and it made me feel wonderful!

I suddenly began to walk on top of the snow and didn't break through anymore. I got to the cabin and started the fire in the fireplace and lit the oil stove.

It was a beautiful night. My father was with me and I felt his presence. He was happy to have me there. I began to cry and touch into my father very closely, probably closer than I ever had in his earth life.

It was a very spiritual experience, one I will remember the rest of my life.

Many parents and children find it difficult to express feelings of love for each other while both are still physically alive. An ADC experience will often present them with an opportunity to finally achieve a deeper level of emotional and spiritual communion.

Lenore, a horse trainer and riding instructor in Arizona, had this exciting ADC 9 years after her father died of cancer at age 47:

This was my wedding day. I was walking down the aisle with my stepfather. I glanced off to my right because a beam of light caught my eye. As I got closer, the light became the form of a man. I knew it was my dad!

As I got up to where he was sitting, he turned around and looked at me. He had a real soft, misty light around him. His eyes were twinkling and he smiled. Then he winked and kind of nodded with approval.

I was so overwhelmed! It was real hard for me to hold back the tears because I wanted to run up and hug him. Then I looked again and he was gone.

I was real happy to see my dad. It was as if he didn't want to miss his baby girl's wedding. I couldn't have asked for a better wedding gift!

There is abundant evidence our deceased loved ones are often present to celebrate the special events in our lives. Such visits affirm not only their approval and love but express their spiritual blessings as well.

Adeline, a homemaker in North Carolina, was asked to convey a message about 9 years after her Uncle Ned died in his 40s:

Uncle Ned was an active alcoholic and a shifter from one thing to another. My family was so afraid that he hadn't asked God to forgive him for his sins before he died.

I was at home by myself one night, in bed reading, and then I turned my bedside light off. I looked at the foot of my bed, and Uncle Ned was standing there! He was in good health and seemed pretty solid.

My mother's name is Millie, and her sister's name is Belle. Uncle Ned was very calm and said, "Tell Millie and Belle that I am all right now. And tell them to stop worrying about me." Then he just gradually faded away.

I was so excited, I couldn't sleep a wink that night! Early the next morning, I got in my car and headed out to tell them. Once there, I got cold feet because my mother and Aunt Belle are very, very orthodox in their thinking.

All day long something was hunching me to tell them. But I was afraid they'd have the papers signed and send me off to a mental institution. So I drove home that afternoon.

The next morning I headed back. When I arrived, Aunt Belle came out of her bedroom and said, "I'm so glad you're here. You'll understand this. Your mother thinks I've had a dream, but I know I was awake!"

She went on, "I was lying in my bed reading my Bible last night. I turned out my light and was getting ready to say my prayers. Suddenly, Ned appeared at the foot of my bed! He looked at me and said, 'Belle, I want you and Millie to stop worrying about me. I'm all right now.' "

When Aunt Belle said that, cold goose pimples went all over me. I said, "Mama, Aunt Belle did not have a dream! The same thing happened to me! I've been wanting to tell both of you to stop worrying about Uncle Ned. He's all right. Stop holding him here. Let him go and do God's work." Then they both cried and cried and cried.

Uncle Ned suffered from the disease of untreated chronic alcoholism, which surely destroyed much of his adult life and his relationships with others. Reportedly, there are many healing centers in the spiritual realms for people who have such illnesses. There, with the help of devoted caregivers, our deceased loved ones are able to undergo emotional, mental, and spiritual recovery and finally achieve the wholeness they didn't have on earth.

Roberta is a homemaker in California. She became a bereaved mother when her 4-year-old son, Timothy, was hit and killed by a car. She was graced with this intimate visit 10 years later:

> I was sitting up front in church because I was in the choir. I wasn't even thinking about Timothy – I was just listening to the speaker.
>
> Suddenly, I felt this warm, encompassing, encircling embrace that seemed to envelop my whole person. It was definitely an embrace – around me and through me – it was internal and external – a very warm feeling.
>
> It was definitely Timothy! It just came to me as an intuitive thought. It was a feeling that I was with him, like I was experiencing his person. It was nothing like you would experience with a four-year-old. This was a very mature person that I felt, yet it was still my son.
>
> I felt it was an expression of his approval and his love. That I was in tune at the time to receive this, and he was able to get through to me.
>
> Since this happened, I have felt even closer to Timothy. This was an affirmation of our relationship, our closeness. It was a spiritual communication but without words.
>
> This feeling hasn't faded – it's a permanent impression. I feel my son and I have an eternal relationship.

Some parents who have experienced the loss of a young child wonder if they will be able to recognize their son or daughter many years later. They ask such questions as "Will my child still be an infant, or will he continue to mature in heaven? Will he know we're his mommy and daddy? Will he still love us?" Roberta's ADC is helpful in answering these questions. Although she didn't see her son or hear his voice, she immediately recognized his unique spiritual essence even ten years after his death. Timothy's visit also assured his mother that his love and affection for her had actually increased as he developed spiritually.

Dana is a computer programmer in Maryland whose daughter, Kristen, died from heart disease at age 14. She was reassured by her mother-in-law, Joanna, who had died 12 years earlier:

> About two weeks after Kristen's death, I concluded that she was in heaven. But I started worrying about who was going to take care of her because I didn't have anyone close in my family who had died.
>
> Then I had a dream of my deceased mother-in-law. I could see her face, and it was like I could reach out and touch her. Although I don't remember her lips moving, Joanna said to me, "Don't worry, Dana. I'll take care of Kristen." Then she just faded away.
>
> I can honestly say that's the first time I ever dreamed of my mother-in-law. It made me feel very good. I felt relieved that there's someone to take care of my daughter.

Our ADC research reveals that family unity is highly valued in the celestial worlds. This affinity seems to include not only our entire biological family, ranging from our great-grandparents to our great-grandchildren, but extends to our in-laws and close friends as well. Undoubtedly, the power of love is the connecting force that binds each of us to one another, forming a true "family circle" both here on earth and throughout eternity.

Shannon is a 29-year-old homemaker in Florida. Her anguish was diminished by her grandfather 12 years after he died of a heart attack:

> My son, Bradley, was born prematurely. He had a lot of medical problems due to his early birth. The doctors were sure he wasn't going to make it.
>
> I was in the hospital chapel praying out loud to the

Lord, "I need help! I don't want my son to die!" Then I felt my deceased grandfather's hand on my right shoulder and smelled his pipe tobacco. It was definitely like he was sitting next to me.

Grandpa Mac had a special blend that he made himself which had a sweet hickory smell. I had never smelled it other than at his house. This gave me a calm, peaceful feeling, and I knew then that my grandfather wasn't going to let anything happen to Bradley.

After about forty-five minutes, something told me to go upstairs to see my son. I said, "Thank you, Grandpa," and the smell of his tobacco disappeared.

The doctors said, "We can't believe this! Your baby has made a complete turnaround! His vital signs are stable and his blood pressure is good." I just broke down and cried. I knew Grandpa Mac had protected him.

Bradley had a miraculous recovery! Though he's hearing impaired, he's a very vivacious five-year-old. He's very curious, very bright, and very articulate when he signs with his hands.

He had never seen a picture of my grandfather. But when I showed him one a couple of years ago, he immediately signed "Grandpa Mac!" I don't know how that kid knew, but he did!

Prayers for assistance can be answered in unexpected ways. According to our research, a deceased relative or friend may be sent as a messenger to comfort us during a time of crisis.

Perhaps Grandpa Mac also visited Bradley several times over the years. This could explain how a little boy was able to identify a photograph of a great-grandfather he had never known.

Victoria is a homemaker in Manitoba, Canada. Her husband and she shared this wonderful symbolic ADC 15 years after their daughter, Gail, died in an automobile accident at age 19:

Last year we went to The Compassionate Friends picnic. It was a bright, sunny day without a cloud in the sky.

At the end of the picnic, we all released helium balloons, and to ours I attached a note to Gail from all of us. The last line said, "Wishing you lots of rainbows, Sweetheart." Then off it went into the atmosphere.

As we were leaving the park, we looked at the clear blue sky, and there was a rainbow from horizon to horizon! My husband and I looked at each other and I said, "Gail got our message and is sending one back to us!"

The park is about twenty-two miles from our home, and that rainbow followed us all the way! As we got back into town, my husband said, "Take a look, honey!" It had become a gorgeous double rainbow! We stood beside the car holding hands, just looking at the sky.

A sentiment often expressed by bereaved parents is "If your parent dies, you lose part of your past; if your spouse dies, you lose part of your present; if your child dies, you lose part of your future." For if their son or daughter dies, the parents also grieve the loss of all the hopes and dreams they had envisioned for their child.

Glendalee, a 57-year-old homemaker in Georgia, realized her father was watching over her 15 years after he died of a heart attack:

I was driving down the highway in my truck. There was a railroad track on my right and side streets coming onto the highway on my left. As I was approaching the city limits, I heard someone say, "Stop the truck!" It startled me, but I didn't stop.

A moment later, somebody said again, "Glendalee, stop the truck!" Then I knew it was Daddy, and it scared me. It was like he was sitting right there next to me. Then he used a name he had called me all my life. He said, "Baby! Stop!" And I slammed on the brakes!

As I did, a car came out of the side street on my left –
it shot straight across in front of me! Then it skidded into
the dirt by the railroad track and stopped. It was a very
scary feeling!

The car had gone completely out of control. It couldn't
have missed me by more than two inches. If my father
hadn't told me to stop, it would have hit the driver's side
of my truck, and I would have been killed!

This is an example of an ADC for protection. In these accounts the experiencer receives a warning of an imminent accident, criminal activity, or other form of danger that might
threaten his or her life.

Jacqueline, a receptionist in Washington, had this moving
experience with her father 18 years after he died of cancer at
age 71:

My husband and I received a music box as a wedding
gift, but it never played. Our neighbor bought it for us because it was very pretty. The man at the store told her it
would never work because it was broken and had only
been glued back together.

On our first wedding anniversary, we were sitting at
our dining table. All of a sudden, the music box began
playing "The Godfather's Waltz" from the movie *The
Godfather.*

Then I saw my dad! He was just as plain as day,
standing right beside me! He looked younger, with dark
hair, like when he was thirty-five or forty. He was beaming from ear to ear with a huge smile on his face. He was
there for an instant and then he was gone, and I started
bawling.

And to this day, the music box continues to play like it
had never been broken!

Unbeknownst to us, there are probably many occasions when
our deceased loved ones are nearby expressing their loving sup-

port. If we learn how to meditate, we can develop our intuitive senses more fully and will be more likely to detect their presence.

Connie, age 45, owns a retail store in Missouri. She was given motivation by her father 19 years after he died of cancer:

> I had been diagnosed as having gallbladder disease and was getting ready to have surgery. As the date got closer, I was getting more and more anxious.
>
> About three or four days before the surgery, I went to sleep really nervous and apprehensive about the whole thing. While I was sleeping, my father came to me in a dream. He had on a long white satin robe and was real serene and peaceful.
>
> He reassured me, saying, "Go ahead with the surgery. You're going to be fine. You're going to go through it easily. Go ahead and have it done." Then he was gone.
>
> When I woke up, I felt calm and secure about having my surgery. I wasn't even afraid after that. And I went through the operation just fine!

ADC research and other sources affirm that our deceased loved ones have very full lives of their own and will generally attempt to contact us only if they have something important to communicate. Presumably they have much better things to do than eavesdrop on our lives or make frivolous intrusions into our affairs.

Jenny owns a cleaning service in Florida. Her father died when she was only 12 years old, and she had this out-of-body ADC with him over 20 years later:

> When my father died, I was very upset. It took me many years, but I thought I had gotten over it. Then some twenty-odd years later, I went to sleep one night as usual.
>
> Suddenly, I was standing in a different place. I don't know where it was – I just popped up there. My father was standing in a clear spot surrounded by fog. He was

very solid and real, and he looked very healthy. The colors were sharp and clear.

I went over to him, and suddenly all these feelings poured out of me. I was mad! I was angry! I was hating him, saying, "Why did you leave me?" I was beating him on his chest.

He let me go on for a couple of minutes, and then he hugged me – I could actually feel his arms around me. Then he spoke calmly to me, very tenderly and lovingly. He said, "I'm here now, and it's time we talked."

My father told me that it had been his time to leave. He said, "When I died I felt so much better!" He had died of lung cancer and had wasted away for several years. He was very happy that he had left, and he was very happy in what he was doing now.

He made me understand that it was the right time for him to go, and he was sorry that I had been so hurt and angry. Then we said good-bye.

I woke up immediately and felt so good – better than I had in twenty years! I felt I was free, like a giant weight had been lifted. I think that was the anger I was holding that I didn't even know I had because I had pushed it so deep. I was finally able to tell my father I loved him and to say good-bye.

Jenny's experience reflects the importance of timing in an ADC of this nature. Apparently, our deceased loved ones can see into our hearts and determine when we are truly ready to release our pent-up emotions of many years. Then and only then would we be receptive to having such a healing encounter with them.

Marla, age 56, is the manager for an apartment complex in the Northwest. She received acknowledgment from her husband, Jack, 21 years after he died of a heart attack:

Before he died, my husband and I were in the process of divorcing because of his drinking and verbal abuse. I was hopeful that things would change and we would get back together again because we had four children.

I also had some feelings of guilt because I was breaking Jack's heart. But so was his alcoholism! I had always loved him and had fond memories, even after he died.

Twenty-one years later, Jack came to me in a dream. It was very wonderful and very vivid – it was so real to me. He had a big, big smile on his face, and he said, "I thank you for loving me and our children. I am fine now. Everything is fine. Thank you for your love. I love you."

I awakened immediately, remembering the big smile on his sweet face. I had an incredible sense of peace and a big smile on my face too.

I walked around in an aura of happiness for about three days. It made me feel so good! I feel Jack had reached a place in his new life where he is at peace now.

Marla's account again reveals the profound healing and growth our deceased loved ones can seemingly achieve by applying the wisdom of their spiritual teachers. ADCs like hers demonstrate that, if we so desire, time and death need not be perceived as obstacles to emotionally resolving all of our estranged relationships.

Laurence, age 58, is retired from the United States Forest Service and lives in Georgia. He was thankful for this warmhearted greeting 27 years after his father died of cancer:

It was June, and I was out in the backyard working in my garden. I was checking my beans and tomatoes, that sort of thing. Then I took a break and was standing under a dogwood tree.

All of a sudden, my father was there right next to me! His face and his shoulders and dark curly hair were just barely perceptible, but he had a very, very strong presence. I knew immediately who it was.

I stood very still. Then I heard my father very clearly say, "I'm proud of you." I had just finished accomplishing some things I had been working on for ten to fifteen years, and I think he was referring to that.

He stayed a little while longer, maybe twenty or thirty seconds, and said, "I have to go now." Then he was gone as suddenly as he had appeared. It was a short, very overpowering experience. Oh golly, I got excited about it!

I immediately went into the house and told my wife. I took her out to the dogwood tree, and of course, there were some tears. I was elated and overwhelmed – very happy that it had happened.

Two statements children yearn to hear their parents say to them with deep conviction are "I love you!" and "I'm proud of you!" As both the previous and the next ADCs attest, it may never be too late to receive recognition and approval from a mother or father.

Ted is a 41-year-old electrician in Florida. He had this joyful reconciliation 30 years after his father died of a heart attack:

My father died just prior to my tenth birthday. My relationship with him was not very strong. I never recall him telling me that he loved me. That bothered me throughout most of my life, though I didn't realize how deeply. I grew up believing that I was not loved – even though other people around me assured me that I was, especially my wife and my children.

I wasn't looking for it, wasn't thinking about him, wasn't searching at the time. But a year ago, I had a dream that my father's spirit came to me. He was sitting at a table, and there was no one else there. He seemed to be very peaceful and very loving.

I had a feeling of total acceptance, as if we were really long-lost best friends who had been separated for many years. My father was not the person I had known when he was alive – he was totally different – he was very loving!

We seemed to converse for a while – it could have been seconds, or it could have been hours. I don't recall any of the conversation, except the fact that he told me that he loved me.

When I woke up, I had a feeling of release – like a burden I had been carrying around had lifted. I was crying, but it was not grief I felt – it was extreme joy!

Now I know my father really did love me, even though he couldn't express it. Before, I had a lot of hatred for him, a lot of anger. But that's gone – it has disappeared entirely. And the knowledge that my father really does love me is still with me.

The fact that Ted's father returned so many years after his death to heal his relationship with his son indicates that our deceased loved ones continue to care about us deeply. This account again confirms that life in the spiritual dimension provides many opportunities for ongoing personal growth. As Ted declared with certainty about his father, "He was totally different – he was very loving."

Marian is a 71-year-old realtor in Florida. Thankfully, her father warned her of danger 33 years after he died of an aneurysm:

I was in bed reading one evening. All of a sudden, I heard my father's voice say very urgently, "Get out of that bed! Get out of that bed!"

I jumped right up and stood there quivering. I walked into the family room and sat down, wondering what was the matter.

I hadn't been there three minutes when I heard a horrible cracking sound. My whole house shuddered, and things were rattling in cupboards and falling off shelves!

I went outside and saw that a heavy limb from my neighbor's tree had fallen on my roof! There had been no wind or storm – it was a fair night.

Then I went back into the house and to my bedroom. There I saw three enormous holes in the ceiling and a large branch projecting over my bed. The entire bed was

covered with lumber and plaster and debris – just where
I had been lying!

It's comforting to realize our loved ones are still watching
over and protecting us even many years after their death. Perhaps they are assisting our guardian angels in such endeavors.

Clearly, the experiencers in this chapter were not in a state
of grief when they had their ADCs. It's highly unlikely, therefore, that they would have fantasized being contacted by deceased loved ones so many years later. This offers further
evidence that these are genuine communications from relatives
and friends who have died.

Can an ADC reveal information that you didn't know before? Examples of receiving evidential material from deceased
loved ones are presented in the next chapter.

CHAPTER 18

Validation:
Evidential ADCs

I believe that Spirit lives on, that it is immortal, and
that we must look to our ancestral spirits to guide us.
—*Susan L. Taylor*

This chapter contains some of the most fascinating and colorful ADC experiences in our files. These accounts demonstrate that your deceased loved ones are still interested in your life and are willing to give you valuable information and advice when you require it. Since you always retain your free will, you can choose to accept or reject their guidance.

An ADC experience is evidential when you learn something you did not know and had no way of knowing before. For instance, you may be told the location of an object that is lost and later confirm the accuracy of the guidance by acting upon it and finding the missing item. In turn, this process assures you that your experience was a genuine after-death communication from a deceased family member or friend.

As the various accounts in this chapter illustrate, all sorts of evidential information can be received from your deceased loved ones. However, their true intention for helping you in this manner seems to be to convince you there is life after death and that they continue to exist and are watching over you with loving kindness.

• • •

The first two accounts are from people who were looking for valuable items that they knew existed but were unable to find on their own.

Ruth, a homemaker in Florida, had this evidential experience with her mother, who died of a heart attack at age 64. An auditory ADC she had with her grandson is described in Chapter 3:

> One day, probably a week after my mother died, my father said, "You know, your mother has $5,000 worth of savings bonds hidden someplace in the bedroom." So I said, "We'll find them!"
>
> We started searching, and we must have worked two hours. We went through every drawer, every box, every closet. We even checked under the mattresses. We looked every place that you could look in the bedroom.
>
> I finally plopped down on one of the twin beds, and my father sat on the other. I said, "Dad, they're not here. They've got to be in another room."
>
> Just then – I mean that quick – I heard Mom chuckle. And she said, "Oh, you dummies! They're in the false bottom of the garment bag." It was in my head, but it was her voice, so distinct.
>
> I got up immediately and walked into the closet. I said, "Mom just told me they're in the false bottom of the garment bag." I reached down, and sure enough, there was a false bottom. And when I lifted it up, there were the bonds – $5,000 worth!
>
> Dad looked at me when I took the bonds out and said, "Ruth, I'm telling you, your mother's here!"

Most people assume they will have ample time to put their personal affairs in order before they die. But if we should die unexpectedly, without disclosing the location of all our valuable possessions, our family members may never be able to find them. In this case, if Ruth hadn't been contacted by her deceased mother, she and her father might have disposed of the garment bag, never realizing it contained the hidden savings bonds.

Muriel works in retail sales in Idaho. Her mother-in-law, Grandma Davis, who died of a stroke at 89, helped solve a mystery:

When Grandpa Davis died, my mother-in-law, Grandma Davis, was left alone. Her family all lived some distance away from her. My husband's brother would visit her and go through his father's things – his guns and his hunting and fishing equipment – and take them out the back door.

But somehow he missed the one gun that was Grandpa's special pride. It was an old army rifle that had a hand-carved stock. It had been carved for Grandpa by a nephew who was quite a renowned artist. My husband loves guns and had a particular attraction to that one.

At Grandma Davis' death everybody looked and looked for that old gun, but nobody could find it. We were all so busy getting things out of the house that I was exhausted and fell asleep for about two hours.

During that time, Grandma Davis came to me. She was at the foot of the bed and looked like she always did. She told me the rifle was between the mattress and the box spring of the bed I was sleeping on. I felt she wanted my husband to have it.

I woke up and called my husband to come into the room. I pulled the mattress up and showed him where the rifle was. He was so shocked and surprised, and he asked me how I knew. I said, "Grandma Davis told me where it was!"

Even when a family heirloom is meant to be handed down to a particular person, sometimes the owner will hide it from everyone, including the intended recipient. Receiving information from the deceased loved one can reveal the whereabouts of a sentimental item and thereby ensure that it will be passed along to the rightful heir.

•   •   •

In the next two accounts the experiencers were able to locate something of value that they didn't know existed before they had their ADC.

Bess is a 55-year-old typesetter and writer in Florida. She heard from her father a few weeks after he died of cancer:

> I had always been able to provide for my family, but I had lost my job, and jobs were very scarce. I was divorced, and the kids and I didn't have anything to eat. We were real hungry.
>
> I was lying on the couch, and my dad came to me. He was real concerned about me and the children and had a serious look.
>
> He told me, "Bess, if you go around to my house and look in that old trunk I've had for so many years, you'll find some money. It's not going to be a lot, but it will help feed your children today." It was his actual voice – I could hear him talking.
>
> Dad looked a little younger and appeared to be in good health. I jumped up, and he faded away just as quick as he appeared.
>
> I went to his house that afternoon and looked through everything he had in the trunk. Sure enough, in a white envelope I found $10! I knew then that Dad was really looking out for us!

Evidential ADCs are validated in a circular way. For example, Bess could not have known to look for money in such an obscure place. Only her deceased father had that knowledge. By following his directions and finding the cash, Bess proved to herself that her ADC experience was real. More importantly, this process confirmed for her that her father continues to exist and has ongoing concern for the well-being of his daughter and his grandchildren.

Gretchen, a 63-year-old homemaker in Pennsylvania, received a fortuitous insight after her mother died of an aneurysm:

My mother left a suitcase of hers at my house before she died. After her death she was very present in my home, and I felt guided by her to go to this suitcase.

I came across my mother's sarong girdle and started to roll it up to throw it away in the trash bin. But it was heavy, and I couldn't fold it easily.

In a flash, I got a vision – it was a mental picture in my mind's eye – of how my mother's mother used to sew a pocket inside her girdle to carry money safely.

Lo and behold, there between the flaps my mother had stitched a pocket! She had matched the design so well, I never would have guessed there was anything there.

I called to my daughter and we sat down on the bed. We heard Mama's happy laugh as we took money out of an envelope in the pocket of her girdle. It contained thirty-six crisp $100 bills – a total of $3,600!

With today's high crime rate, many people find it necessary to hide valuables in unlikely and obscure places. But it's better not to count on having an ADC to help us locate the hidden treasures of our deceased loved ones. Instead, thoroughly examining their most mundane belongings could be very profitable.

In these next three accounts the experiencers received information they hadn't known before.

Denise is a former telephone operator in Florida. She had this sleep-state ADC with her husband, Louis, who died at age 53:

Louis had been a career soldier for twenty-eight years. He had just come back from a tour of duty in Vietnam, and he died suddenly a week later from pneumonia.

About nine months after his death, I was asleep one night, and I was aware that Louis was talking to me. He was laughing and laughing – he was so happy! He said, "Hey, Dee, you'll never guess who's up here! He hasn't changed a bit!" So I asked, "Who is it?"

Louis said, "I can't believe it! Father Antonio is here! When I asked him what he was doing here, Father said, 'What makes you think you're the only one who can make it to this place?' " Father Antonio had that kind of humor, and he and Louis were real good buddies. Then I woke up.

The next day I had a telephone call from another priest, a dear friend. He said, "I have some very bad news to tell you." I said, "Oh, I already know. Father Antonio died." He asked me, "How could you know that? He just died last night!" I said, "Louis told me in a dream."

During the course of an ADC we may learn something we didn't know before and cannot immediately verify. Later, when this news proves to be accurate, it provides confirmation that our experience was real.

Tricia is a clothing designer in Florida. She was 18 years old when she attempted to tell her family that she had seen her mother, who had died of cancer:

Right after Mother passed away, I was in my bedroom. All of a sudden, I felt a presence. I had a little night light, so I rolled over and turned on the switch.

I saw my mother standing there! She had on a blue velvet dress that I'd never seen before. When she died of cancer, she weighed only fifty-seven pounds. But when I saw her, she was beautiful and healthy and happy!

I remember jumping up and screaming! Then I ran into the other room to tell my family that my mother wasn't dead. They thought I was being hysterical and having hallucinations. Finally, they calmed me down, and I began thinking they were right.

Some time later, my aunt and I were going through my mother's hope chest. I came across a blue velvet dress and started bawling my eyes out.

My aunt said, "What's the matter?" And I said, "This is the dress my mother had on when I saw her!" My aunt said, "That's the dress your mother made to get married in. She didn't have enough money to buy a wedding dress, so she made this blue velvet one herself."

Once again, an ADC account illustrates how important it is to trust our intuitive experiences. After Tricia had encountered so much discouragement from her family, it's worth noting that a seemingly unimportant detail, such as the dress her mother had been wearing, later convinced her that her experience was authentic.

Jeanette, age 41, is a businesswoman in New Hampshire. She was in a dilemma 1 year after her father died from a chronic illness:

> My sister, Debbie, was on drugs. She was living in Minnesota, and I was in New Hampshire. She would call me up and tell me that her baby had no food. She would ask me for this and that, and I would always send her money. I was making myself crazy because I knew what she was really doing with that money.
>
> One night Debbie called me all drugged out. She wanted $500! I wanted to help her, but I didn't want to give her any more money. I just didn't know what to do!
>
> I was so upset, I went to bed crying. I said, "Please, Daddy, come to me. I don't know what to do. You've got to help me!"
>
> My father came to me in my sleep and he was smiling. I remember saying, "Daddy, this isn't anything to smile at!" He said, "But you have the solution. When you wake up you'll know it." Then he hugged me and held me for a long time.
>
> The next morning I realized, "Oh, I know! I'm going to tell my sister to send me all her bills. I'll pay them myself." The solution was right there! I know my father gave it to me, except he let me believe I was thinking of it myself. There's no way I would have thought of that – just no way!

So Debbie sent me her current bills and I paid them. Then she got really mad at me and never asked again.

An ADC may provide a creative solution for an old problem, just as Jeanette was given an effective method for dealing with her sister's drug abuse. Her strategy can also be applied successfully to anyone who has an alcohol, gambling, or other addiction or to those who have difficulty managing their personal finances wisely.

In each of the next four accounts the experiencer received information that was primarily intended to benefit somebody else.

Lydia, age 70, is a retired nurse in Florida. Her brother-in-law, Graham, gave her a precise message after he died of heart failure:

Graham passed away when he was eighty-nine years old. I guess his heart just gave out. I had this experience with him before I knew he had died.

I felt his presence in my kitchen. He said to me, "Tell Vera," who is my sister, "to look real good around the desk in her living room. Take the drawers out and look in the back."

I wrote a letter to Vera and explained my experience to her. Then later my niece called me. She told me they went through the desk and found about $3,000 in $50 bills he had hidden away!

Obviously, Graham wanted Vera to find the money so it wouldn't be thrown out accidentally. All through his life his main interest seemed to be money, but I think he was more concerned about his wife's security.

How many inheritances have been discarded because no one knew of their existence? But a much larger legacy is contained within this account than finding $3,000. Graham gave a priceless gift to three people – his sister-in-law, his wife, and his daughter – the knowledge that life is eternal and that he continues to exist and care about them after his death.

Kitty, a 65-year-old homemaker in Alabama, did a favor for Leland, a family friend who had died in an accident:

> Leland was our friend, and we bought our home from him. He was a mail carrier and was killed one morning in his mail truck.
>
> The next morning he appeared in my bedroom! While standing there, he told me to tell Frances, his wife, that he had an insurance policy she didn't know about. He said, "It's in our bedroom, in the top drawer of the chest under the paper. Tell Frances where it is." And then he disappeared.
>
> My husband, Cliff, walked in the room and I told him what had happened. He said, "Well, let's call and tell Frances." I said, "She'll think I'm nuts!"
>
> So my husband went down and told Leland's brother, Reed, to look in the top drawer of the chest under the paper – that he might find an insurance policy there. But Cliff didn't explain what had happened to me.
>
> Sure enough, they looked and there was an insurance policy just like Leland had told me! Reed called and thanked my husband, but we never told them how we knew. They just wouldn't have understood.

Kitty and her husband proved that it's well worth taking a risk to deliver an ADC message, and they found a clever way to do it. Without realizing it, you too may have already received a message from a deceased loved one through a good neighbor.

Becky, a 36-year-old legal secretary and writer in Virginia, was formerly a staff member of a Ronald McDonald House. There she befriended a 10-year-old African American girl, Amira, who was dying of bone cancer:

Two months after Amira's death, I dreamed I was with her in a park. It was a very beautiful, sunny day. Amira was in a violet and white African ceremonial dress with a turban and everything.

She was ecstatic to see me. She sort of giggled and picked up her dress, saying, "Look, I've got my leg back!" Her right leg had been amputated before she died. Amira was beaming! She wanted to show the world she was whole again.

Amira asked me to tell her mother that she was happy and was learning a lot of new things. She said she would see me again someday. Then she waved good-bye, and that was the end of the experience.

I called her mother on the phone and told her about my dream. I related to her what her daughter had been wearing. Apparently Amira had an outfit exactly like that at home, one which I had never seen. It was a violet and white ceremonial dress from Africa that someone had given her. Her mother said it had been Amira's favorite!

Some ADCs are validated only if they're shared with other people. When Becky delivered the message to Amira's mother, as promised, she learned the significance of the beautiful outfit her young friend had been wearing. This, in turn, proved to Becky that her experience had been real. And her description of the dress gave Amira's mother even greater confidence in Becky's ADC.

Debra is a 48-year-old psychologist in Florida. She assisted her grandfather with some unfinished business after he died very suddenly from a heart attack:

After my mother called and told me my grandfather had died, I lay down in bed to pray for him and say good-bye. With my eyes closed, I received a message from him telepathically that was very strong and very specific.

Grandpa said, "In my apartment there is a credenza. In the left-hand top drawer there is a yellow legal tablet.

It contains a list of stocks and bonds. Some need to be sold immediately. It is imperative that your father get this information!"

He was very intense and very eager to impart this knowledge. There was no endearment at all – he was strictly business. This was very much in character for my grandfather.

I got up and called my mother and told her my experience. A few days later, I found out my father had gone to Grandpa's apartment and looked in the credenza. The legal pad was exactly where Grandpa said it would be. It contained a list of securities, just as he had told me.

I don't know what my father did about those stocks and bonds – we never discussed it. The only thing my father ever said was, "There must be something to this, Debra, because you had no way of knowing about that list."

It's likely Debra entered a semi-meditative state while praying for her grandfather. This can be a very effective way to have an ADC experience, and it will be discussed further in the last chapter.

Each of the remaining accounts contains evidential material that is more complex.

Kelly is a nurse in the Southwest. She was given detailed information by her 2-year-old son, Cody, just 6 weeks after he died from a gunshot wound while playing with his father's handgun:

Cody came to me in a dream. He appeared happy and healthy. I saw him as a child, but he seemed older. He talked to me and related to me almost like he was an adult.

He said there was something wrong with his tombstone – that it was on a little girl's grave who had died two weeks before he did. And he told me that his name was backwards.

The next day, I went out to the cemetery, and there

was no tombstone where Cody was buried. I called the monument company and asked them when they were going to put the stone on my son's grave. They said it had already been placed out there two weeks earlier.

Then I went to the caretaker of the cemetery and asked him where the newest gravestones were. He took me to a grave, and there was Cody's tombstone.

I asked the caretaker whose grave it was. He looked at his chart and said it was a little girl who had died on October 1st. Cody had died on October 14th.

All the other tombstones were facing in one direction, but this one was turned around facing the other way. To Cody it must have looked like his name was backwards!

Finally, the monument company came out to the cemetery and put the tombstone on Cody's grave correctly.

It's remarkable that a young child could communicate such a complicated message. Yet when his mother discovered the mistakes that had been made at the cemetery, all of Cody's statements turned out to be accurate.

Lucille is a 39-year-old hotel housekeeper in Florida. An ADC experience inspired her to embark upon a process of self-discovery:

A man came to the foot of my bed one night. I was scared because I didn't recognize him. He said, "Mary, your mother loves you." I was adopted, and "Mary" was the name I was given when I was born. My adoptive parents changed it to "Lucille."

He continued, "Your mother is looking for you. Start looking for her. Find your mother! I love you."

I remember asking him who he was just before I couldn't see him anymore. And he said, "You'll find out." The next thing I knew, he was gone. I was still scared, yet I had tears of happiness. I was glad to know that my birth mother was looking for me.

This gave me the incentive to find my biological

mother. I was always dreaming about finding her, but I didn't want to hurt my adoptive parents.

Then I went to a club for adoptees, and I found my mother with just one phone call! She asked, "How did you find me?" I told her an elderly man came to the foot of my bed. I described what he looked like, and she said, "That's your grandfather!"

I learned when Grandpa was dying, he told my mother, "Find your daughter. Find your baby." He wanted to rest in peace knowing we would be together again. My mother and I agreed to meet the following day.

When we met, she showed me a picture of my grandfather, and that was the man who had been standing at the foot of my bed. Grandpa had the same suit on in the photograph that he wore when he came to me. Then I knew my experience was real!

It seems our deceased loved ones can see far beyond our limited earthly perspective and envision possibilities that are not readily apparent to us. Our willingness to follow their loving guidance may open doors and create opportunities we never dreamed existed.

Ann Marie, 39, is a secretary and bookkeeper in Oklahoma. She was heartbroken when her daughter, Brittany, was still-born:

I was at full term and had been in labor off and on for about a week. I went to the doctor's office, and he couldn't pick up a heartbeat. And when I went to the hospital, Brittany was pronounced dead.

She was my only child. I had waited for her for ten years, and I had a hard time letting her go. I was wondering who was taking care of my daughter and if she was all right and safe.

This dream was about three months after Brittany died. The first thing I remember was a bright light. There were a lot of people and there was singing.

All of a sudden, I saw a lady holding my daughter. Brittany appeared to be at least six-to-nine months old. She held out her arms to me and called, "Mommy!"

I didn't recognize the woman who was holding her. She was an older lady, pretty good sized, and her hair was braided up. I asked her who she was, and she told me she was my Grandmother Robinson. Then my experience ended.

Afterwards, I talked to my mother and told her about it. My Grandmother Robinson died when I was only one or two years old. I never knew her and I had never seen a picture of her.

Then my aunt came to visit and brought some family photos so I could see them. I picked Grandmother Robinson out right away! She looked exactly the way I had seen her a couple of weeks earlier – same dress, same size, same hair. I had never seen that picture before!

This was God's way of telling me that my daughter is okay. I've always taken this as God's gift to me.

Grandmother Robinson's choice of physical appearance and attire was seemingly not coincidental. This ADC suggests she had knowledge of the photograph that would later make it possible for her granddaughter to confirm her identity.

The final account in this chapter was reported by Mitchell, a 45-year-old private investigator in Vermont. He had a very persuasive encounter 26 years after his father died of pneumonia:

On the morning of March 14, 1989, at 2:34 a.m., I was awakened from a deep sleep to see my deceased father standing at the foot of my bed. My father and I communicated with one another by mental telepathy.

He looked as real as the day I last saw him! I asked, "Are you all right, Dad?" He replied, "Yes, son." Once again I asked, "Are you sure you're okay?" He answered by nodding his head up and down in an affirmative way.

For years I was confused and upset that my father had deserted me when I was eighteen years old. His sudden death from pneumonia left me with many unanswered questions.

I then asked, "Why did you die and leave me alone? Why didn't you say good-bye?" My father replied, "Son, you had to grow in order to become strong and independent and to face life and what challenges it had to offer you. I felt as though I was hindering that process."

I said, "Dad, I love you." My father started turning away and stated, "Yes, son, I know." I asked, "Where are you going? Why are you leaving me again?" He said, "My son, I must go now." While stopping briefly, he turned, looked back with a beautiful smile, and said, "Count the days." Then he walked out of sight.

Several days after my experience, I began thinking about my father and tried to analyze his words, "Count the days." A thought came to me about the number of days my father had lived on earth.

So I loaded my computer and searched the calendar back to my father's date of birth. I counted the days he lived on earth up until his death. The total amounted to 16,305 days.

My father died at age 44, and I was also 44. So I wondered if I had lived longer than my father. Just for the fun of it, I proceeded to count the days from my birth up until the morning of my vision. The sum total was 16,305 days, the same amount of days my father had lived!

Long ago I had asked for a sign, and boy, did my dad show me! I felt very loved. This reassured me that he definitely lives on after death. I'm not afraid of dying anymore because I know there is something hereafter.

It was only when Mitchell used his intuition that he discovered the meaning of the mysterious clue he received from his father. This was the perfect assignment to appeal to his analytical nature, and it provided a key piece of information regarding the similarity of the two men's lives.

These have been a sampling of the many evidential accounts in our files. The ones who benefit the most from having this kind of ADC are the experiencers. When they learn something they didn't know and had no way of knowing before, they receive indisputable evidence that they were contacted by someone who has died. These accounts also furnish convincing documentation for others that ADCs are actual communications from deceased loved ones, just as the 2,000 people who were interviewed stated.

Can you receive more from an ADC than just information or guidance? Are you being watched over and cared for in other ways? The next chapter illustrates that many people have been protected by the timely intervention of a deceased loved one.

CHAPTER 19

Special Delivery:
ADCs for Protection

The body is only a garment. How many times you have changed
your clothing in this life, yet because of this you would not say
that you have changed. Similarly, when you give up this
bodily dress at death you do not change. You are
just the same, an immortal soul, a child of God.
—*Paramahansa Yogananda*

Nearly all ADCs are inspired by the ongoing love and concern your deceased relatives and friends feel for you. It is,
therefore, understandable that they might attempt to protect
you from time to time, especially if you are facing imminent
physical danger or some other threat to your well-being.

This chapter contains accounts from people whose lives
were protected, and perhaps even saved, by the intervention of
a deceased loved one. That is, they had an ADC experience
at the exact moment such loving assistance was required
and were safeguarded during a serious or possibly fatal situation.

In each case, they received warnings that protected them
from motor vehicle or other accidents, harm from criminals,
house fires, industrial injuries, undiagnosed health problems,
and emergencies involving infants and young children.

There is no stronger personal evidence that an ADC is real
than having your life actually protected or saved by one. And
imagine how fulfilled your deceased family members and
friends must feel when they accomplish a successful intervention.

• • •

With the exception of the final two accounts, the ADCs in this chapter are arranged according to how long after the death of a loved one they occurred.

Wilma, age 54, is a retail store owner in Kansas. Luckily, she had this ADC with her father 1 month after he died of a heart attack:

> My husband had broken his leg. Being we're farmers with children, I had all these chores to do. One evening I was hurrying to town after dinner to buy some groceries. I was by myself in my car and had my mind on a thousand things.
>
> I was coming down a hill at a pretty good lick when my father said, "Wilma, quick! Turn here!" It was as though he was sitting right next to me, and his voice was just as clear as a bell!
>
> I turned the corner and went one mile south, then back to the east, and one mile north, all the time thinking, "What in the world am I doing? I'm in a hurry and I'm going three miles out of my way!" It made no sense, and I felt like a darn fool!
>
> Later, on the way back, I saw one of my neighbor ladies. I thought she was having car trouble, so I stopped. She said, "I was so relieved when I saw you turn! The bridge is out!"
>
> It's a flat wooden bridge with two big cottonwood trees hanging over it and a lot of shrubs. It collapsed with no boards sticking up or anything. I know I wouldn't have seen it until I was on top of it!
>
> I had been just a quarter of a mile from the bridge when my father told me to turn. I would have been going 60 miles per hour when I hit into that empty space! Had my father not warned me, I probably would have been killed!

It's interesting that Wilma's father directed her to drive all the way around the bridge without revealing his reason for doing so. This subtle and indirect method is sometimes used in ADCs for protection when there is sufficient time to divert the experiencers from harm's way without unduly alarming them.

Pattie, age 33, is an insurance underwriter in Nebraska. She learned her father was still interested in her safety 5 months after he died of Parkinson's disease:

> I was driving home from work in heavy traffic. We were going 55 miles per hour, bumper to bumper, on the Interstate. I was sitting down low in my seat with just one finger on the bottom of the steering wheel, and my mind was kind of wandering.
>
> All of a sudden, I heard my father's voice in my head as he said sternly, "Sit up! Put both hands on the wheel! Put your seat belt on because you are going to have a flat tire!" I heard him clear as a bell.
>
> I bolted up in my seat, put on my seat belt quickly, and placed both hands on the steering wheel. I probably went half a mile when "Booooom!" The tire exploded into shreds! But I was ready for it and able to pull over to the shoulder of the road safely.
>
> I hate to think what would have happened if I hadn't been ready for that blowout!

Pattie's father used a more direct approach in cautioning her to prepare for an imminent emergency. You'll notice a marked contrast in the various ways people are alerted by a deceased loved one in the remaining accounts in this chapter.

Alicia, age 39, is a nurse in California. Her mother provided critical directions 9 months after dying of cancer:

> I was awakened during the night, and when I looked up, my mother was standing in my doorway! Her facial expression was one of urgency and concern and indicated something was very, very wrong.

She walked into my daughter's bedroom and came back out. She motioned for me to go in there, and then she just disappeared.

I got up and went into my daughter's room. When I got to her crib, she wasn't breathing and her lips were blue! Tiffany was only nine months old and had gone to bed that night with a bottle. She had bitten off the end of the rubber nipple and was choking to death! But, fortunately, I managed to get the piece of rubber out of her throat.

If I had not gone into my daughter's room at that time, she probably would have died! There's no doubt in my mind that my mother came to warn me.

How many other tragedies might be prevented if more people were open and receptive to having ADC experiences and trusted them? In the course of our research, we spoke with several people who unfortunately failed to act upon the guidance they were given and later came to bitterly regret it. We urge everyone, especially parents of young children, to immediately respond to their intuitive feelings and ADCs whenever they have them.

Jeff is a 23-year-old telephone repairman in Florida. He had this lifesaving encounter after the death of his 19-year-old friend, Phil:

Phil died the day after Thanksgiving. He fell asleep behind the wheel of his car and hit a telephone pole.

Approximately two years after that, I was coming home about 12:30 at night after working all day. I was driving through some S curves and fell asleep.

Suddenly I heard this scream, "Wake up!" My eyes opened, and I looked over at the passenger seat. Phil was sitting there smiling! He was glowing – light was radiating from his body – and I could see through him. It really startled me to see him.

Then I looked forward just as I was entering another S

curve. I was approaching it at 45 miles per hour, going straight at a lake! I turned just enough to make it around the curve and stopped the car.

This experience was totally and completely off the wall! I wasn't expecting anything like it – it blew me away! Phil saved me from having the same experience he had. He saved my life!

A number of people who have died in a particular type of accident seem to have a desire, or possibly a mission, to protect their loved ones from a similar death. Perhaps their intervention is a means of making amends for having treated their life a little too casually or carelessly while they were physically alive.

Ella is a music teacher in Virginia. She was rescued from a dangerous situation by her husband, Rusty, about 3 years after he died in a parachute accident at age 29:

I was flying my plane down to Columbia, South Carolina. My baby was asleep in the back seat. I got into icy conditions and had an emergency situation. My engine was loading up badly, and I had to land within five minutes. But I couldn't find an airport!

I was only 500 feet above the ground and just holding my own. Suddenly, I felt Rusty grab me and say, "Look out the window of the right seat. Get over here and look out the window!" I said, "All right, all right, all right!" I had to crawl over to the right seat without boggling the wings.

I looked out the window and thought, "There's nothing out there." Rusty screamed at me again, "Behind you, way behind you!" I looked out underneath my tail, and I could just barely see the airport. I had passed it!

When I landed on the runway, I just greased her on. She didn't even make a ripple or a tiny bump. I pulled her over and parked, opened the door, and fell out – my knees couldn't stand. And that's when I fell apart!

It can be extremely difficult to find a small airport when flying at such a low altitude in bad weather. Without Rusty's help, Ella might have been forced to crash-land her plane.

Noreen, a nurse in Wisconsin, had a serious communication from her mother, who was 83 when she died of old age:

> I was at the stove stirring pudding. It was quiet in the house because the kids weren't home yet. All of a sudden, I realized I was having a conversation with my mother, who had departed three years before.
>
> She stood right next to me in a familiar blue and white checkered dress. She told me to tell Louise, my sister, to get to the doctor right away – it was imperative that she do so. Mother said, "I'm telling you because you will be able to convince your sister to do it."
>
> I immediately went to the phone and called Louise at work. I said, "Mother just told me that you should get to the doctor at once! Please do it. It must be important!" My sister said, "I'm fine, except I have a scratchy throat."
>
> Louise went to the doctor, and they immediately put her into the hospital for tests. They found she had ulcers in her esophagus that were near the cancerous stage.
>
> When the doctor asked Louise why she had come in, she said, "My mother told me." But she didn't tell him that Mother had been dead for three years!

Sometimes a deceased loved one is seemingly unable to make direct contact with the person who is in immediate danger. In such cases, he or she may be able to notify another relative or friend, who will hopefully deliver the urgent message promptly.

Bernice is a writer in the Northwest. Her son, Gene, gave her some strong advice about 3 years after he took his life at age 32 when he was terminally ill with Hodgkin's disease:

The Captain of the *Golden Odyssey* sent us an invitation to go on their Mediterranean cruise in the spring of 1977. My husband wanted to go, and he asked me to make the reservations.

The next morning I got all dressed up to go to the travel agency. Halfway to the car, I heard my son, Gene, say, "Mom, you must not take that plane to Athens."

My son's voice was very calm, but he made me feel we mustn't go. So I turned right around and went back in the house. That night I told my husband what had happened. He accepted it, and we didn't make the reservations.

On the night we would have taken the plane from Los Angeles to Athens, I sat in our living room and felt sad that we weren't going.

The next day the same plane took off from Tenerife in the Canary Islands and collided with a Dutch KLM airliner. It was the greatest passenger plane crash in history – 581 people were killed!

This account suggests that our deceased loved ones may have foreknowledge of some human events and, if appropriate, can alert us to life-threatening situations. Perhaps they are telling us indirectly that it is not yet our time to die, as near-death experiencers are frequently told. The implications of this theory are far-reaching because they support the belief that each of us has a spiritual purpose for our life and enough time to fulfill it.

Andrew, age 42, is an engineer in Washington now. He had this auditory ADC with his mother 3 years after she died of heart failure:

I was on my way home from work. There was very little traffic, and I was going down the expressway in Chicago about 55 to 60 miles per hour. There was a semi in front of me, and I was getting ready to go out in the left lane to get around it.

All of a sudden, I heard a voice calling "Andy!" It sounded urgent – it was real loud and clear. I glanced around but didn't see anybody.

Then I heard the voice a second time. So I took my foot off the gas and let the car slow up. I looked around again, but I still didn't see anything.

When I turned forward and looked out front, the semi truck was falling over to the left. I naturally put my foot on the brake as the truck slipped all the way over on its side and slid down the highway.

If I hadn't heard that voice and slowed up, I would have been right alongside the truck when it tipped over! It was a fifty-five-foot semi, and I wouldn't have been able to get around it in time. I definitely would have been underneath it!

Afterwards, when I thought about it, I knew it was my mother's voice. It was obvious my mother was there to protect me, watching over me like a guiding light.

A considerable number of after-death communications for protection involve potential motor vehicle accidents. This isn't surprising, however, when we realize that the average person is most likely to be at risk while traveling in an automobile or truck, or especially when riding a motorcycle.

Marsha is a 35-year-old owner of a print shop in Missouri. Her life was saved by her friend, Josh, 5 years after he died when his truck was hit by a train:

I was driving home in a hurry late one night from my parents' house. I got to the train crossing, and the gates came down. I thought, "Oh, great! Now I will be sitting here for twenty minutes!"

I waited for a good three minutes and still no train. Finally, I decided it must be one of those little pokey, pesky maintenance cars that sometimes cause the gates to go up and down and up and down.

So I looked in the direction they usually came from

and didn't see anything. The radio was on pretty loud, and I didn't hear anything either. So I started to drive around the gates.

I had just cleared the first gate when I saw the light! A train was right there – no more than 20 to 30 feet from me! The headlight looked as big as my car! Time stood still – I froze and couldn't move! I just sat there watching it come.

Then I heard Josh scream at me very loud and clear, "Drive this car!" I knew it was him – I recognized his voice. It sounded as though he shouted from the passenger's seat. But I didn't respond.

Then physically I felt a foot stomp over mine on the gas pedal! I actually felt pressure on my foot, and the gas pedal went right to the floor! I heard the tires squeal, and my truck shot forward!

I looked in the rearview mirror and watched the train roar by. I said out loud, "Thanks, Josh!" Then I began to shake, so I pulled over for a couple of minutes.

The next day I had a big bruise on my right foot!

Just as Josh had been killed when a train hit his truck, so Marsha might have died the same way without his help. Though it's unusual to have physical evidence after an ADC, such as a bruise on your foot, it's not unique. This was also reported by a woman who tripped and started to fall and later discovered bruises on her arms where her deceased husband's hands had caught her from behind.

Vivian, a homemaker in California, didn't hesitate to follow her father's guidance 6 years after he died of heart failure at age 72:

It was morning and I was ready to get up and start my day. Then I heard my father's voice say, "Vivian, your mom is in serious trouble!" I asked, "What kind, Dad?" And he said, "Financial." I could hear him like he was speaking out loud. I knew if my dad told me this, it had to be true.

I realized that the young man who lived next door to my mother was very attentive to her. Bud was in his early twenties, and my mother was in her seventies.

I called my mother and asked her whether Bud had ever asked her for money. She got furious with me! So I called my sister, and we started going over Mom's bank account.

We discovered that Bud was altering her checks. She would give him a check for $5.00, and he would write in an extra zero or two – and make it for $50.00 or $500.00! Or she would give him unsigned checks, and he would sign her name. He had taken my mother for about $4,500!

I called the police and found out Bud was on parole and had been in trouble before. So I had him arrested, and he went back to prison.

ADCs will sometimes alert us to various criminal activities that could threaten us physically or financially. While Vivian's mother was the victim of a common swindler, other experiencers report they have been protected from more violent crimes.

Jan is a pediatric nurse in Arizona. She received very specific instructions from her husband, Ronny, who was 20 years old when he died in an automobile accident:

This was about eight years after my husband's death. Our son, Wally, became very ill. I had him under a doctor's care, but he was not getting any better.

I woke up in the middle of the night and felt my late husband's presence at the foot of my bed. Through telepathy Ronny said, "Take Wally to a dentist or he will die!" After he knew I understood his message, he left.

The next day I called a dentist, and he checked Wally over. He diagnosed him as having a systemic infection because some of his teeth had been injured in an accident. And after my son received the appropriate care, he recovered completely.

The accuracy of the messages people receive during ADCs is truly amazing. How many parents would consider taking their sick child to a dentist for medical treatment when a physician isn't able to diagnose the cause of the illness?

Rosemarie, a 42-year-old administrative assistant in North Carolina, was given a direct order 11 years after her grandmother died of cancer. Another experience she had very shortly after her grandmother's death appears in the chapter on sleep-state ADCs:

> I had just started a new job. As I was sitting at my desk one morning, I heard my grandmother say, "Go home!" I looked at my watch, and it was only 10:00. I thought to myself, "I can't go home because it's not lunchtime yet. I can't just walk out now!"
>
> A minute passed and she said again, "Go home!" Only this time it was louder. She kept saying it for about five minutes. Grandma would not leave me alone! So I grabbed my purse, ran out the door, and drove home real fast!
>
> My daughter, Michelle, was ten years old and home by herself since it was during the summer. She met me at the door and said, "Mom, I was trying to call you. They said you had left. A man was trying to break in the back door!"
>
> Michelle had run to her bedroom and was hiding until she heard me coming in the front door. She was scared to death and shaking! The man apparently ran away at the time I drove up.
>
> Immediately, I jumped in my car and drove down the street. I saw the man, called the police, and gave them a description. They picked him up later and arrested him.

Some ADCs for protection are so urgent that they demand our immediate attention. Apparently, our deceased loved ones have an overview of our life and can detect an emergency situation we're not aware of. It's vital that we learn to trust their warnings and act upon them at once. Doing so may save someone's life, possibly our own.

Audrey, a business consultant in Florida, was spared possible harm 13 years after her grandmother died of cancer at age 80:

> I was living by myself in a studio apartment in Queens, New York. It was on the fourth floor, and my windows overlooked the fire escape. I was afraid because somebody could come in one of those windows. But it was a hot summer night and my air conditioner wasn't working. So I had the windows open.
>
> I went to sleep, and about 4:00 in the morning I heard my grandmother say, "Get up and close the windows!" She wasn't mild or soft – she was like a drill sergeant!
>
> I jumped up and closed the windows. As I did, my shoulder hit a heavy wood carving that crashed on the floor. I thought, "Oh, my God! That poor woman downstairs. She's really going to be upset with me!" Then I went back to sleep.
>
> The next morning, I went shopping. As I turned the corner, there was my neighbor from downstairs. I said to her, "I really want to apologize to you. Last night I knocked something over."
>
> She said, "No! No! It was a good thing you woke me up. There was a man on the fire escape! He could have come into my apartment!"

An ADC can protect more than just the intended experiencer. This intervention was unusual because a deceased loved one was aware of a potential danger and provided a warning that set off a chain of events which ultimately safeguarded two women's lives.

Catharine, a 48-year-old homemaker in New Brunswick, was alerted to an emergency by her great-grandmother, who had died of heart disease:

Along about 2:30 in the morning, I heard someone call my name, "Catharine!" I woke up, and I could smell a little smoke. I reached and put my glasses on and looked toward the window. I could see orange through the curtain, and I thought, "It's too early for the sun to be coming up."

I got out of bed and pulled the curtain back. The barn was on fire! And the end of our house was starting to catch fire too! All I could see out the window was flames!

I screamed to my sons, "The house is on fire! Get up quick! We've got to get out!" My older boy grabbed a fire extinguisher and ran outdoors in his underwear to try to put it out. But he said it was no use. We just got out with the clothes on our backs. Nothing was saved.

A few days later it came to me who had called my name that night. The voice was that of my great-grandmother, who had been dead for twenty-four years!

Most ADCs for protection are short and to the point, giving only essential information. Sometimes we will hear just our name or nickname being called to attract our attention or warn us of danger.

Ed is a retired tool and die maker in Arizona. He was 44 years old when his work was interrupted by his mother 27 years after she had died of pneumonia:

I was a foreman in a factory in Los Angeles where I operated a machine to cut envelopes. On this day I had set the die on a ream of paper and shoved it under the press to make the cut. Then I saw that it was set too close to the edge and would slip off.

So I started to reach under the press to reset the die, and I heard someone say, "Edmund, don't!" My mother was the only one who had ever called me "Edmund." At work I was always known as "Ed."

I looked to my right, and there was my mother! She was standing there looking at me. She was solid, but I only saw her from the waist up. She had an aura around her – she was very bright.

Mother seemed concerned about me and had a look of anxiety. Then I looked at the machine and realized that if I had done what I had started to do, both my arms would have been crushed to the elbow under 48,000 pounds of pressure!

I looked back at my mother, but she was gone. When I realized what I could have done had my mother not warned me, I got the shakes so bad I had to take an extended rest to quiet myself down.

Imagine Ed's feelings of gratitude after his ADC. In a moment of grace, he was protected from severe injury and reminded that his mother was still part of his life so many years after her death.

Florence is a 61-year-old homemaker in Florida. She heard from her father not just once, but twice, long after he died of heart disease:

This was eight years after my father died. I had just had my car serviced at a dealership, and my ten-year-old son and I were heading home. I usually would have taken the New York State Thruway and gone 70 miles per hour. However, I suddenly had the feeling that my father was in the back seat of the car. I felt his loving presence very strongly.

My father said, "Please, I want you to go home on the back roads. Go no more than ten miles an hour. Go real slow so that I can enjoy the plants." My father's hobby had been gardening. It was a beautiful day, and all the spring flowers were in bloom.

When I was about three or four blocks from home, I thought I was getting a flat tire. I got out and looked, but all of them seemed okay. So I got back into the car again.

As I started driving again, there was an old man walking along the sidewalk. He was very nervous and excited. He called out to me, "Please, don't move! Your wheels are coming off!"

We were only blocks away from a gas station. My son ran up there, and they came back with a tow truck. They found that the wheels had been rotated, but when they were placed back on the axles they had never been tightened. All four wheels were very loose!

Later I realized if I had driven on the thruway at 70 miles per hour, one of the wheels could have come off! There could have been a severe accident involving myself and possibly a lot of other people. Obviously my father saved us from a catastrophe!

This is another example of employing a diversionary technique to avoid frightening someone. The same method was used in Florence's next ADC, which is the final account in this chapter:

Sixteen years after my father's death, I was in New York City on my way to visit a friend in New York Hospital. I was walking down the street, approaching a brownstone house that was being ripped down.

My eyes were directed to a workman who was using a sledgehammer on the roof. But I dismissed that and kept on walking.

Then I felt my father's presence and heard him say, "Stop! Look at that stoop." The front steps were the same kind we had on our house in lower Manhattan when I was little.

He added, "Think about the way I used to bounce you on my knee when you were a child. Stop!" This time it was a very strong command. With that, I stopped. There were people walking behind me, and my stopping prevented them from going around me.

Then suddenly the heavy metal part of the workman's sledgehammer landed right at my feet and broke the concrete sidewalk! The two children behind me screamed! It was frightening for me to realize that my skull could have been cracked wide open!

An older man in back of me said, "My goodness, why did you stop? There was no reason for you to!" I said, "I had a feeling that my deceased father was with me and told me to stop." He replied, "Well, your father certainly saved your life and maybe those two little girls behind you too!"

Again, Florence's father cleverly distracted his daughter from a serious physical threat without unduly alarming her. And on both occasions more than one person benefited from his guidance.

It's a tremendous expression of love to protect another's life from the pain and tragedy of an accident or possibly from death itself. Such an intervention certainly fulfills a deceased loved one's promise of "I will always be with you."

Are some people persuaded by a deceased loved one not to commit suicide? The next chapter features ADCs that saved adults and children from taking their own life.

CHAPTER 20

Saving Grace:
ADCs for Suicide Intervention

Blessed are they that mourn:
for they shall be comforted.
Jesus of Nazareth

It's natural to grieve a variety of losses during your lifetime that may evoke very painful feelings of sadness, depression, and fear. Unfortunately, if you spiral downward in consciousness and allow yourself to become overwhelmed by despair, to the point of feeling hopeless and helpless, you might consider taking your life.

At those times a deceased family member or friend may return to persuade you that suicide is not an appropriate or acceptable choice. He or she might remind you "this too shall pass" and passionately affirm that life is worth living.

These suicide interventions are a specialized form of ADCs for protection that occur at the critical moment someone truly needs encouragement. They seem to be somewhat common experiences, and each person who has had one is certain that a deceased relative or friend was directly responsible for saving his or her life.

This is the most profound category of ADC experiences in our files. These powerful accounts can serve to uplift and inspire those who may be contemplating suicide and deter them from acting upon their feelings of self-destruction.

• • •

In the first four accounts the experiencers had strong feelings of depression that caused them to contemplate suicide as a means of eliminating their emotional pain.

Danielle is a 16-year-old high-school student in New York. She reported having this influential ADC more than 3 years after her grandmother died from cancer:

> I was thirteen years old that summer. I was very depressed. I was sitting on my bed crying and thinking of suicide. I called out to my grandmother, "I need help now! I need you now!"
>
> Grandma appeared next to me, right at the end of my bed! She actually looked like an angel in a very pretty white robe. I saw nice pastel colors around her. Pastel colors always remind me of heaven and the Lord.
>
> She said, "Everything is going to be okay. Say a prayer before you go to sleep. I love you." She was very supportive, and when she reassured me, I felt a warmness through my body.
>
> I told her I loved her and I thanked her. My gut instinct was saying, "Everything is going to be okay!" Then I said a prayer and just fell asleep.
>
> Since then I have felt very good about myself. I have become mentally and emotionally stronger because of my grandmother.

We selected a child's experience for the first account in this chapter to emphasize the alarming increase of teenage suicides in our society. Many adolescents attempt suicide as an escape from their feelings of depression and worthlessness, tragically fulfilling the adage "Suicide is a permanent solution to a temporary problem."

Marcie, age 30, is a retail sales clerk in Washington. She was 18 years old when she was calmed by the loving kindness of her father about 5 years after he had died by suicide:

I was going through a really hard time emotionally. I was very, very depressed. I was down and out, probably like my dad had been before he took his life. I felt so totally alone and just wanted to be with him.

One day, I was sitting on the floor crying uncontrollably. Suddenly I felt as if someone hugged me, but no one else was in the room. Then I heard a "clink" on the hardwood floor. I went over and picked up a penny that had the Lord's Prayer on it.

I smiled and said, "Thank you, Dad." I had given that same penny to my father before he died to keep in his pocket, to know I was always thinking of him.

I believe in my heart my dad wanted to show me he was still there, that he still cared. I really feel he put the penny there because he wanted me to know that I wasn't alone.

Marcie was only a teenager at the time, and her deep depression could have easily caused her to follow in her father's footsteps. Since we teach by example, the lesson of suicide can regrettably become a family legacy that is passed along to future generations. Once a loved one has taken his or her life as a means of escaping suffering, this option can appear desirable to other family members as well, especially children.

Holly, age 34, is a bookkeeper in British Columbia. She regained her will to live during a series of encounters she had with her father 13 years after he died of a heart attack:

I was thirty-two and at a very, very difficult time in my life. I had made a decision that it wasn't really worth going on. I had come to a point where I was trying to decide the quickest and easiest way out.

I used to have a lot of tears when I went to bed. Then one night I physically felt I was being hugged. But I ignored it and just sloughed it off. However, it continued to happen for three or four nights. I got to a point where I was waiting for this to happen, wanting to see if it was only my imagination.

Then one night, as I was lying in bed with my eyes closed, Dad's face suddenly appeared! He looked just the way I remembered him the last time I saw him. And he said to me, "Don't do this! You have a greater purpose in your life. You have to stop how you're thinking right now. You're on the wrong track, and you have to change."

I had no previous experience with anything like this. It was such a shock! I said, "Is this you? Are you my dad? What's happening here?" Then I actually felt his hand taking my hand, and he said, "I am here and I've come to help you."

Now, anytime I need encouragement, I just close my eyes and can hear my dad saying, "Go for it! You can do it!"

Sometimes it takes a close call with suicide to realize that life is a very precious gift not to be wasted. Initially, her father's loving intervention and his forceful message gave Holly the support she needed. But ultimately, it was her own change in outlook that made the lasting difference in choosing life over death.

Walt is a 42-year-old actor, writer, and truck driver in Florida. He underwent spiritual renewal 3 years after his grandfather died of emphysema:

I was working for a newspaper under stressful conditions. I got very depressed and was thinking of committing suicide.

One night I thought I was awake when my grandfather came in and sat on my bed – I even felt the bed move. He put his hand on my leg, and I actually felt him! He was happier than I had ever seen him, and he was wearing an olive green suit.

Grandpa said, "What's wrong with you, Walt? You're

not like this. You have always been very happy and very
confident." It was my grandfather's voice – he had a New
England accent.

I was surprised that he was there – he was supposed
to be dead! When I realized it was my grandfather, I completely woke up, but then he was gone.

It was like "Wow! My grandfather came all the way
from the other side to cheer me up!" Nobody around me
did that, nobody alive. I felt cared for – somebody was
concerned for my well-being.

I knew my grandfather came to me because he loved
me. He loved me enough to communicate at a time when
I really needed someone. He reminded me about an attitude that I had forgotten, and his coming brought me
back to the way I used to be.

If we allow ourselves to become as isolated and filled with
stress as Walt did, we are in danger of falling prey to our fears
and negativity. His account demonstrates the gentle power of
an ADC to heal our thoughts of self-destruction and inspire a
healthy will to live. What greater gift can a deceased loved one
give than to reach across time and space to remind us that our
life has enormous value!

The next three accounts involve people who were feeling
suicidal because they were grieving a broken relationship.

Sally, age 33, is a nurse in California. Her life was radically
changed 15 months after her mother died:

I had been treated for depression on and off since I
was eighteen. Clinical depression and alcoholism run in
my family, especially with the women.

My sister, Peggy, had been treated for depression
since she was sixteen. She was an alcoholic and died of
an overdose of prescription drugs when she was twenty-
one. My mother, who was a recovering alcoholic, had
been extremely depressed her whole life. And finally, at
age fifty, she committed suicide too.

After breaking up with my boyfriend, I was overwhelmed and couldn't continue with the pain I was feeling. I was in a deep depression and decided that I wanted to die. So I drank a whole bunch of alcohol, told my cats good-bye, and wrote a note to my family before I fell asleep.

Just before waking up in the morning, I had a dream that I got a phone call from my mom. I recognized her voice as she said, "Sally, don't do it! Don't do it!" She was loving, but pleading. That was all she said to me, but it was really powerful!

I used this experience to turn my life around. Immediately I got up and enrolled myself that morning in an outpatient alcohol rehab program. Now, a year later, I have a positive attitude about life and how good it can be.

The legacy of suicide nearly claimed another victim. When depression and alcoholism can be traced throughout a family, its members run a higher risk for self-destruction. Sally's ADC and her courage to change enabled her to break this deadly family pattern.

Michael, age 30, is the manager of a liquor store in Georgia. He found a new purpose for living when his grandmother came to him:

My girlfriend had left me, and I was extremely depressed for three weeks. I contemplated suicide and was at the end of my rope. I was trying to decide what I should do with myself. I was so tired of feeling depressed – it was so painful to me.

That night, I had this dream right before I woke up. I was all alone in a very empty place. It was like a great hall that had no beginning and no end, no doorways and no windows. It was total emptiness.

My grandmother came up to me. She put her arms around me and kissed me on the cheek. She told me,

"Your life is worthwhile. Don't give up your life because of someone else. You have everything to live for and many things to do. Go out and be yourself. You'll love again, so live and enjoy yourself!"

I woke up and I felt better than I had in three weeks. This experience did me a world of good. I no longer felt the pain inside.

I had never met my grandmother before. I had only seen two pictures of her in my life. But I knew of her accomplishments and I knew how she had died. She had committed suicide about forty years earlier!

Taking my own life was not worth the pain and suffering I would have put myself through and everybody else around me. My grandmother came because I needed somebody to tell me that. She knew what her death had done to my mother and father.

In a way she was saying, "Don't do what I did. Live your life because it's worth it. Take the chances while you have them here. If I had the opportunity to do it over again, I wouldn't have committed suicide."

Who would know more about the importance of physical life and the consequences of suicide than Michael's grandmother, who had taken her own life forty years earlier? It's highly significant that so many people who committed suicide have come back to motivate others to make wiser choices.

Deirdre, age 31, is a computer specialist in Virginia. She was only 21 years old when she received an affirmation of life from her boyfriend's grandmother, who had died by suicide 6 months earlier following a long struggle with cancer:

I became very depressed about my relationship with my boyfriend, Terry. I started asking myself about my life's purpose, and I felt an inability to cope with my confusing thoughts and feelings.

I was in bed and felt like I had hit rock bottom – emotionally, I was at my lowest. I cried uncontrollably for a while, thinking about terminating myself. I just cried and cried until I couldn't cry anymore.

About 5:00 in the morning a baby-blue misty light appeared in the hallway and moved into my bedroom. It was oval shaped, about three feet high and a foot wide, and was three feet off the ground.

I closed my eyes, and Terry's grandmother started talking to me in my mind. It was just like the conversations we used to have when she was alive.

She said that my family and Terry's family would not understand why I had terminated my life. And that life was too precious to give up. She reassured me that I was loved and would truly be missed. She told me that suicide was not the answer. She had made that mistake herself, but I should not make that mistake too.

It was like she encompassed me and surrounded me. I felt a warmth inside of me that I had never felt before. She gave me an inner strength, and I felt that I could do anything that I wanted to do at that point. Then the light was gone.

The loss of a love relationship is never a justifiable cause for committing suicide, despite the amount of pain we may be feeling at the time. Suicide is a denial of our spiritual identity and our purpose for being here. It is a total rejection of our future and the people, the experiences, and the lessons that life holds for us.

Deirdre's story has another positive outcome. She and Terry reconciled their differences and have now been married over ten years.

In the next two accounts the experiencers were having severe difficulties in their marriage that caused them to regard suicide as a solution to their problems.

Katharine is a 43-year-old jewelry artist in Florida. She was given a very strong reprimand about 19 years after her great-aunt, Mildred, died of old age:

I was a twenty-four-year-old student in London. I had been married for two years and found out that my husband was having an affair. I was really devastated! I was having second thoughts about pursuing my education, and the whole situation had me very, very depressed.

I went to the tube station and was feeling that life was not worth living. I thought it would be nice and quick and easy to throw myself in front of a train. I remember moving closer to the edge of the platform. I heard the train coming, and I was getting ready to jump.

All of a sudden, somebody tapped me on my left shoulder, and a voice distinctly said, "Think of your mother, child!" The voice was stern and sharp. Then I had a flash of my Aunt Mildred's face, just her head and shoulders. She knit her brow and was scolding me.

The minute that happened, an old battered train came through the tunnel. I thought, "Oh, my gosh, how silly this is!" I quickly ran up the stairs of the station and took a bus home.

I felt overwhelmed because of how stupid I had been. My mother had just had major surgery, and my death would have set her back considerably. I was so ashamed for even thinking of killing myself. I'll never consider it again, never, not in a month of Sundays!

Intense feelings of rejection, abandonment, and loneliness are common during the breakup of a marriage and may produce reckless thoughts of suicide. But when we are immersed in our own grief, we rarely consider how our death will affect those who love us. At such times, our self-centeredness may easily cause us to forget that each of us is a spiritual being who has a special purpose or mission for our life.

•   •   •

Tony is a 46-year-old park ranger in Florida. He experienced a series of interventions from his father, who died of cardiac arrest:

About two months after my father's death I was not yet divorced, but I was separated from my wife. At the time my depression was pretty severe, and I became suicidal.

Depression has been handed down through heredity and runs in my family. My uncle had committed suicide. My dad was gone and my uncle was gone, and I figured I'd be with them. I was thinking about doing it with a shotgun I had.

Several times during a three-month period, in the middle of the night, my dad called my name, "Tony! Tony!" It sounded exactly like him – it was his voice.

Each time I would smell the odor of his cologne, Mennen After Shave, which was more or less Dad's calling card. I felt like I had been visited, but I never actually saw him.

Each time, right at that instant, there was a feeling of calm, like everything was okay. It was like he was trying to tell me, "I'm still here for you if you have any problems."

These experiences changed my mind because they made me realize how foolish I was. My dad gave me a nudge, and I think that's all I needed. I sold my shotgun and started doing more positive things with my life.

I went back to school and started going to church every Sunday. Now I am active with my congregation, and I am presently helping with an outreach ministry for the bereaved.

We all feel compassion for a young child when his mother or father dies, but we may overlook the fact that when an adult loses a parent, he too becomes a bereaved child. Some of the issues may be different, but the sense of loss and feelings of grief can be just as overpowering.

Like Tony, many people must grieve more than one loss at the same time. We are more vulnerable then to being overwhelmed by feelings of despair that can lead to thoughts of suicide. But we must never count on having an ADC to protect us from ourselves. Our only true safeguard against suicide is to make an unshakable inner commitment to living our life to its natural completion.

In the next two accounts the experiencers were struggling with the grief of widowhood when they had an ADC experience.

Bobbie is a 29-year-old noncommissioned officer in the Air Force in Virginia. Her husband, Scotty, had also been an NCO in the Air Force before he died of a brain tumor:

> I was in such pain over Scotty's death and losing all of our dreams. I was basically feeling we both had been cheated. I felt like I had been cut in two, and no drug on this earth was going to stop the pain. There were a couple of times suicide seriously crossed my mind because I was hurting so bad.
>
> Sometimes when I would be in the middle of a real intense crying jag, I would get a comforting from Scotty. He would say, "That's okay. Cry, it's good for you!" His mood was loving concern, and usually at the end of my crying, I could literally feel him holding me.
>
> But when I would even start to think of ways of committing suicide, it was almost a stern lecture. He'd say, "That's not going to solve the problem! That's not going to get rid of your pain!"
>
> When I'd be down in the pit, Scotty would say, "Get your butt in gear! Don't just sit there and wallow in self-pity! Don't just sit around doing nothing!"
>
> I would argue with him, saying, "That's easy for you to say, you're dead!" He'd say, "Yeah, so? You're alive! Why don't you start acting like you're part of the living and not part of the dead!"
>
> Scotty always felt life was for living. I think these experiences are examples of him being there for me when I needed him most. Now, as I continue to heal and face life on my own, I am able to let him go.

Apparently, Scotty was able to distinguish between Bobbie's normal grief and her suicidal emotions. Therefore, he wisely provided a balance of gentle nurturing and tough love according to her needs.

Deep grief is a natural and healthy process when we lose a loved one. But if our thoughts turn to feelings of self-destruction, we need to remember, as Scotty said, that suicide will not solve our problems or remove our emotional pain. A much better choice is to join a bereavement support group or obtain professional counseling.

Leigh is a resident of Mississippi. She was widowed when her husband, Ralph, died of a heart attack at age 50:

> About one year after Ralph died, I was lying on my couch crying. We had separated a couple of times the year that he died, and I was feeling a lot of guilt that Ralph's death was my fault. I felt like my leaving him had put more stress on him and perhaps caused his death.
>
> I had decided which way I was going to do it – I had it all planned out. After Ralph died, my medical doctor suggested I take a tranquilizer and sleeping pills. I had plenty of them on hand.
>
> But right before I planned to do it, I went to the funeral home and made my own funeral arrangements, even down to the pall bearers and what I wanted to wear.
>
> I had already written a couple of letters, one to a friend of mine and one to my stepdaughter, apologizing to them for committing suicide. I had also written a letter to a friend about what I wanted done regarding a dog and a cat I had at the time. All of that was lying on the table beside me.
>
> I had been drinking beer and was trying to get myself drunk enough to do it. I was crying real hard, sobbing, when I heard Ralph's voice very distinctly say something like "This is not the way it's done. Don't do that! Hang on! It's going to be all right." Then he said that he loved me.

I don't care if anybody believes it, but that was Ralph Taylor's voice, and that's the God's truth! It was so real, it was almost as if I could feel his breath on my ear!

Immediately, I jumped up and switched the lights on and looked around each room of the house. I stopped my plans right then and went and tore the letters up.

Even though I didn't stop thinking about committing suicide until maybe a year later, I didn't do anything else about it.

Of all the planned suicides we've heard, Leigh was closest to actually taking her own life when she had this ADC. But what if Ralph had not intervened at just the right moment? Today, eleven years later, Leigh is a happy and successful registered nurse.

The next three accounts are from bereaved parents who felt life was not worth living following the death of their child.

Sondra is a nurse in Saskatchewan, Canada. Her son, Greg, came back after he died in an automobile accident at age 16:

This was exactly three months to the day after Greg's death. I couldn't take it any longer – I had to be with my son. I made plans to end my own life. I went to bed, and in my prayers I asked God to allow me to go and be with Greg.

Later that night, I woke up and there was a real warmth on my right cheek, like a kiss. Then the strong smell of Greg's Polo cologne just filled me. The message I got was, "Mom, I'm okay. Get a grip, Mom!"

I lay there awhile and just couldn't believe it! I kept breathing in Greg's cologne. It lasted maybe two minutes, and then it faded.

In the morning, I contacted my minister. He said that God had allowed Greg to come back to tell me that I was needed here and that he was safe.

After this experience, my thoughts of suicide ended. That was a turning point in my slow recovery because now I know my son is okay.

The death of a child has been called "life's ultimate tragedy." Many newly bereaved parents are so filled with pain that they may contemplate suicide as an instant way to be reunited with their deceased son or daughter.

Kate is a homemaker in New York. An indirect communication saved her life after the death of her 19-year-old son, Darryl:

> While in the Marines, Darryl developed leukemia and spent eleven months in and out of hospitals before he died. I was extremely depressed with his death. I was saving up pills, thinking that I couldn't go on any longer. I had enough of them to kill an elephant!
>
> I didn't have any religious beliefs, but I had asked for a sign many, many times. I wanted desperately to believe that my son still existed.
>
> One afternoon my husband took a nap. When he got up, he said, "I dreamed about Darryl." I asked, "What happened?" And he said, "Nothing really. We just hugged." Then I asked, "Did he say anything?" My husband said, "Yes. Darryl said, 'Life is worth living!' "
>
> I was so overwhelmed and so happy to have heard from Darryl! That was my sign he was all right. At last, I had hope that there is something more to life. And with that, I took all the pills and flushed them down the toilet!
>
> My husband's experience gave me the hope I needed and the willingness to go on, in spite of all my pain. I feel God reached down and picked me up out of all that misery and started my healing process.

The timing and healing power of ADC messages, even those that are delivered through others, are truly astounding. Over and over again, they indicate that we live in a far more compassionate and loving spiritual universe than we had previously envisioned.

The final account is from Gwen, an artist in Maryland. She had this out-of-body ADC with her 22-year-old son,

Christopher, who died when his neck was broken in a motorcycle accident:

> The day after Christopher's funeral, I was feeling so awful. I was in a terrible state! The next day, while everybody was out, I was going to take sleeping pills in order to be with my son. That's how low I was.
>
> That night I had a dream. I was in a place that was very light, and there was soft music playing in the air. I've never heard such instruments or such music – it was beautiful!
>
> Stretching out from me as far as I could see was this big table covered with a white cloth. On the table were gold dishes with food. Everything was very attractively arranged like you would see on an ocean liner.
>
> There were a lot of people there walking around very slowly. Some were helping themselves to the food, and they all looked very happy. Everybody was dressed in long robes of different colors. It was such a beautiful, peaceful, happy scene!
>
> Then I heard Christopher say, "Mom," and when I turned, he was standing there! He had on a white robe and a large gold cross on his chest. He was all shiny with light and seemed very happy. It was such a joy to be with my son again!
>
> Christopher had a big plate of food, and he held it out to me as he said, "Mom, this is for you." He seemed very proud to be giving me this food. Then Christopher smiled and turned his head to each side to show me that his neck was no longer broken.
>
> I woke up knowing deep in my heart that I had actually been with my son. And I threw the sleeping pills away at once! Christopher saved my life – I'd swear to it! I'll believe it until the day I die. And I feel when it's my time, he'll be there for me.
>
> Whenever I'm down, I think of this experience, and it lifts me up again.

Gwen was truly blessed to have had this moment of grace with her son. Very likely her visit with Christopher took place in heaven, where they joyously celebrated the feast of eternal life.

The implications of suicide interventions are far-reaching. All the experiencers in this chapter and thousands more are still alive today because they believe they were contacted by a deceased loved one and were willing to heed his or her lifesaving message. Yet how many others who also felt suicidal had such an ADC but dismissed it for some reason and chose to take their life anyway?

Imagine the joy our deceased relatives and friends must feel when they are able to save our life through their intervention. They tell us that physical life is a gift, a priceless opportunity to learn our spiritual lessons of unconditional love. And they emphasize that the same teachings we choose to reject during our earthly existence will still have to be mastered, though with much more difficulty, after we die.

Are ADCs exclusively personal experiences, or can they be shared by others? The next chapter contains reports of two or more people being contacted by a deceased loved one while they were together at the same time and place.

Confirmation:
ADCs with a Witness

I think death is a tremendous adventure –
a gateway into a new life, in which you have
further powers, deeper joys, and wonderful horizons.
—*Dr. Leslie D. Weatherhead*

Almost all after-death contacts are made to only one person
at a time, whether he or she is alone or surrounded by others.
On some occasions, however, two or more people, who are together in the same place at the same time, will perceive their
deceased loved one simultaneously. We call them ADCs with a
witness or shared ADCs.

Descriptions of these shared encounters may be nearly
identical or quite different, depending upon the individual perceptions of the experiencers. The value of having an ADC in
the presence of a witness is that you can receive immediate
and direct confirmation from another person that your experience is authentic. Such validation is especially important if
you are doubting your senses or questioning your sanity at the
time.

Reports of shared ADCs provide credible evidence that
after-death communications are genuine experiences with deceased loved ones and not products of overactive imaginations.
These witnessed encounters furnish convincing testimony that
ADCs are objective and real events that two or more people can
perceive and respond to independently of each other.

•   •   •

In the first four accounts the experiencers and witnesses had identical ADCs that they related to each other immediately.

Christina is a hostess for a restaurant in Michigan. Her only children, Jon, age 10, and Kelsey, age 7, were murdered by their father, who then took his own life:

> About three months after Jon's and Kelsey's death, my mother and I were flying from Detroit to Florida to attend The Compassionate Friends' national conference in Tampa.
>
> I was sitting in the window seat next to my mother, and I was acutely bereaved and crying. As we passed through the clouds, it was very sunny with a real heaven-like atmosphere. I felt so close to my kids at that time.
>
> All of a sudden, my mom said, "Christina, look above your head!" When I looked up, there was a perfect miniature rainbow arching over my head! It was just like a regular rainbow that you would see outdoors. It extended from ear to ear, about six inches above me. This rainbow was so magnificent! It stayed there for a good five minutes.
>
> Mom and I were crying because it was a definite sign! We were convinced that the rainbow was a symbolic tribute from my children because my little girl, Kelsey, drew rainbows all the time. We both felt Jon and Kelsey were sending a message to us that they were all right.

In this instance, Christina's mother was the witness who saw the beautiful little rainbow first and brought it to her daughter's attention. This special gift from her deceased children was both timely and prophetic for Christina because her attendance at the TCF conference became the turning point in her bereavement.

Lloyd is a retired chemist in Vermont. He enthusiastically participated in this greeting from his friend's mother, Anne, who died of heart failure at age 80:

Anne's daughter, Shirley, and our friend, May, and I were returning home from Anne's funeral. As we came in the kitchen door, Shirley said, "You know, it's funny, I feel as though Mother is right here!"

All of a sudden, the kitchen was suffused with a fragrance as though there were a million roses blooming at once! All three of us stood transfixed. Time stood still, and I just lived for the moment. It was glorious! It was a great, uplifting feeling.

But there are no roses in Vermont in September! And being of a suspicious mind, I went sniffing around and looked in all the corners. There was just no place that marvelous, encompassing odor could have come from. After a few minutes the scent gradually faded.

We checked with each other to see if we had experienced the same thing. Sure enough, we all had smelled the roses at the same time!

Shirley said, "Just as we came in, I was thinking, 'I hope we have done everything Mother wanted.'" As far as we could tell, her answer was given. It was as if Anne had said, "Yes, Shirley, and here is a gift for all of you because you have been so nice to me."

That's my story. I am basically trained as a scientist, and I look for answers. I could find no other explanation that fit, and I was intellectually convinced. After that my soul said, "Yes, that's a fact!"

Because all three people smelled an aroma of roses in the kitchen simultaneously, each one was able to validate the experience of the others. In fact, of the twelve types of after-death communication, sentient and olfactory ADCs are the most commonly shared.

Emma is a counselor in Alaska. She and her husband, Gerald, became bereaved parents when their 19-year-old son, Stan, died following an automobile accident:

During the days after Stan was buried, my husband, Gerald, and I had feelings that we didn't share with each other – because we weren't quite sure what they were.

About the fourth day he told me, "I feel almost like it's a pulling, like I need to go to the cemetery." That's exactly how I felt. But I kind of dreaded going because it would mean that it really had happened and all this was true.

Gerald and I looked at each other and immediately got in the car. We drove to the cemetery about twenty-five miles from where we live.

We were walking to Stan's grave, and as we got near, I felt this sense of our son's arms around me. A sense of Stan's love came into me.

I looked at Gerald and he said, "Stan is here! I feel him, I sense him, I feel his love!" This was exactly what I was feeling at that moment!

My husband and I grabbed ahold of each other, and it was like Stan was hugging us. The sense of his love was so strong, the feeling just permeated us!

We were so grateful for being able to feel that. We knew in our hearts it was an embrace from our son and a saying of good-bye. I believe Stan came back to let us know that he loves us as much as we love him.

I know our son isn't gone – I know he still lives on. This experience made me know it to my very soul.

This account demonstrates how valuable it is to hear some-one speaking about his or her ADC at the very moment it is happening. Because Gerald had sufficient courage to admit he was sensing their son's presence, Emma received immediate confirmation that her own experience with Stan was real and not just a result of her grief.

Tammy is a computer operator in Washington. She was given new hope after her 9-week-old daughter, Melanie, died of SIDS:

Melanie's death really broke my heart. I was so bitter and angry and couldn't believe that this had happened. I couldn't understand why – it was just so unfair! And I was so scared that she wouldn't go to heaven because her christening was to be on June 9th, and she died on June 6th.

We buried Melanie on June 8th. When we came back from the cemetery, I was the first one to enter the house. As soon as I opened the door, the house smelled of roses – a very strong aroma. I didn't say anything for fear the others might say I was going crazy.

When the others came in – about ten people – everybody else started smelling the roses! Somebody said, "Oh, Melanie's here! The house smells of roses!" Only one person didn't smell them, and she had never seen Melanie when she was alive. The aroma was there for a few seconds, and then it was gone.

This experience reassured me that my precious baby is okay and she's with God in heaven.

An independent witness spoke first and confirmed the same aroma Tammy was smelling. It's very significant that only the ten people who had known Melanie when she was alive shared this olfactory experience, while the one person who had never seen the baby before wasn't able to perceive the fragrance of roses.

Many bereaved parents of infants who died before they were baptized fear that their child will not be granted entrance to heaven. This account and others in our files suggest that their concerns are quite unnecessary.

In each of the next four accounts two people participated in the same ADC experience but didn't realize this until they spoke to each other after it was over.

Lauren is a behavior therapist in Florida. Her 53-year-old brother, Donald, died by suicide:

Donald had a low back injury and a limp, and his body was always contorted. He had had two surgeries and was consumed with unbearable pain for three years before he died.

During his memorial service, I looked out the window and saw Donald walking towards the church! His body was not solid, and I could see the trees behind him. He looked a bit younger and seemed to be whole – and he didn't have his limp anymore!

He was wearing a plaid shirt that he liked and a pair of trousers. He looked very peaceful and happy, like he was out for a stroll. Donald walked up to the window as if to beckon me to come with him. Then he just disappeared.

After the service my sister-in-law, Joyce, said, "Did you see Donald?" I was quite surprised and said, "Yes!" She said, "I saw him too!"

This was probably my brother's way of saying goodbye. It was an impactful experience that brought a natural kind of closure to my grief.

How will we ever know that we're not the only person having an ADC if we don't take the risk of telling someone else about our experience? Fortunately, both Lauren and Joyce had the courage to promptly reveal they had seen Donald. And perhaps others at his memorial service saw him too but were reluctant to admit it.

Blair, age 45, is a business executive in Florida. She obtained confirmation from an unexpected source after she had a meeting with her father, who had died following a series of strokes:

I was feeling very sorry for myself, very much alone in the world. I remember sitting in a chair in my hotel room praying for my father the night before his funeral. There were two other people in the room – my son, who was five years old, and a friend who was there for moral support.

As I was praying the lights in the room seemed to grow dim, and all of a sudden, there was my father! He seemed very, very solid. Though he was in his eighties when he died, now he appeared to be more like a man in his sixties.

There were colors radiating from him and surrounding him – a combination of bluish white, rose, and gold. He stood there and told me, "Be strong and take care of your mother. Remember, I love you. Good-bye." Dad's facial expression softened considerably when he said, "Remember, I love you." It lasted only a few seconds, and then he left.

My little boy, who was in bed, got up. I thought he had been asleep. He ran to me and said, "My granddaddy! My granddaddy!" I said, "Your granddaddy is gone." And he said, "No! My granddaddy was right here!" So my son saw him too!

Our research indicates that young children are far more open and receptive than adults to having ADCs. Therefore, it's best not to argue with a child who insists he has seen, heard from, or perhaps even spoken with a deceased loved one, because to do so might cause him to doubt all his future intuitive experiences.

Wells, a 42-year-old psychotherapist in Florida, was present when his friend, Jean, made a generous visit after dying of cancer:

As a psychotherapist, I work very hard at remaining psychologically clean. I'm in the business of helping people stay that way or regain that way. I try hard not to indulge in fantasies.

One evening, about three months after Jean's death, I was in a support group. Alice, a friend of Jean's, was doing some intense work. She was really in a lot of emotional pain and was struggling with herself to face some issues.

As I was sitting there listening to Alice, I felt the hair on the back of my neck stand up, literally! All of a sudden, there was a presence in the room. I looked up and saw Jean sitting on the floor next to Alice. I was awestruck!

Jean had a concerned expression like you'd have about a friend who was really hurting and troubled. She was listening very intently to Alice.

I thought it very appropriate, given the intensity of Alice's pain, that Jean would show up to make sure things were working out all right. She was there for Alice. She just sat and listened, changed posture a couple of times, and then she left.

When the group was over, one of the guys, who was also a very dear friend of Jean's, hung around. We looked at each other, and I said, "Did something happen for you tonight?" And he said, "Yes!"

We compared stories, and he had also seen Jean and experienced her presence at the same time I did. She was seated on the floor for him in the same place that she was seated for me.

Seeing Jean was a completely spontaneous experience and one that I know happened. It was so very powerful! It's not something I imagined or dreamed up.

Wells and his male friend were not only mutual witnesses to each other's ADC, but they also had the privilege of observing Jean's ministry of love to Alice. How often does a deceased loved one return to assist us if we require emotional and spiritual support? Probably far more frequently than we realize!

Leslie, age 39, is a volunteer worker in Virginia. She had this happy reunion with her father 4 months after he died of cancer:

I had just gone to bed and turned the light off when I saw my father standing in the doorway! All the lights were out in the house, yet I could see him very clearly because there was a glow around him.

I kept thinking, "This is really Daddy! This is really him!" I was so excited that I sat up and said, "Daddy!" I wanted to go over and touch him, and I started to get out of bed.

He smiled and said, "No, you cannot touch me now." I began to cry and kept saying, "Let me come to you." He said, "No, you can't do that. But I want you to know that I am all right. Everything is fine. I am always with you."

Then he paused and said, "I have to go look in on your mother and Curtis now." Curtis is my son, and he and my mother were in the next room. I got up and followed my father to the hallway. But he disappeared – he just faded away.

So I went back to bed and kept saying to myself, "This is just your grief. Daddy wasn't really here." Then I finally fell asleep after tossing and turning for quite some time.

The next morning I got up, and Curtis, who was three, almost four at the time, came out in the hallway. He said, "Mommy, I saw Granddaddy last night!" My mouth fell open and I said, "You did?" He said, "Yes! He came in my room. He was standing by my bed."

How could a three-year-old come up with that? I questioned him, "Were you dreaming?" He said, "No, Mommy. I had my eyes open. I was awake. I saw him!"

So then I knew that Daddy had to have actually been there. There was no way to refute what had happened. It was a wonderful experience for me because I learned that love continues on.

Again, a young child validated his mother's experience and convinced her that it was real. This account is slightly different than a typical ADC with a witness because Leslie's father visited her first and then went on to see his grandson in a separate room.

When two or more people participate in an ADC together, they won't necessarily have identical experiences. Such variations can be attributed to a combination of their intuitive abilities, receptivity, and individual perceptions. The next four accounts are from people who shared an after-death communication at the same time and place but whose personal experiences were significantly different from each other.

Ginny is a dental hygienist in Georgia. She received validation of a joyous ADC she had with her sons, Mike, who drowned at 17, and Philip, who had died at birth 13 years earlier:

> Three weeks after Mike's death, I was attending a baptism in church. All at once, I felt a hand slide across my shoulders from the right to the left, and I heard the voice of my son speak to me, "I am here, Mom." I knew it was Mike, and I thought I had flipped out!
>
> About that same time, I felt a very firm hand on my left shoulder. Then a voice I had never heard before, slightly more mature than Mike's, said, "We're both here, Mom." And I thought, "Oh, my goodness! I have completely gone overboard and I'm ready for the funny farm!"
>
> I looked at my fourteen-year-old daughter, Mandy, sitting next to me, and she looked at me. She had tears running down her face. Mandy said, "Mama, do you feel Mike?" She said she didn't hear him or see him but she felt his presence.
>
> This was my confirmation that I had not imagined it. Truly both my sons had touched me and had spoken to me. I believe that with all my heart!

Just when Ginny was about to dismiss her experience as a flight of fancy, her daughter was able to verify that it was factual. More importantly, this bereaved mother learned that her two sons, who had never known each other in physical life on earth, had found one another in the spiritual dimension.

Deanna is a 35-year-old counselor in Florida. She and her mother were together a few hours after her brother, Charley, died in a motorcycle accident at age 32:

About 6:00 the next morning, my mother and I were sitting in the kitchen talking about my brother. My mother looked at me and said, "I know that Charley is here. I just felt him touch my cheek!" Then Mom put her hand on her cheek as if she had just been kissed.

Then I saw Charley standing in front of me laughing and smiling! He was somewhat transparent, but I could see he was wearing a striped polo shirt, shorts, and his sandals. He looked at me with a sheepish expression – his little shy smile – and he had his hands in his pockets.

I heard him say, "Please tell everyone how much I love you all. Especially tell Mom that I love her."

Then he asked that we stay close to his children, who were three and five at the time. He said, "The kids love you a lot, and you know that I trust you with them. Please take care of them for me. They will need you all."

I remember my heart opening, and a rush of emotion poured from me to my brother. Then Charley was gone.

This is an excellent example of two people having separate and distinctly different personal experiences during a shared ADC. While Charley's mother felt her son's hand touch her cheek tenderly, his sister, Deanna, actually saw him and received his important message telepathically.

Lois, a homemaker in Nebraska, witnessed a very nurturing moment shortly after her husband, Ray, died of a stroke at age 33. An earlier experience of hers is in the chapter on auditory ADCs:

When my husband, Ray, passed away, our four sons were between eight and thirteen. The three older boys knew that their father had not been well and understood what had happened. But our youngest son, eight-year-old Jesse, was frightened and disoriented.

Ray was always very compassionate with the boys and always talked to them about everything that happened. He went camping with them and discussed problems with them. He spent a lot of time with his sons.

Two mornings after Ray died, I walked down the hall of our house. As I approached the master bedroom, I saw Jesse sitting on the side of the bed with his father! His dad had his arm around him and was talking to him. Ray looked natural like he normally did. He seemed to be calm and reassuring.

Ray was aware I was there too. He looked and kind of smiled at me, then gestured for me to go back down the hall. So I went around the corner and waited for about fifteen minutes.

Jesse finally came out of the bedroom. Apparently, Ray had explained to him what had happened, and he seemed to feel a lot better. Jesse said, "Daddy told me that he has gone and won't be coming back and not to worry about him. Everything will be all right." Jesse seemed much happier than he did before.

The fact that this happened didn't surprise me very much. After that, our boy was able to accept his father's death and go on.

Because Lois was a witness to her son's intimate talk with his deceased father, she was able to be immediately supportive when he willingly shared his experience with her. Unfortunately, all too often in our society, children have their ADCs invalidated when they risk telling them to others.

Andrea and her former husband, Oliver, are bereaved parents in Florida. They were greatly comforted by their 25-year-old son, Douglas, after he died in a motorcycle accident. Another account of hers appears in the chapter on symbolic ADCs:

Douglas was our only child, and his father, Oliver, and I had been divorced since he was twelve years old. After his funeral service, I broke down really bad. While Oliver was holding my hand, we were crying in the funeral car on the way to the cemetery.

All of a sudden, such a calm came over me that I stopped crying. It was Douglas! He was kneeling in front of us, and he had his right hand on my knee and his left hand on his father's knee. I could feel the pressure and the warmth on my leg.

It was like I could reach out and touch Douglas, but I didn't. He had on the clothes that I had picked out to have him buried in, a light blue shirt and off-white pants.

There was such a peacefulness about him, and it gave me that same peace, that same comfort. I saw a light around his whole being – it was a soft, white glow. He had a smile on his face and was very contented, very peaceful.

I told his father, "Douglas is here! I see him!" I looked at Oliver, and he looked at me, and tears rolled out of his eyes. Oliver leaned his head back and said, "I know, Andrea. I feel him too. Douglas is here!"

Then our son looked at both of us and said, "I'm all right. I love you, Mama. I love you, Dad." It was telepathic and just as clear as could be. Then he gradually went away.

What a beautiful, peaceful feeling I had as I sat through the rest of the services at the cemetery. I knew Douglas was all right, and I didn't cry anymore.

I'll never forget that experience! I can close my eyes and still see it perfectly. I know there's life after death – my son proved it to me!

Douglas displayed perfect timing in contacting his parents on the day they needed him most. Although Andrea saw and heard her son and even felt his touch, Oliver was also reassured when he sensed his son's presence. What a difference it would make in our bereavement process if each of us could have such a life-affirming experience so soon after the death of a loved one!

Many animals have physical senses that extend well beyond the range of human abilities. This is particularly true for cats and dogs, whose sense of sight, hearing, and smell are far more acute. It's not surprising, therefore, that animals are able to detect our deceased loved ones more readily than we can. In the next three accounts pets were the witnesses when an ADC occurred.

Rene, age 39, is a legal secretary in the U.S. Virgin Islands. She was not the only one to perceive her father, who came back after he died of cancer:

> Within a month after my father died, I was aboard my sailboat one night, alone with my dog, Heidi. I was reading a book when all of a sudden I had a strong feeling that my dad was there. It was a warm, loving, and very peaceful feeling.
>
> I could not see him, but I sensed his presence very strongly. I intuited that he came to tell me he was fine and that he loved me more than anything in the world. He somehow conveyed all these wonderful feelings to me. My father was saying good-bye, and I had a sense of release.
>
> This was definitely not a product of my imagination, because while all this was going on, Heidi started running around and looking in the direction where my father apparently was. Heidi was real happy and excited, barking and wagging her tail like she could see my dad! Then she jumped up and sat real close to me.

Though Rene sensed the presence of her deceased father and felt his emotional mood, Heidi may have actually seen him. The dog's unusual behavior validated Rene's ADC and removed any doubts she might have had about its reality.

Tina is a vocational teacher in Washington. She was involved in this rather humorous episode about a year after her 47-year-old brother, Rudy, died in an industrial accident:

> I was in the kitchen doing my housecleaning. All of a sudden, our cat shot out of the family room! Her hair was standing on end and she was hissing. She was going so

fast she couldn't get any traction on the linoleum floor – she was kind of running in place.

At the same time, our little dog was backing out of the family room, barking and growling with his hair standing up! They prompted me to look, and when I did, I saw my brother, Rudy, sitting in the rocking chair! He was smiling at me.

I was so happy to see him! He was sitting there in a pair of blue jeans and a red plaid shirt, just as he had done many, many times when he was living. I had a calm, reassuring feeling that Rudy was okay. Then he faded away before my eyes.

I was a hard-nosed nonbeliever until I had this experience. I didn't think anything like this could ever happen. If it hadn't been for the reactions of the animals, I would have thought that my mind was playing tricks on me.

In this and the next account, the animals seemed to react with fear when they saw or sensed the presence of the deceased human being. Perhaps they were startled by the suddenness of his arrival or some aspect of his appearance.

Jackie, age 47, is a senior systems analyst in Tennessee. She, her husband, Dwight, and their two pets responded to this encounter with her Uncle Leonard 4 days after he died of cancer:

My husband and I were in the kitchen watching television. Suddenly our cat ran out of the room and our German shepherd got in the corner and started shaking. Dwight looked at me and said, "We have company!"

We could both feel my uncle's presence. It was like being around a high-tension wire – an electrical charge was in the air. Dwight and I knew he was there and we talked to him. We told him everything was okay and it was all right for him to go on.

We knew Uncle Leonard was just checking on us. More than letting us know he was okay, he was trying to see how we were doing. His presence lasted about twenty minutes, and then we could feel the charge in the air diminish.

At that point, the dog got up and came to us, and the cat returned to the kitchen.

Pets often perceive a deceased person before their owners do, making them very reliable, objective witnesses. In another account, a woman reported she saw her large dog standing on his rear legs, apparently supporting himself by leaning his front paws against her deceased father, whom she didn't see though she felt his presence.

Many people have asked us whether deceased pets ever return to visit their masters. Yes, they do! We've heard several reports of ADCs involving beloved animals, including dogs, cats, a rabbit, and even a horse. We'll gladly devote an entire chapter in our next book to this subject if we receive enough valid accounts.

On several occasions we were able to interview two people who had shared the same ADC. As you'll notice in the final two accounts of this chapter, the testimony of one person is essentially a mirror image of the other.

Benjamin, age 21, works in the publishing business in Iowa. He and his wife, Mollie, age 20, reported having virtually identical ADC experiences with his mother just a few days after she died of cancer.

Here is Mollie's account:

The night of his mother's funeral, my husband, Ben, and I went to her house and visited with his family. We were there quite late.

As we got back in the car, I looked at the front door. I saw his mother standing in the open doorway waving good-bye to us! She looked like she normally did – it was definitely her! She looked very peaceful, very healthy, and younger.

In times past, when we would visit her, she always

stood by that door and waved good-bye. So this was just like she had done many times before.

I looked over to Ben and said, "Did you ...?" and he started crying real hard. I realized we had both seen his mother at the same time, but Ben wasn't able to speak. As soon as I looked over to him, she was gone.

I think the reason I was allowed to see his mother was for confirmation for Ben so he would know she was not a figment of his imagination.

And this is Benjamin's account:

The day of my mother's funeral, my wife, Mollie, and I visited my cousin and her husband at Mother's house. We stayed well into the night, and then Mollie and I got into the car. I put the key in the ignition, and as I did I looked up.

About ten yards away, I saw my mother standing in the doorway behind the clear glass storm door! She would always stand in the doorway out of kindness and courtesy to make sure we had gotten safely to the car. This was a common practice of hers – I had seen it a thousand times.

The inside door was open so the light from the house was illuminating Mother from the back, and the porch light was illuminating her from the front. She appeared to be in good health and was very solid. She was there waving good-bye. She seemed relieved – less tired, less stressful. I got the definite impression that this was a "don't worry" type of message.

Instantly, I had a tremendous physical feeling, almost like being pinned to the ground. It was like a wave came over me and went completely through me from head to toe. It seemed like an eternity, yet it seemed like a split second. I tried to speak but I couldn't.

At the same time, Mollie said, "Ben, I just saw your mother in the doorway!" I bowed my head and said, "So did I," and I began to cry. That was the first time I had shed any tears over my mother's death. I have never wept so hard in my entire life. And I felt a sense of relief, like "good-bye for now."

Benjamin's ADC allowed him to unlock his grief and release his pent-up tears. But more importantly, because Mollie was present and had seen his mother too, she was able to furnish immediate confirmation that his experience was authentic. Had he been alone at the time, he might have dismissed this sacred moment as simply a stress reaction caused by his mother's recent death.

The accounts in this chapter clearly demonstrate that ADCs with a witness, or shared ADCs, are objective experiences rather than subjective ones. That is, the deceased family member or friend had an objective reality that was perceived simultaneously by two or more people who were together at the same time and place. Their independent testimony provides the most convincing evidence yet that after-death communications are genuine contacts by deceased loved ones, exactly as the 2,000 men, women, and children who participated in our research assert.

The next chapter is a collection of longer accounts that are among the "best of the best" after-death communication experiences in our files. You are invited to read them with the eyes of your heart and listen to them with the ears of your soul.

CHAPTER 22

A Necklace of Pearls:
The Best of the Best ADCs

> Death is a transition.... Joni Eareckson Tada will walk and
> run again. Helen Keller will see and hear. The child who died
> of cancer will have rosy cheeks and a strong body. The man
> crippled with arthritis will stand upright. The woman who was
> disfigured in a fiery car crash will have a face without blemish.
> —*Dr. Billy Graham*

We've saved the "best of the best" for last. Each ADC account in this chapter resembles a perfect, lustrous pearl that glows with its own inner light. And when strung together, a magnificent necklace of incomparable value is revealed.

All the experiencers drew strength from being contacted by their deceased loved one, which produced lasting emotional and spiritual healing. Every report is a complete short story that requires no additional commentary.

Deeply moving accounts like these often brought tears of joy to our eyes. They lighted our way with inspiration and transformed our research into "heavenly work" during the seven years we conducted the interviews. We feel honored that so many people entrusted us with such intimate and sacred experiences.

You may want to read this chapter slowly to savor every ADC fully. All the stories contain a healing power within and beyond the mere words on the page. Allow their spiritual essence to nourish and uplift you, for each one contains a pearl of great wisdom that may speak directly to your heart.

Laura works for a community college in Washington. She was devastated when her 6-week-old son, Anthony, died of SIDS:

It had been a traumatic year. My mother had died in March, and I was having real difficulties with her loss. It was a very hard winter. I was living in Montana then, and my husband and I were separated during the six weeks of Anthony's life.

I didn't even know what sudden infant death syndrome was at that time. It was never explained to me even after my baby's death. I felt I was in a void – it was like a nightmare.

Part of my despair was that Anthony had not been baptized. Someone had planted a seed in my mind that all babies who aren't baptized would burn in hell forever. I was agonizing over this, and it was awful. I was frantic because the guilt was more than I could bear.

When I came home from the cemetery after his funeral, I went into my bedroom and turned the lights off. I sat on the bed for quite a while and emptied my mind of all thought.

I went to a very tranquil place. It was like I was on a raft on still water, and the water became like a mirror, and I started feeling peace. Then beautiful rays of light came down towards me, and a stairway became visible.

Suddenly, Christ appeared in an awesome form and size! I had gone to church all my life and been close to God and close to Christ, and I knew this was Him. He was solid and real – He was magnificent! He had long hair and was clothed in a long, white robe.

Christ started descending the stairs and came all the way to the bottom. He extended His arm and had Anthony cradled in it. Anthony was whole again! He was perfect! He was my baby!

The message I got was "Anthony's all right. He is home and he is safe." Now I knew my baby was with Christ! Then they faded away and disappeared.

This answered the one big question that had been tearing me apart. It relieved my agony of not having him baptized. Since then, I've never worried about where Anthony is – I know he has a special place with Christ.

Stewart is an instructional designer in the Southeast. He had difficulty accepting the death of his 2-year-old son, Danny:

Danny was in a wet diaper when he sat down on a metal air vent in the floor of our living room. He touched a lamp that had a short in it, thus completing a circuit, and was electrocuted.

I was called at work and went quickly to the hospital. At the emergency room, they asked me to wait in a small, private room. They had been working on my boy feverishly from the moment he was brought in and had tried everything – with no effect.

A nurse came in and I could see concern on her face. It was her duty to break the news to me that Danny had died. When she left the room, I broke down in the most uncontrolled sobbing from way deep inside me that I have ever experienced.

Finally, I regained my composure, and the nurse asked me if I would like to go back and see my son. They were very kind to me. I went to the emergency room, and they left me alone with my little boy's body. It was just perfect except for a small wound on his forehead. The feeling of finality was devastating.

I wanted to take action and do something! I wanted him back! And I got this idea, "This doesn't have to be final. I know of many instances when people have been revived – I've heard those stories. This doesn't have to be! I don't have to accept this. I'm going to call Danny back!"

Just at that moment, an intuitive impression came into my mind that Danny was speaking to me. That impression was "Daddy, don't do that. I'm okay. It's all right." It was as clear as if it had been a voice of words. But he spoke more maturely than he could have as a two-year-old boy.

I was still for the moment. I did not understand why it
should be "all right" because for me it was not all right.
Nevertheless, I took that communication as authentic
and I accepted it. I thought, "Well, Danny knows best. It's
his body. If he says it's okay, then it's okay." And I relaxed
after that.

I know if it hadn't been for that communication, the
grief would have been even more difficult to bear. It got
me over the hump. I was put at peace, what peace there
could be at the time.

Johanna is an elementary school teacher in Massachusetts.
She and her family had cause for celebration 8 years after her
daughter, Margaret, was killed in an automobile accident at
age 20:

My husband and I planned to go to New York City for
Easter weekend. We wanted to visit our daughter, Robyn,
who was a student at New York University and also attend the Easter Sunday Mass at St. Patrick's Cathedral
which would be celebrated by the Cardinal. We asked
Robyn to check if we would need tickets. She said she
had called and was told that we wouldn't.

When we were in New York, Easter was a strikingly
pleasant, brilliant day, and so we all walked to St.
Patrick's from our hotel. As we approached the Cathedral, we could see quite a crowd – I couldn't even estimate the number of people!

I walked up to the nearest policeman and asked if we
needed tickets to attend the 10:15 Mass. He said, "Tickets? Of course you need tickets! People have had
months to get tickets. There's no way you're going to get
into this Mass without them!" Of course, we were quite
dismayed.

Within a minute or so, a man stepped forward from the
crowd and said to me, "Take my tickets," and he handed
me an envelope. As readily as he appeared, he just
seemed to disappear. The crowd was amazed. I opened

the envelope, looked inside, and there were four tickets! One was white, and the other three were yellow.

We went to the side and waited a good half hour. Finally, we were allowed in the main door. The white ticket was for a seat in the center of the Cathedral.

We used the three yellow tickets and were escorted down the aisle to our assigned seats in pew 39. And directly to our right, close by, was St. Margaret's altar!

I was joyfully overwhelmed that our daughter, Margaret, had sent us an exceptionally strong message on Easter saying, "There is a life after death, there is a heaven, and I will see you again."

Randall is a university professor in California. His view of life was permanently altered 2 weeks after his 4-year-old son, Timothy, died in an automobile accident:

Each day was frayed with terrible anxiety and depression and shock. I was struggling between a state of denial and the fear of accepting the reality that my son was gone. I couldn't cope with the idea that he wasn't going to be here anymore.

I went back to work as soon as possible after Timothy's funeral. Each day when I came home, I dreaded coming into the yard, knowing he wasn't there and knowing I would have to face that reality.

One day when I got home, I walked in and sat down in the chair at the fireplace looking towards the front door. I know I was awake. Just then, Timothy came through the door! The door didn't open – he just came through it!

He appeared to be very tangible, very real. He looked exactly like he did before he was killed. But he was dressed in white and had an aura of brightness. He was very cheerful and exceedingly happy. He was clothed in light – light seemed to pervade the whole area. It wasn't a halo – he just seemed to give off great brightness and whiteness.

Timothy came and stood before me and said, "I am not going to be coming back. I am gone and you must know this." He was very emphatic. The tone of his voice and his inflection were real.

I leaned forward in the chair, and Timothy said, "I'm all right and everything is fine." And then he disappeared – he just vanished from where he was standing.

From then on, there was no more denial. I knew my son was gone and wasn't going to come back. Even though I couldn't see him anymore, I could face it because Timothy assured me that he was, in effect, alive.

The sadness was there, the pain was there, but there also was a feeling of joy and hope mixed with my sadness. And I began to heal.

Mary Lou is a 57-year-old spiritual counselor in South Dakota. She was able to achieve resolution of many long-standing issues while having this insightful experience 21 years after her father died of cancer:

My six children all came home this summer with their spouses and their kids. One night we were sitting around the kitchen table talking. About midnight I was tired and went up to bed, but they said they were going to stay up a while longer.

So I went to sleep, and about 2:30 I felt a finger tap me on the top of my head. I knew it was my dad because when he was alive that's how he would get my attention. I sat up and heard him say internally, "Go downstairs! Go downstairs!" So I did.

I stood in the kitchen listening to my kids talk about their childhood. I sensed my father's presence and knew he was with me. My kids were saying they certainly hoped that their children felt secure and nurtured and loved. Then I chirped in and said, "I sure hope you all know that I loved you when you were small!"

There was silence – just a dead silence. A couple of

their faces even got red. I thought, "Okay, Dad, this is why I was supposed to be down here." If my father hadn't been there, I probably would have been devastated. I immediately went upstairs and back to bed.

In the morning, in a twilight state, I heard my dad say, "It is time to let go of the guilt! You have felt guilty all these years for not doing as well as you thought you could for your children. How much more could you have done?"

Then I was shown some of the scenes from when my kids were younger. My husband, who had been a recovering alcoholic, came home drunk one day after being sober for ten years. From then on it was just downhill. He lost his job because he was drinking like a billy goat, and I ended up working at this dumpy little factory so the kids could eat.

Three of my children had cystic fibrosis, and I developed breast cancer. There wasn't a whole lot left of me each day, yet somehow I held it all together. But I still felt guilty because I wasn't always available for my children. Guilt is such an insidious thing, and I didn't even realize how deeply I had carried it all these years.

I was reminded by my father that the three children with cystic fibrosis are still alive and well, and my youngest is earning his second degree. And my ex-husband is sober now.

Then my father said, "You're a good person. You were a good person then, and you're a good person now. Let go of the guilt! You did the best you could!"

This was an immense relief! I had a healing! I absolutely let go of the guilt and don't have it anymore. And this wonderful, joyous experience helped to heal all of us.

In the morning, a couple of my children apologized, saying, "Oh, Mom, we didn't mean to hurt your feelings." I said, "Don't worry. It was the greatest thing that ever happened to me!" Then I told them about my experience with my father, and we all were able to talk it through.

Beatrice is a civic leader in Oregon. She was left with a lingering question, like many children have, when her mother died of cancer unexpectedly at age 67:

> My mother was a real strong-minded lady while I was growing up. She wasn't nearly as loving to me as she was to my sister, and I always wondered why. She often seemed cross towards me and sometimes had me crying an awful lot. When she died suddenly, I felt really bad and thought, "Oh, no! Now I can never talk to Mother again!"
>
> About a month later, I awoke all of a sudden and sat up. My mother was standing at the foot of my bed! She was very real and very solid. She was all well and looked about thirty years old. She was so pretty and so young with an absolutely beautiful face.
>
> Mother was just complete happiness! She was holding her arms stretched out on each side expressing joy. She was smiling at me with all the love that she could give. She told me, "I really loved you, and I wish you had known it more." It was love, love, love! It was a great reconciliation!

Neil is a retired mail carrier in Mississippi. His 19-year-old son, Ken, died suddenly in his sleep from heart arrhythmia:

> For about a year and a half, I couldn't turn Ken loose because I couldn't believe that he was gone. I figured if I could just hold on to him someway, I could bring him back.
>
> I always planted beautiful flowers at my son's grave and kept them watered. One day, I was at the cemetery pulling weeds out of them. I was kneeling down when, out of the clear blue, Ken's voice came to me. It was happy and real joyful.
>
> I heard him externally, so loud and clear, like he was standing there, and I felt his presence. I raised up on my

knees and looked around, but there was nobody else in the cemetery.

Ken said, "Dad, it's me! I wish you would turn me loose so that I could enjoy where I am. You and Mom always taught me and brought me up to be with God. Now you're keeping me from Him and from enjoying heaven.

"I cannot reach the fulfillment that God wants for me because you're holding me back. I would appreciate it if you would just turn me loose and let me enjoy it here." He told me that he was perfect in God's sight. And he described how beautiful and how peaceful it was there.

I just busted out crying because I couldn't believe it. Then I realized, "Who am I to hold him back from what God would want him to do?" So I said, "All right, Ken. This is it then. Son, I'm going to turn you loose and let you go." I'm not saying it was easy, but I knew that it was the right thing to do.

I had almost hated God before. Then I just sat there and cried and asked God's forgiveness. And when I did, the whole burden in my heart raised up off of me – it felt like a ten-pound ball leaving. All the pain left, and I felt so much peace in my heart. This reaffirmed my whole faith, and since that day I have drawn a lot closer to God than I had ever been.

When Ken came to me, it all changed. This put everything into perspective. From that day on, it's been better. It still hurts but not like it was. Now I can look at Ken's picture and say, "Son, I love you," and go right on with my day.

Emily, an office manager in New York, was deeply concerned about her brother, Leon, after he died of cancer at age 49:

Leon was not a religious man, and when he was dying of cancer, I decided I would try to get him to accept Jesus into his life before he passed over. The Lord had made a big difference in my life, and I wanted my brother to be with Him too.

But when Leon died, he still had not accepted the Lord into his life, and that really worried me. I was so fearful he was in hell, and I just couldn't accept that. I prayed about it a lot, and I told everybody how worried I was. I had many, many other people praying for my brother too, and each day I asked for some sign that Leon was finally with Jesus.

About five months later, I was driving home from my sister's house one afternoon. It had been raining hard with thunder and lightning, when suddenly the storm started to clear and the clouds separated. A vivid ray of sunshine came down through the clouds, and when I looked up off to my right, my brother was there with the Lord!

They were life-sized – very, very real, very solid and distinct and three-dimensional. They were very close, shoulder to shoulder, and I only saw the upper portion of them. Leon was facing me, the Lord was wearing a robe and facing him, and they were both smiling. My brother appeared younger than when he died and looked very healthy. Nothing needed to be said – Leon was with the Lord, and that's all I wanted to know.

That was so wonderful! I was so relieved to finally have my answer, and I was so thankful. It was absolutely total relief for me because I knew Leon was finally at peace and with Jesus.

I had assumed you could not be saved once you died. I suggest that anyone who is under the same assumption I was to not give up their prayer vigil. I think prayers finally made it possible for my brother to be with the Lord.

I gained an awful lot from this experience, and my own walk with the Lord became that much stronger. Anything is possible through the Lord. I believed it before, but now I know there is nothing that is impossible!

Valerie is an office manager in Massachusetts. She was called upon to assist another person after her only child, John, died of cystic fibrosis when he was 18 years old:

I continued to go to the cemetery even though I always felt that John wasn't there. But it was an outlet for me to be there once in a while and reflect.

I never interacted with other people at the cemetery – I just went to put a flower down. Usually I was in my own thoughts. But this particular time, I felt John was talking to me.

He came through to me suddenly and said, "Mom, somebody needs you." This intense feeling kept coming over me – something was pushing me away from his grave.

It was John, and he kept saying, "Mom, you don't need to be here. There's somebody that needs you." It was very brief, it was telepathic, and I was being pushed and led.

I walked away from my son's grave and came upon a man who was kneeling by another grave. Led by John, I said, "Excuse me, I'm sure you're planting flowers here because somebody special in your life has passed away."

The man turned around, stood up, and said, "Yes, it's my son." He looked at me like "Who are you?" And I said, "I'm sorry to bother you, but I saw the pretty flowers and just wanted to say hello, and I'm very sorry."

I could still feel John standing nearby. And there was another soul with him, but I didn't know who it was until the man started to talk about his son.

He said, "My son, Troy, was murdered. He had muscular dystrophy and was on crutches to help him walk. He was very smart and intelligent."

The father talked about how angry and hurt he was and the pain he had about his son's death. He kept elaborating on the men who had killed his boy. He was so upset he wasn't with his son when he died. Finally, he put his arms around me and started to cry.

Then I heard John say, "That's why you're here, Mom! You've got to tell him that when those men were strangling his son, when they were in the act of killing him, Troy left his body. There was no suffering. The pain was gone.

"Mom, the only ones who are suffering are the people down there who are alive. You are the sufferers! Troy is with us now and he's okay. And he feels sorry for the men who killed him."

I repeated everything John told me. The man just looked at me and asked, "How do you know this?" I said, "Because my son who died just told me." And I shared with him other experiences that John had given me, showing me there's a life after death. Troy's father was so elated that he hugged me and kissed me.

John was right! Somebody needed me – somebody needed both of us. I'm so glad we were able to help this bereaved father.

Cynthia is a clinical social worker in Florida. She was given a gentle prompting shortly after her profoundly retarded 8-year-old son, Aaron, died of kidney failure:

Aaron was my only child. My relationship with him was more intense because he was never able to do anything for himself his entire life.

Two or three months after Aaron died, I was trying to go to sleep. My husband asked me to rub his back because he'd worked very hard that day and was extremely tired. But I just didn't want to do it because I felt a little bit angry at him. Truthfully, I was angry with everybody at the time. So I said, "No."

While I was lying there, I heard a little voice say, "Do it, Mommy!" I sat upright in bed because it was so clear. I knew exactly whose voice it was – it was Aaron's! I was shocked because my son had never learned to talk! So then I did rub my husband's back.

Because of this message, I realized I needed to listen and be more understanding of what my husband was going through. I needed to help him in his grief and with his sense of loss.

Scott is an 18-year-old high-school senior in Ohio. His friend, Marty, died of congenital heart disease at age 17:

A couple of years ago, I was really bad off. I was on drugs and didn't care about myself or anyone around me. After I attempted to commit suicide, I went to the hospital to get my head straightened out.

When I got out of the hospital, Marty was there for me from day one. He was by my side to make sure I was okay and that I stayed in the right line. But after he died, I grieved a lot and started sliding downhill again.

About three months later, I was lying in the dark on the couch in the living room one night. I looked at the clock and it said 2:05. All of a sudden, I saw Marty about ten feet away from me! I could see him like it was daytime!

He had on a white T-shirt and blue jeans. I sat in shock as he looked at me and smiled. I couldn't believe it! One part of me was scared, but I was so happy to see him I stood up.

Marty came over to me. Everything was light around us, but I don't know where it came from. He said, "Don't be upset, okay? I'm happy. Go on with your life! Don't keep your mind stuck on me. It's nice for you to remember me, but just go on."

When Marty was alive he didn't smile much, but he did this time. It looked like he was more at peace with himself and more happy. I gave him a hug, and I could smell his scent and feel his body heat – it was Marty! I could even feel his breath when he was talking – it was the weirdest thing. Then I sat down and closed my eyes. The last thing I remember is falling asleep.

This experience lifted me back up again. It totally changed me. I knew he was okay and that he was happy. And now I could be at peace with myself. Marty might be dead, but he's always around me – I know that. I feel he is saying, "I'm here. I will always be here for you."

Now I have a friend who is in the same position I was in when Marty was alive. I do for him what Marty did for me, and he's completely off drugs now. Maybe one day my friend will do this for somebody else.

Arlene, a homemaker in Illinois, had this spiritual reunion nearly 2 years after her 27-year-old son, Russ, was murdered:

My husband and I became chapter leaders of Parents of Murdered Children. We were very involved with other parents whose children had also been murdered.

Many times at our meetings I said, "The first thing I'm going to ask God when I see Him is 'Why? Why do these good, decent young children have to be murdered? Why do You allow that?' " It's the same for a lot of bereaved parents – they are always asking "Why?"

One night, I dreamed I went to heaven. The Lord was there. He was all-encompassing – He was everything! My first question to Him was "Why? Why did you allow Russ to be murdered?"

The Lord said, "Arlene, there's your son. Go and let him welcome you." So I looked to the side and saw my son!

Russ was standing there smiling with his arms held out to me. He was in a dazzling white robe, as white as pristine snow with sparkles in it. There was a happiness in the expression on his face – I had never seen his face like that in life. His face was radiant – he just glowed!

I ran over to Russ, and we put our arms around each other and hugged. I just wanted to hug him and squeeze him. My son said to me, "Mom, welcome to this place." Then with my arm around his waist and his arm around mine, we went to this beautiful setting of green trees and blue sky. No words were spoken and I forgot all about my question, "Why?" Just being there with him was sheer joy!

Then we walked up a little hill, and I felt I was going to see something wonderful on the other side. But I didn't get to see it because I woke up.

Since this experience, I have no longer been concerned about the question "Why?" I think the Lord was telling me that it's not important how we die and not to worry about the "Why?" What's really important is that we live the best way we know how with what the Lord has given us.

Rob is a mechanical contractor in the Midwest. He felt his life had been utterly shattered when his 26-year-old daughter, Bonnie, was killed:

Bonnie had been murdered, and I was full of self-pity and hate. I felt there was no God and no justice. I was obsessed with wanting to kill this guy, the man who killed my daughter.

It was the day we buried Bonnie. We came back to the house and had a lot of people here. I had to get away, so I went out to the backyard.

Suddenly, Bonnie's presence was so strong I felt if I turned around I would see her. Then a thought seemed to come from the back of my head. I could almost hear Bonnie's voice.

I heard her pleading with me, "Dad, please! You have to pray for him!" I said, "You don't know what you're asking! I can't do it! I have always believed that if you pray for someone it's almost like forgiving them. I can't bring myself to do that!"

Then Bonnie said, "Not for him, Dad. For you!" She was pleading with me that I had to do this for my own sake, for my own sanity. I got the feeling she was begging me, because the way I was going, I would probably have killed somebody or gone insane. Then she was gone.

I stood there trying to make sense out of this. There was no doubt in my mind that this was a communication between my daughter and me – no doubt at all.

Then I went into the house. My wife was in the bedroom with a woman we know. I held hands with them and said, "Bonnie just told me to pray. I have to pray for him." And we said the Serenity Prayer.

About six to eight months later, I was ready for a straight jacket because I was still constantly thinking of ways to kill this guy. Finally, in complete desperation, I went to Bonnie's grave one night. I was standing there, trying to make some sense of the whole thing. Suddenly, this thought came from the back of my head, flowing right through me.

I heard Bonnie say, "I'm not here, Dad. I'm not here in the ground. Daddy, please don't worry. I'm fine." She was very strong, very calm, very loving – almost like a wise grandmother talking to a grandchild.

Then she said, "Just go home and help Mom. Get off your butt and move! That's how you get things done! And remember, Dad, pray for him!" Bonnie was trying to help me from cracking up, and then she disappeared again.

After that, some friends in the twelve-step program of Alcoholics Anonymous helped me. And my wife helped me too. This was the beginning of putting my life back together.

Finally, the desire to kill left me, and I refuse to live in that world of revenge anymore.

Jennifer is a homemaker and bereaved mother in Wisconsin. She was overwhelmed with sorrow when her 21-month-old son, Allan, died of pneumonia:

After Allan died, I was thinking about him every day – every day that he was gone. When I went into labor ten months later to give birth to my new baby, Gerry, I was still thinking about my Allan. Even when I took Gerry home, I didn't feel happy.

One day, I was sitting in a chair holding Gerry. He was cranky and fussing and crying as I was rocking him. I held him in my left arm and patted him on the back, but nothing helped.

Then I felt a pressure against my right leg. Allan was standing there with his little arms crossed on top of my leg, looking up at me and smiling! He said, "Sing to baby, Mommy. Sing to baby."

So I began humming even though I didn't feel like it, and the baby quieted down. When the pressure on my leg was gone, I stopped humming. Then I felt the pressure again in the same way, and Allan was back! Again he said, "Sing to baby, Mommy." So I started singing to Gerry, and Allan left.

I had been wondering all that year if Allan was happy, and where he was, and if he was all right. So when he came back to let me know he was happy, I felt a lot happier too. And I've been singing and humming to my Gerry ever since.

Diana is an equestrian instructor for handicapped children and adults in Pennsylvania. She was inconsolable when her 4-year-old daughter, Lisa, died of unknown causes:

A few days after Lisa's funeral, I was awake and lying in bed early in the morning, wondering how I was going to face the day. I became aware of a mist, like a thick golden fog, in the left-hand corner of the room. It gradually took the shape of a man sitting on a stool, and the whole picture was from floor to ceiling.

He was the size of a real person and had on a white robe tied with a brown hemp belt and sandals. I knew He was Jesus! He had long hair that was gray and black, and He was the color of every man. He was all colors.

There were aspects of Him that bordered on being Oriental, there were aspects of Him that looked Scandinavian, and there were aspects of Him that had African feelings. He was very global, universal. I couldn't see through Him, but He was not three-dimensional.

I could see my daughter sitting sideways on His knee. Lisa was wearing a long white dress and was looking up into His face with an absolutely beatific smile. There was light and joy emanating from her eyes and face, and there was an exchange of energy flowing between them.

Jesus was looking directly at me when He asked, "Would you have her back if you could?" What I saw was so beautiful and so glorious that I didn't want to do anything to interfere. I remember thinking, "How could I want Lisa back when I see how happy she is?"

Suddenly, my bedroom door burst open and my two little sons ran into the room. The whole scene of Jesus and Lisa disappeared – the beautiful picture just wasn't there anymore.

I had been paralyzed after Lisa died. This experience gave me the strength I needed to do what had to be done.

I'm so grateful I was allowed to see another place in the universe, for I realized there are worlds other than the physical. Death ceased to be a frightening and sorrowful experience, for I knew that Lisa's spirit still exists.

Samuel is a retired civil service worker in Alabama. He was brokenhearted by the death of his 19-year-old grandson, Dennis:

Me and Dennis were very, very close. I can just see that boy from the time he was crawling, and I was toting him around in my arms. He followed me everywhere I went. I sometimes believe that I cared too much for him. I loved my other grandkids, but Dennis was my heart.

He was a very sweet kid, and he didn't have any ugly

ways. He just wasn't that type of boy. He was just quiet-like, and I never heard him cuss. He even got on me about drinking and smoking.

Dennis got involved with the law, and they picked him up for a little misdemeanor – he had some books that didn't belong to him. They said they locked him in the jail and that he tried to hang himself, which he didn't completely do. They found him and carried him to the hospital about 2:00 in the morning. About 4:00 that same morning, he had a heart attack and passed away. It hurt me so bad.

It was maybe two or three months afterwards. In my dream, Dennis was right there in front of me, walking straight to me just as real as ever.

I grabbed him and was hugging him, and he was hugging me. The very words that he told me were, "Granddaddy, I don't want you and Mama worrying about me. You all don't worry about me because I'm all right." I heard his voice – it sounded just like Dennis.

I was holding his hand, and all at once, I woke up. I was almost in shock – it was just so plain! Up until that dream, I felt I was better off dead.

That kind of eased me up a little bit, and I've gained a little more will to live. Now I feel things will get better and I can go along. There must be a life after death, since that happened so plain to me.

Carlita is an elementary school teacher in New Mexico. She had this wondrous out-of-body ADC experience with her daughter, Serena, who was miscarried during the 5th month of pregnancy, and her son, Carlos, who was stillborn 14 months later:

For about six months after I lost my son, I was in very deep, deep sorrow. I didn't understand why – why me? I was just miserable and very close to wanting to end it all.

One night in a dream, I was where I envisioned heaven to be. I was in a beautiful pasture that was filled with beautiful flowers. An angel came to me and said he had something very special to show me.

The angel was holding a six-month-old baby boy in his right arm and was holding the left hand of a little girl, who was walking like a toddler. The girl was tiny, but she could talk.

She said, "Mommy, I am Serena, and this is my little brother, Carlos. We are fine. We are very happy. We love you very much, and we don't want you to be sad anymore. We will all be together someday."

They were both dressed in white robes. Serena had tiny little sandals on her feet and Carlos was barefoot. They had this beautiful glow, this perfect light around them that came from their heart center.

I asked the angel, "Can I get close to them?" and the angel nodded "Yes." It was like the angel was their babysitter for the time being.

I remember sitting on the grass and putting Carlos on my lap, as Serena came close. I was crying and loving them both. I just wanted the children to know that I loved them and that their daddy loved them too.

I wanted to be there and watch the children as long as I could. I was able to hug them and kiss them one more time. Then they walked away with the angel, and I had this inner peace as I woke up.

What is so wonderful is that I learned the children have features of both me and my husband. Serena looks a lot like her father, and Carlos seems to look like me.

Dave, age 42, lives in Ohio. He received encouragement after his grandmother died of a heart attack when she was 83 years old:

Baba, my grandmother, was an old-line, traditional Roman Catholic who went to church every day. She was a very spiritual and a very prayerful woman who said five rosaries daily.

At fourteen years of age, I entered the seminary to study for the priesthood. My grandmother was my best supporter. She was so proud and so happy that I was going to be a priest.

But nine years later, I left the seminary. So Baba's dream did not come true. Though she was disappointed, she still loved and cared for me until she passed away the following year.

Two years later, at age twenty-six, I again felt a call to the ministry and was ready to go back and continue my studies for the priesthood. Two or three days before I reentered the seminary, I had the most vivid dream of my life.

I was transported to the home where my grandmother had lived, and I saw Baba in the corner of the room. She appeared as I remembered her, with her hair in a bun, wearing a little silk dress and the apron she always wore.

As she moved towards me, she took on a whole new appearance, almost as if her skin was translucent, and light was flowing from her body. Her outward appearance changed to a very beautiful, young, and vibrant entity filled with light.

Baba hugged me. I'll never forget that hug because it felt so warm. She whispered in my ear, "David, I have prayed that you will be a priest. I will always pray for you and help you. You will be a good priest." Then she kissed me on my left cheek, moved away, and disappeared.

When I woke up, I knew in the core of my being that I had just had a reunion with my grandmother! Baba came across time, space, and the universe to tell me she was so happy for me. I felt at peace and had no worries or fears or doubts about going back to the seminary.

I was ordained four years later in 1981 and have had a very positive priesthood. I know my grandmother has been with me and has been praying for me throughout this whole time.

Kathryn, age 60, is a teacher and homemaker in Virginia. She was filled with hope by her father-in-law 12 years after he died of cancer. An olfactory ADC she had with her mother is in Chapter 5:

This experience happened about a month after my daughter's cancer operation. Krista had ovarian cancer, and it was discovered just two months after her graduation from college.

It was such a shock! Her cancer was very advanced and had metastasized to a number of other places. Krista's prognosis was extremely poor, and this was an inordinately emotional time for all of us.

Krista was to have been married in May. When we found out in April that she was ill, the wedding was canceled. Our nephew's wedding was also in May. My husband and I attended the wedding, stayed about twenty minutes at the reception, and then quickly headed for home.

As we were driving, we were very quiet. I was leaning back on the headrest with my eyes closed, deep in thought, contemplating how drastically our lives had changed in only a month's time.

Krista was catastrophically ill, and nothing was as it had been. I was thinking, "This is so hard to believe. These are the kinds of things that happen to other people, and you never think they are going to happen to you."

Suddenly, I was literally overwhelmed by the presence of my father-in-law! He was simply there. I could hardly get my breath, I was so overtaken by his beingness. It was a powerful, comforting, wonderful presence that belonged absolutely to my father-in-law and no one else.

Tears of joy rushed to my eyes. He was enormously loving, and I felt his compassion. It was breathtaking! I didn't know such things could happen.

He managed to bring his essence to this encounter so

that I knew who was there. Then these words were impressed into my mind, "Katy, honey, you can stop worrying now. Krista is going to be all right. In fact, she's got it made! We've been able to do a great deal here." I didn't hear his voice. It was as if my father-in-law was sending a telegram into my head.

My daughter did proceed to get well – so quickly, so amazingly! She had chemotherapy treatments and radiation, but she didn't have the terrible reactions that people generally have. Her recovery went very smoothly.

Krista came out of this almost like being born again. She wanted to do everything differently. She did ultimately marry, but she married someone else. Finally, at about her tenth-year checkup, her doctor proclaimed her recovery to be a miracle!

Meredith is a 43-year-old homemaker in Saskatchewan. Her sweetheart, Vic, provided a helpful service 7 years after he died of cancer:

I was going down the stairs one day, and I tripped and landed on my ankle. I felt this horrible pain! I went to the hospital and they x-rayed it. The doctor said, "You've got a hairline fracture." He gave me some crutches and said I should stay off my feet for six to eight weeks.

The next night, I went to bed and had this funny dream. I was in a setting that was very peaceful. I looked up and Vic was there! His expression seemed to be very caring and very understanding – a sort of quiet affection.

Vic said, "I want to take a look at your foot." I said, "Well, I don't think you can do anything about it. You're not a doctor." He told me, "Just stretch out your leg and give me your foot."

He took my foot and moved it in and out, and I heard something click. That was it, but there was no pain. Then Vic said, "When you get up, you should be able to walk on it. But take it easy because it has to heal."

I woke up immediately and had to go to the washroom. Without thinking, I accidentally stood up on my feet and realized, "It doesn't hurt!" To my surprise, my foot felt fine – and I could walk! So I said, "Thanks, Vic!"

I figure God sends people that you've cared about to help you out.

Paulette is a nurse in Alaska. She was grief-stricken when her 14-year-old son, Nicholas, died:

Kids believe they are going to live forever – they don't think about the finality of death. My son, Nicholas, was afraid of going to a big high school. He told a friend he was going to take some pills, just enough to make himself sick, so he wouldn't have to go to that school. But he went too far and died.

The night after Nicholas died, I went to bed and heard noises in his room. I felt pulled to go there, so I got up and went to his room and sat on his bed. I said, "Okay, here I am. What is it that you want from me?" I was so angry with him!

It was like Nicholas's very soul was there – his presence dominated the whole room. He said, "Mom, I'm so sorry for what I did. I didn't mean to do it. I'm so frightened!"

I said, "Nicholas, go find Grandpa. He'll take care of you. It will be all right. Just find him." My father and my son both died on Labor Day weekend, fourteen years apart.

Afterwards, I didn't understand what had just happened. I became so scared I ran upstairs and got into bed, still shaking.

When I got up the next morning, I thought, "What have I done? Nicholas didn't even know my father!" I was so afraid I had said the wrong thing, and I was angry at myself over that.

All that day I kept saying, "Nicholas, you have to send me a sign that you're all right. I need this desperately! How am I going to go on living if I don't find out you're all right?" I went to church and prayed to know that Nicholas had found my father.

The next evening, my friend came over and said, "Paulette, have you been outside? You should go out there – there's something I've never seen before."

I went out and saw a double rainbow in beautiful colors! I knew it was my sign that Nicholas was all right and that he and my father were together.

I got exactly what I needed, and all through my son's funeral I didn't cry. How can you cry when you've been given the greatest gift that anybody could receive – the knowledge that your child is at peace.

Lewis, age 42, is a disabled Vietnam veteran in the Midwest. He had this crucial ADC soon after his father died of a stroke:

I was a corporal in Force Recon at a Marine Corps base in Vietnam. We were preparing to go out on a mission.

That evening, I went out to take a walk and pray. I noticed a haze twenty-five feet in front of me, like a human form coming closer and getting larger. I came to an abrupt halt and dropped to position on the ground, ready to fire.

Then I recognized my father's voice saying, "Lewis, you've made me very proud. But where you are going on this mission, you will need your full willpower to return. You will need your belief in yourself." My father was really worried. Then he said, "I know you have willpower, but if you don't have enough, I will see you here." And he just vanished.

Around 0330 we headed out. On the second day we were ambushed. Twelve of us went out, but only three came back. I was wounded in the chest, and the second guy had a minor wound to one arm, and the third guy was hit in the leg. They carried me almost eight miles to an LZ, and then I was medevaced out.

I remember coming to for just a few minutes and the doctor saying, "He doesn't have a chance to live." Then he went on to other patients. I blacked out and had the feeling I was between here and there. Then I heard a male voice say, "It's not time to give up!" I wanted to believe it was my father, but I wasn't sure.

I came to in a hospital in California many weeks later. I still carry seven shell fragments in my chest. I know it was not my time to die.

To me this experience meant that my father cared a great deal about me. He had a great love for me, and that love carried on after his death. This proves to me that even after your death, you still remember the ones that you loved on earth.

I know several men who had an experience like this when they were in the field. Like me, they were once non-believers. But they are still afraid to put it out to the public because a lot of people will make fun of you and say you are crazy.

Grace is a magazine publisher in Indiana. She had reason to smile again several years after her daughter, Kim, was killed in an automobile accident at age 17:

About six years after my daughter, Kim, died, I had to fly to Chicago to attend a meeting of The Compassionate Friends. I was absolutely terrified of flying! I decided that the only reason I got there in one piece and the plane didn't crash was because God wanted me to be at that meeting.

On the way home, we were sitting in the plane on the tarmac at O'Hare. I was certain that the odds were not with me, and I was growing increasingly anxious. I convinced myself that the minute the plane got in the air it would crash.

With growing fear, I glanced up, and Kim was in front of me in the aisle! She was just standing there, laughing in a happy way, like she was saying "Oh, Mom." I was very surprised!

I could see Kim's long, blond, curly hair, and she was dressed in white diaphanous clothing, almost like she was bathed in light. She wasn't as defined as a living person – she was more like a translucent, light-filled presence. She had a certain solidity, but there was a floaty, ethereal quality to her.

Kim smiled and said, "Not this time, Mom. You still have things to do." Her attitude was that I had nothing to worry about – that everything was fine. And then she was gone.

This message was totally opposite to anything I was prepared to believe at that moment. If my mind had been playing tricks on me, the scenario would have been very different. If this had only been my imagination, Kim would have looked very grim. And she would have said, "I'll see you in a few minutes, Mom," because that is exactly what I was expecting to happen.

Almost right away, I decided that probably no one would ever believe this. But that didn't matter because it was my experience, and it was very real. This was my precious moment with my daughter, which belongs to me.

I've gained an absolute certainty there is a life after death. And now I am no longer afraid of flying!

Adele is a television producer in the Northwest. Fortunately, she followed the guidance of her 9-year-old son, Jeremy, after he died of leukemia:

My son, Jeremy, died the day after Mother's Day. Three weeks later, just before I woke up, I heard him ask, "What are you going to do with my money?" I said, "What money?" And he said, "All the money that you saved for me."

I had totally forgotten about Jeremy's savings account, and I didn't even know where he had hidden his savings book. I asked what he wanted me to do with it because obviously it must have been very important to him.

Jeremy said, "I want you to go see Malcolm." Malcolm is a friend of mine who is a diamond wholesaler. I said, "Well, whatever is in that account isn't enough to go see Malcolm!" And Jeremy replied, "Yes it is! Just go see Malcolm, and you'll understand what I'm talking about. When you see it, you will know. You will think of me." Then he was gone and I woke up.

Although I thought this was kind of crazy, I looked around the house for my son's savings book but couldn't find it.

Several days later, I happened to be in the same building as Malcolm's wholesale jewelry store. So I popped in there and started looking around. I saw a beautiful butterfly necklace with a diamond in it. It suddenly clicked what Jeremy had said, "You'll know it when you see it. It will remind you of me."

My heart started pounding and I got kind of nervous. I asked Malcolm how much the necklace would cost. After some figuring and some bantering back and forth, he told me $200. I told him I would come back later.

My heart was still pounding when I went back to my office and called the bank. I explained that I couldn't find my son's savings book and wanted to know how much money was in his account. In a few minutes, I was told the amount was $200.47!

I went back to Malcolm's store after work and bought the butterfly necklace with Jeremy's money. Now I don't go anywhere without it. I can touch it and say, "My son gave me this for my last Mother's Day with him!"

Daniel, a social worker in Minnesota, had this illuminating series of ADC visions on four consecutive nights following the death of his 28-year-old wife, Kathy, from cancer:

When I went to bed the night after my wife died, I was just so tired and drained. As I tried to relax, my mind raced with thoughts. Suddenly, a radiant picture of Kathy popped into my head. Her image was there even when I opened my eyes. I felt such a peace and sense of presence.

Kathy was so beautiful, with perfect features, wearing a brilliant, white flowing dress. She was more radiant than any time I had ever known her! She had her beautiful, long brown hair again, as she had prior to chemotherapy and radiation. I was so absorbed by her striking beauty!

We talked telepathically, and Kathy said she was very, very happy and that she had met her grandpa and grandma and other relatives too. I told her I loved her and how glad I was that she had gone on and didn't have to suffer anymore.

We enjoyed each other for quite awhile, and I thanked her for being there for me. As her image faded, I recalled that Kathy had promised to be with me when I needed her.

The second night, after the wake, I felt numb as I lay down in bed. Thoughts started running nonstop through my mind – wonderings about Kathy and if everything we had done for her was okay. Again, I felt her presence and had a beautiful vision of Kathy wearing an even brighter and lighter flowing gown. Light radiated around her, behind her, and from her.

She said she had met some more friends and relatives and was very busy. I told her she should go meet St. Francis, since he had meant a lot to her, and she said she would.

We talked about the kids, and Kathy assured me that she would be nearby and not to worry. She thanked me for taking care of her, and I thanked her for trusting me with her care. Then I just drifted off to sleep.

The next day we buried Kathy, and my mind could not comprehend all that had happened. As I went to sleep that night, again this wonderful vision of Kathy returned. She appeared more and more radiant and bright, almost as if a pure light was taking over her body.

I asked her what heaven was like, and she replied, "I am so happy here. There are no barriers between us. We can experience totally the goodness we have in ourselves and the goodness we behold in each other. We grow through the experience of coming to know totally the goodness that is in each one here. Our capacity to know goodness is increased, and we are freer yet to know greater goodness in others we meet. I can't wait for you to know this love and freedom!" We continued to share our thoughts until the vision faded.

The fourth night, as I lay down to sleep, the vision returned. With my eyes open or closed, it was there just as before – except there was less of Kathy visible and more bright light.

She said, "Come with me. I want to show you something," and I somehow stepped into the vision. We moved down a little path to the base of a big valley, with two tall, rugged mountain ranges on each side leading to a summit up the valley far away.

"This is life," she said. "The paths are many through the valley, and you will meet many people. Each will have their own ideas of what is right and wrong, so just enjoy them for who they are. Some of us get to go to the front of the line. Others have to spend a lifetime working their way along the paths to the top."

Then Kathy's features slowly disappeared into a bright, white light at the head of the valley. She was totally enveloped in that light, and the light just disappeared into a similar light at the top of the mountain.

It was not as if Kathy was leaving me – it was as though she was in the light, she was the light, and there were no bounds to that light. The light radiated from her to me, and the experience of that light would never leave because now it is a part of me.

There was no sense of loss when the visions stopped. These experiences were so vivid and real and reassuring that I had no doubts or questions about them. They seemed complete and whole in and of themselves.

Rosalyn is a 39-year-old chemical dependency counselor in Washington. The healing power of prayer and forgiveness were dramatically revealed to her:

Uncle Mickey came to live with us when I was seven years old after my parents divorced. He was an active alcoholic, and my mother was trying to help him out. But he sexually abused me during the two years he lived with us, and this was emotionally very traumatic for me.

By the time I was seventeen, I was an active alcoholic myself. And at eighteen, I was very heavily into drugs. I drank and drugged for years, and then I sobered up.

In order to stay sober, I had to go back through my past and look at the people, places, and things that had harmed me. I had to be as honest as I could about the effect those things had on my life. I also needed to make peace with my uncle because I chose to believe that if he had been sober he wouldn't have abused me.

So I wrote Uncle Mickey a letter and told him how I felt and told him that I held nothing against him. But I don't know if he ever received it. Over the years, I asked the Lord to let my love cover that sin for my uncle.

In the spring of this year, I was sleeping and woke up. I turned over and Jesus and Uncle Mickey were next to my bed! I only saw their heads and shoulders, and there was a light behind both of them.

There was an overwhelming presence of love and a seriousness too. The Lord was asking me a question that I heard in my mind. There was authority and power and yet a gentleness in His voice.

Jesus asked, "Do you hold anything against this man?" I told Him, "No, I don't." Then Jesus turned and looked at my uncle and said, "Neither do I hold anything against him." I knew then Uncle Mickey was at peace and was with the Lord – and that he was free.

A couple of days later, I got a letter from my mother that said Uncle Mickey had died.

Glen is a mail carrier in the Southwest. He had this spiritually transformative ADC with his son, Ron, age 21, who was murdered, and with Ron's mother, Helen, who had died of cancer 16 years earlier:

My son, Ron, was killed on a Monday night, but I didn't find out about his death until Tuesday morning. The next day, because it was a homicide and I was the next of kin, I had to go down and identify his body.

That's probably the hardest thing I ever did in my life. This image of him lying on the table in the morgue remained whenever I would think about my son. It would come speeding to the front of my consciousness, and that's all I could see – this ugly, dirty picture of my boy.

On Thursday, I woke up about 4:00 in the morning and raised up and looked at the alarm clock. Suddenly, Ron was there standing in front of me! It was like there was a floodlight in back of him, but I could see all of him clearly. He was dressed in a T-shirt and blue jeans.

He looked solid, he looked real! When he smiled at me, I knew he was in perfect health. His teeth were all beautifully formed and totally white. Before he was killed his teeth were chipped and discolored.

Then he brought his mother, Helen, to me. When I buried her body sixteen years earlier, I buried her in my mind too. I didn't believe in God, and I didn't believe in an afterlife or heaven. I didn't believe in anything except this life.

Ron and Helen were holding hands. She looked perfectly healthy with all of her hair. She had lost her hair to chemo and radiation treatments. Now she looked like I remembered her when we were first married. She was in a flowing dress and looked very pretty.

I said, "Helen, I'm sorry. I forgot...." And she said to me, "I understand, Glen." She understood that I had forgotten about her. Then she was gone, and I could hear myself sobbing.

Ron smiled again, and I realized that my son was in heaven or that he was going to go to heaven. I filled up with a glow – I've never known a feeling like that before. I felt like I was going to bust all over – I felt so good!

All of a sudden, I believed! I knew that God, Jesus, the Holy Ghost, the saints, and everything that I had been taught was true! I just knew it!

Then Ron said, "No hatred, no anger, Dad," and he repeated it, "No hatred, no anger." I think he was trying to tell me he didn't hate anybody and wasn't angry with anybody. And he didn't want me to hate or be angry with anybody either.

Ron also said, "Don't worry about me. I'm happy." That made me feel good, and I asked him if he would be there to meet me when I die. He said, "Hey, Dad, I'm just a rookie here. I don't know!"

Then my present wife, Linda, who was sleeping beside me, woke up and touched my arm. That ended my experience with Ron. Even though I could no longer see or communicate with my son, I felt so euphoric, so at peace.

A month or so later, I thought, "What if it was the devil that did all this?" Then I kind of slapped myself in the face and said, "Hey stupid, why would the devil do something like that to turn you away from him?" Satan had me in his grasp for about forty years. Now I know that God is a lot stronger than the devil.

After Ron was murdered, I was going to terminate the man that killed him. I was going to make sure that man's life was ended. Now I don't feel that way anymore. I feel sorry for him because he has to live every waking minute with the fact that he murdered my boy.

You can't believe how happy I am that my son is in heaven with his mother! This experience changed my life. It opened my eyes. It made me know that there is a God and there is a heaven and He created all of us.

CHAPTER 23

Love Is Forever:
Reflections on ADCs

Death is but a transition from this life to another existence
where there is no more pain and anguish. All the
bitterness and disagreements will vanish, and
the only thing that lives forever is love.
—*Elisabeth Kübler-Ross, M.D.*

There are two significant aspects of our grief when a loved
one dies. One is our concern for the continued existence and
well-being of our deceased family member or friend. The other
is our personal sense of loss and the tremendous emotional pain
we feel as a result of a loved one's absence from our daily life.

Those who are bereaved often ask many questions about
their deceased loved one, including "Is there really a life after
death? Does he still exist? Is she okay? Is he happy? Does she
still love me and know that I miss her? Will I ever see him
again?"

The firsthand accounts in this book offer answers to all of
these questions. Over and over again, ADCs confirm that there
is a life after death and our deceased loved ones continue to exist. Those in a heavenly realm are healed and whole and happy
in their new life. From there, they continue to love us and are
genuinely concerned about our well-being, as they watch over
us with compassion and understanding. And we can trust that
our separation is only temporary, knowing we will eventually
be reunited with them when we make our own transition.

But perhaps you have been wondering "What about all those
people who have never had an ADC experience with a de-

ceased loved one?" This question was often raised during our workshops for bereaved parents. For instance, a bereaved mother would ask with a pleading look in her eyes, "Why haven't I heard from my son?" A bereaved father would appeal to us with an anguished voice, "Why hasn't our daughter contacted me?" Similar concerns were expressed by widows, widowers, and bereaved children.

Does this imply that a deceased child, spouse, parent, or other loved one doesn't care enough about his or her family's pain and suffering to establish after-death contact? Are these grieving people somehow less worthy of having ADCs than others who do have them? Have they been abandoned when they most need comfort and reassurance?

Some adults appear to be more open and receptive to having ADC experiences. Perhaps they had one as a child and their parents believed their account, or maybe such events were freely reported and openly discussed within their family as they grew up. In either case, their intuitive senses were acknowledged, validated, and reinforced, rather than being dismissed. Presumably, these people would be more likely to have similar spiritual experiences throughout their lifetime, and in fact, they frequently do.

During our research, we observed that prolonged, deep grief and strong emotions like bitterness, anger, and fear often seem to block people from having ADCs. Yet this is not always the case, as some accounts in this book have demonstrated. Nor is it necessary to believe that after-death communications are possible, since many skeptics have reported having had one. Therefore, why don't nearly all people have ADC experiences?

It is our understanding that your deceased loved ones will repeatedly attempt to communicate with you for months or even years after their death. It's as though they are "knocking on your front door" or "ringing your doorbell," but if you don't hear their signals, you can't respond and allow them to enter your life. Sooner or later, they will probably move on and await reunion with you when you make your transition into the light.

Is there anything you can do now to increase the likelihood

of having an ADC experience? Actually, you have already completed your first step by reading this book and learning that millions of people have reported being contacted by a deceased loved one. If you have concluded that their experiences are genuine and ADCs are a natural and normal part of life, then you have opened your heart and mind to the possibility that you too may have one in the future.

The fastest and easiest way to have an after-death communication experience seems to be to ask or pray for a sign that your deceased loved one still exists. Examples of this were covered in the chapter on symbolic ADCs, *Butterflies and Rainbows*. If you ask for a sign, it's important to be observant and patient because it may take a while for you to receive it. Though some ADC signs are obvious and clearly understood, others are more subtle. Above all, learn to trust your intuition, for only you can identify your sign and find personal meaning in it.

Another method is to ask or pray for your deceased loved one to communicate with you while you are sleeping because it is then that you are most relaxed, open, and receptive to having a visit together. You may visualize his or her face while sending loving thoughts before you fall asleep. But don't be discouraged if this technique doesn't work right away. Instead, if necessary, repeat it with positive expectancy over a period of weeks or months.

The most effective action you can take is to learn how to meditate. You can purchase simple, easy-to-use books and audiotapes on meditation at your local bookstore. For faster results, you can attend a short, inexpensive course on meditation taught by a competent teacher in your area. Be sure to ask for references, just as you would for a physician, an attorney, or any other professional.

Meditation offers many healthful benefits. If you are bereaved, it will allow you to sleep more restfully, improve your appetite, and reduce some of your depression and emotional pain. Additionally, it will soften any anger, resentment, despair, or other strong feelings you may have. It will also help facilitate your healing process, especially if you meditate once or twice a day for about twenty minutes.

Meditating daily is a loving way to nurture yourself. As you become more comfortable with these deep-relaxation exercises, your focus will gently shift from the outer, material world to the spiritual dimension. Whether you are bereaved or not, you will gradually open and develop your intuitive senses. It's likely that this process will increase your ability to have an ADC experience while you are awake or asleep, and possibly, in time, you may have one while you are in this peaceful state of relaxation. Since ADCs cannot be willed or forced to occur, it is simply a matter of allowing them to happen by training yourself to be more sensitive and intuitive. For those who have a strong religious faith, deep prayer and contemplation offer similar opportunities for spiritual growth.

If you sense the presence of a deceased loved one while you are awake, consider the possibility that he or she may be trying to communicate with you verbally. Simply sit down, close your eyes, relax your body, take a few slow, deep breaths, ask to be given a message by telepathy, and open your mind to receive one. Remember, it's possible to have an entire two-way conversation this way.

This same communication technique may be used while you are having any other kind of awake ADC experience, ranging from an auditory ADC to a symbolic one. But be certain to apply common sense if you receive any information or guidance that feels uncomfortable to you. Just because someone has died doesn't mean he or she has become a fully enlightened and all-knowing being.

Through meditation, many people learn, usually for the first time, that they have an identity or existence that is independent of their physical body. During progressively deeper meditations, they often discover that they are more than their body, more than their feelings or emotions, and more than their thoughts. Gradually, they realize that they are an eternal spiritual being or consciousness, one who is far more than their previous limited self-concept of a mortal human. This new awareness provides a greater sense of inner peace and joy, which typically transforms their life from one of deprivation and competition to one of cooperation and abundance.

Throughout history, men, women, and children have asked "Who am I? Why am I here? And where am I going?" Countless religions and philosophies, both ancient and modern, have sought to answer these profound questions.

Most religions have taught that some vague, undefined part of us, usually called a "spirit" or a "soul," leaves our body at death and continues to exist in another realm of being. Our ADC research and that of other, similar phenomena provide evidence that every person is a spiritual being who is temporarily wearing or inhabiting a physical body. Each of us is a spirit or a soul who occupies a body while we are here on earth in order to function within this dimension of reality. What we call "death" is merely the act of leaving our earthly body permanently. This perception affirms "I am not a body that has a soul. I am a soul who has a body." Thus people don't die; only physical bodies die.

We might consider our body to be our "earth suit." Without it we could not hold this book, answer a telephone, or interact with the physical world in any way. We would pass through walls and all other solid objects and most likely not be seen or heard by anyone. In short, we would be in the same position as a deceased loved one who is complete in every way but just doesn't have a physical body any longer.

Our earth suit is as necessary for life on this planet as a space suit is for astronauts while they perform tasks outside their spacecraft high above the earth. Unfortunately, many people, having worn their earth suit during their entire lifetime, believe "I am my body. Without it I will no longer exist!"

A physical body may also be compared to an automobile, for both are "vehicles" we use for traveling through life. A few are defective when they are new and break down quickly, while some receive poor care from their owners and deteriorate rapidly or are destroyed in an accident. However, most vehicles require only regular maintenance and minor repairs. Naturally, all cars and physical bodies eventually wear out and have to be disposed of. But when this occurs, we needn't perceive that the driver of a car or the wearer of a body ceases to exist as well.

Most of us, even though we may already believe in the reality of life after death, still express ourselves as though we don't. For example, we usually say things like "Our son was buried last week" or "Grandma was cremated three days ago." Others may state "My father died of heart disease" or "When I die, I want to be buried with my husband."

But if we truly agree that everyone is an eternal spiritual being, such thoughts and language regarding death completely deny the fact that only our physical bodies die and only our bodies are buried or cremated. As Elisabeth Kübler-Ross has said, "Death is like taking off a heavy winter overcoat in the spring when we don't need it anymore. . . . Our physical body is only the shell that encloses our immortal self." Therefore, we need to differentiate between the spiritual being, who is eternal, and his or her body, which has died.

Our choice of words is very important because language reinforces how we think and feel about a subject. We could affirm our faith in life after death and be more clearly understood by others if we would be willing to express ourselves in a manner that is consistent with our beliefs. For instance, we could say, "Our son's body was buried last week," or "Grandma's body was cremated three days ago." And "My father's body died of heart disease," or "After I make my transition, I want my body to be buried beside my husband's body."

Using new expressions like these may feel awkward at first, but they will more accurately reflect our belief in an afterlife. Such phrases would also be far less confusing to young children than being told "Mommy is in heaven," while at the same time the adults around them are crying and behaving as though they had literally buried her in a grave for all eternity.

Wakes, funerals, and burial and memorial services are all appropriate rituals to commemorate the lives of our loved ones whose bodies have died. These events provide an opportunity to honor their accomplishments and share our special memories of them. They are a perfect place and time to joyously celebrate their transition as they go toward the light on their journey home.

Based upon our ADC research and many other sources, it's reasonable to conclude that each of us is enrolled in an enormous university that may be called "the school of life." Whether we know it or not, every one of us is both a student and a teacher. The classes here are exceptionally diverse, but the spiritual curriculum, which is basically the same for everybody, is designed to teach us all to love everyone unconditionally, including ourself. When we attain a sufficient degree of spiritual awareness, we automatically begin to feel an inner prompting to serve others. The seductive materialistic goals of wealth, power, fame, and status are gradually replaced with the spiritual values of love, compassion, forgiveness, tolerance, acceptance, generosity, and peace.

You may have noticed that many spiritual people choose to enter the helping professions, though others may express their spirituality in more conventional occupations. For example, many near-death experiencers serve as professional caregivers or volunteers who work with the terminally ill and the bereaved. But their form of service is secondary to their desire to help others overcome the fear of death and to enjoy life more fully. Clearly, it isn't the type of work we choose that is important, but rather it's our attitude and feelings about loving and serving one another.

Near-death experiencers also stress the importance of the pursuit and application of knowledge, especially self-knowledge and wisdom. They intuitively desire to learn more about the spiritual significance of life and the natural laws that govern it. Some people who have had ADCs or NDEs develop interest in a specific religion, while others choose to study metaphysics.

The common denominator for all spiritual seekers is that they increasingly realize that the materialistic goals and addictions of their culture are like salt water. The more they drink, the thirstier they become – because more is never enough. The familiar slogan "He who dies with the most toys wins" is eventually seen as an empty promise, a road that leads only to spiritual impoverishment. Instead, they consciously embrace the ideals of a spiritual pathway and drink its pure, fresh water, which revitalizes their body, mind, and spirit and ultimately leads them to inner peace.

If life on earth really is a vast school, one designed to teach us the spiritual values of unconditional love and service, then what is death? Why do some children die so very young, while others become adults and live for many years? It could be that some souls require only a few course credits to complete their education or serve as teachers for others, while most must attend many courses and master many lessons. Regardless of how long someone has lived on earth, death could be perceived as a "graduation" from physical life and, therefore, an occasion for celebration and joy rather than a time of sorrow. The following ADC account suggests that this may be true.

Ruthanne, a retired health educator in Maryland, had this experience with her uncle:

> Before he died, my Uncle Frederick was bedridden with emphysema. He was my last living older relative, and we were very close.
>
> One day, he and I were talking about his impending death, and I said, "Why don't you go ahead and let go? Your wife, Adelaide, will be waiting for you." He said, "Really? Do you think so?" I said, "Yes. Death is like a graduation from the school of life."
>
> After he died, I went to his funeral Mass. I was seated in the third pew with my cousins. During the service, I turned to watch the casket being wheeled in from the back of the church.
>
> About ten feet above his casket, I saw Uncle Frederick. He was wearing a black graduation gown with a mortarboard! He was joyous and happy, just exuberant! He was whole and solid, with an inner glow.
>
> He took his cap off and was waving it, saying, "You're

right! You're right! It's just like you said!" Uncle Frederick's personality was just beaming through! He was jumping up and down, which is something he would have done in his younger days. Then he said, "Did you know that everyone can come back to watch their own funeral? I'm here to tell you that it's true!"

Aunt Adelaide was right next to Uncle Frederick, and the whole family was behind them. I saw all these people I recognized – my parents, my grandparents, and other relatives from both sides of the family. They were in solid form, but mainly I just saw their faces. It was like a group picture.

I put my hands over my face because I began laughing and crying with joy. But everyone else thought I was upset and sobbing. My cousins were saying, "Oh, Ruthanne, it's okay, it's okay." I wanted to say, "You folks don't know how okay it is!" But I didn't think anyone there would understand.

How comforting it would be if all people everywhere had their "spiritual eyes and ears" open and could see and hear their deceased relatives and friends welcoming the arrival of another family member who has recently made his or her transition. How very differently they might regard life on earth, their purpose for being here, and the nature of death if they perceived these matters from a spiritual viewpoint.

Ruthanne's account and others in our files indicate that our deceased loved ones may elect to attend their own funeral. Some might be curious to see who comes, to learn what the mourners are feeling, and to hear what is being said about them. Of course, this occasion could also furnish them with an opportunity to console those who are grieving by assuring everybody that they continue to exist.

Imagine their happiness and fulfillment if all the people they tried to contact at their funeral were open and receptive to the concept of after-death communication. How might they feel if their loved ones could see them and hear them and receive their messages of comfort and hope? They could then convince everyone that they were totally healed and whole and happy and had entered a beautiful new world, a heaven, that is filled with love and joy. The mourners would learn that death is only a temporary separation and that they would be reunited in the future. As was true for Ruthanne, their tears of grief would be turned to smiles, for they would receive personal confirmation that there is indeed a glorious life after death that awaits all of us.

Some people who have had a prolonged near-death experience or explored the afterlife during a number of out-of-body journeys report that it is composed of an unlimited number of subtle gradations or levels. These apparently extend from the highest, brightest, celestial realms, which are filled with love and light, down through a midrange of grayer, darker levels, to the lowest worlds, which are virtually devoid of all light, love, and emotional warmth.

These realms may be thought of as levels of consciousness or levels of love. That is, the external "landscape" matches the spiritual awareness or ability to love on the part of the inhabitants who dwell there. Those who truly love God and seek to serve others live on the higher, brighter levels, which are filled with indescribable beauty, while those who are very selfish and self-centered have condemned themselves, at least temporarily, to the lower, darker regions.

This is a description of a vertical model of the spiritual afterlife, but if you prefer, there is also a horizontal one. Consider heaven being in the center, surrounded by a nearly infinite series of concentric circles. As you move outward, the light and love decrease until there is only outer darkness.

Some near-death experiencers report having had a "life review" in the presence of a compassionate, nonjudgmental Being of Light. They state that their entire life was replayed in a panoramic display, down to its smallest details, and that they had to relive all their actions, all their thoughts, and all their feelings. During this event, they realized that their material accomplishments on earth counted for very little compared to how they had treated others, because love and kindness were the true yardsticks for measuring the overall success or failure of their life.

They were also shown that the times they had reached out to people with genuine concern and compassion were the special moments that had "made the angels sing." Conversely, if they had been unkind and had harmed others, either intentionally or unintentionally, they had to experience the results of all the suffering they had caused. This awareness dramatically revealed to them that we are all interconnected and illustrated how negativity creates a ripple effect, which in turn causes further pain for others.

It seems likely that each of us, with the possible exception of young children, will have a life review when we enter the light. We will evaluate or judge for ourselves the degree to which we were loving, unkind, or perhaps even cruel to others. It appears that our own thoughts, feelings, and actions will determine the level of existence we will initially inhabit. That is, we will be neither rewarded nor punished after we make our transition. Instead, we will ultimately go to the place we have rightfully earned according to the amount of love, compassion, and kindness that we have demonstrated during our life on earth.

Since we all have free will, we can choose to remain "asleep" spiritually and be victims who blame everybody and everything for our circumstances. Or we can "awaken" and live our life in accordance with spiritual principles. If we have learned little or nothing on earth, we cannot expect our life in the spiritual dimension to be much different.

What is heaven like? According to some accounts of NDEs, out-of-body ADCs, and other sources, no words are adequate to describe the beauty, joy, love, harmony, light, and heightened sense of aliveness of the heavenly realms. The communities include magnificent cities and beautiful countrysides. The flowers, plants, and trees have colors and a vibrancy beyond any that exist on earth. Sparkling, refreshing waters are found everywhere, and birdsong, rapturous music, and butterflies fill the air. Even our deceased pets, whom we have loved on earth, will be waiting for us.

While new arrivals may rest as long as they wish following their transition, heaven is filled with purposeful activity. There are majestic buildings of great architectural grace. There are schools of learning, libraries, halls of healing, spiritual centers of all kinds, and infinitely more. The inhabitants value knowledge greatly and are encouraged to pursue subjects of their own choosing. These cover virtually all topics, but the favorite ones reportedly are the arts, music, nature, the sciences, medicine, and all manner of spiritual studies, which they in turn try to pass along in the form of inspiration to those still living on earth.

As souls evolve spiritually, they aspire to advance to ever higher levels of consciousness. There, just as here, spiritual growth is most quickly attained by serving others. The residents, with expert guidance from highly evolved teachers and masters, select their own form of service and receive extensive training. Many compassionately choose to help souls who dwell in the lower realms, including those who exist in the lowest, darkest regions.

No one, regardless of the cruelty or malicious crimes he or she may have committed on earth, is ever forgotten or forsaken. When someone feels heartfelt remorse for having harmed others and demonstrates even a glimmer of spiritual awareness, immediate assistance and encouragement are available to help that soul move forward and begin the arduous ascent to the higher levels of life after death. However, that person must be willing to accept full personal responsibility for all the hurt, all the pain, and all the suffering he or she has caused others, which apparently is an extremely painful process emotionally, mentally, and spiritually.

Throughout this book, we have intentionally used the word "deceased," which implies "departed from physical life," rather than the word "dead," which indicates finality and the end of existence. If after-death communications are authentic contacts from deceased family members and friends, then certainly our loved ones are still very much "alive." More than that, their messages assure us again and again that life is continuous. From this perspective, it can be said that all of us are living in eternity now!

Physical life always has purpose and meaning. It is intended to be a spiritual learning experience, an opportunity for change, personal growth, and transformation for each of us. But no one can presume to know what another's lessons might be or how successfully that person may be accomplishing his or her individual spiritual courses. Death is merely the final stage of physical life, when we have completed our earthly school, cast off our body, and graduated. The assurance of an afterlife that ADCs, NDEs, and OBEs provide can inspire us to overcome our fear of death so that we may be free to embrace life spontaneously and joyously.

As you have read this book, you have undoubtedly noticed that after-death communication experiences offer much more than consolation for the bereaved and evidence of life after death. They also contain many teachings on how to live our life in a more satisfying and fulfilling way. This is because their essential message is about the importance of love, especially spiritual love. This was summed up perfectly in an ADC that a Canadian woman had with her deceased father, who had been a very successful, wealthy, and powerful man before his body died of cancer at age 49. He told her plainly, "It's not what you have, but what you do with your life. The only thing that matters is love."

In our complex, modern-day society, it may appear to be very difficult to love everyone "unconditionally." But we can certainly practice being kinder and gentler to one another. Expressing loving kindness and forgiveness toward everyone we encounter will definitely enhance our life and contribute to the world becoming a more peaceful place.

Widespread belief in the reality of ADCs has the potential to change the world. What if everyone knew that we are all eternal spiritual beings who are only temporarily wearing a physical body while we are attending a school for our spiritual enlightenment? How might this perception, if universally acknowledged, affect how we regard ourself, others, and life in general? Such global awareness could enhance our understanding and acceptance of one another, knowing we are all equal participants in the same sacred spiritual journey. Surely, we would then treat everyone and the planet Earth with far greater respect and reverence.

Chapter 1 contains an ADC experience that Maggie had with her 15-year-old daughter, Joy. It feels appropriate that the final account in this book is from Joy's father, Lee, who is an engineer in Illinois:

It had been more than a year, and I was still struggling with my daughter's death. I had completely hit bottom. So, shortly after Christmas, I asked Maggie to start praying with me that I would get a sign that Joy still existed.

On Valentine's Day, we decided to stop by the parish house for a good-bye party for the priest, Father Pat, who was leaving. He had found all the photographs that had been taken during his tenure and put them out on a table.

I was looking through the photos and casually picked up a little 3″ x 5″ color picture that was really artistic. It was a double exposure that I learned later had been made by a professional photographer.

The double exposure effect showed a picture taken from the rear of the church, with the congregation standing and facing the altar. Completely superimposed over this picture was another picture of a large statue of Christ, facing the back of the church with His arms open wide and His palms facing forward. He seemed to be blessing the entire congregation.

A little blonde girl was turned slightly sideways and appeared to be in the palm of Christ's right hand, looking up into His face. Suddenly, I realized it was my daughter, Joy!

I couldn't believe it at first, and I started getting goose bumps all over. I asked Father Pat if we could have this picture, and he said, "Certainly."

This was my sign! This was the boost that I needed to believe there is a loving God. It brought my faith back from zero to stronger than it ever was before.

Maggie and Lee sent us an 8″ x 10″ copy of this photograph, and it has provided ongoing inspiration for our work. Thank you Joy, Maggie, and Lee. And thank you Elisabeth Kübler-Ross for the loving ways you have enriched the lives of so many of us.

During the seven years we conducted our research and wrote this book, we became convinced that spiritual love transcends all barriers of time and space, including death. We believe after-death communication experiences demonstrate conclusively that these bonds of love are never broken because life and love are eternal.

EPILOGUE

Joy:
A Promise

When the earth shall claim your limbs,
then shall you truly dance.
—*Kahlil Gibran*

If you have read this book with your heart-mind, you recognize the truth of the vast spiritual reality that exists beyond this physical world. The accounts will have seemed familiar, as if you had known about them before. They serve as a window to a wondrous, unlimited dimension that is your eternal home. It is from there you journeyed to the school of life on earth and to there you shall return after your lessons are completed.

When your spiritual eyes and ears are open, you may behold the infinite beauty that awaits you and hear the celestial music that nourishes your soul. These transcendent moments of grace will remind you of your identity, in case you forget and become blinded by the glamour and deafened by the din of the material world.

There is no death of the spiritual being you truly are, only a change, a transformation, as you release your physical body. Like an immortal butterfly emerging from its cocoon, you will be free to soar as high as your wings, your consciousness, can carry you. Upon returning home, you will celebrate reunions with your loved ones who preceded you, and you shall know the meaning of joy.

The greatest power

in the universe is love.

Now it's your turn ...
we want to hear from you!

This is the first of a series of books we're planning to write about after-death communications. If you've had an ADC and are willing to share it, please mail your account to us. Your ADC experience will be helpful to many other people.

Write your experience(s) in detail in English and include your name, address, and home phone number. Also, please indicate the best time for us to call you. We'll select the ADC accounts we feel are most suitable for our books. If we choose yours, we'll interview you by telephone if you live in the United States or Canada.

We want to receive more ADCs like – or unlike – the ones in this book, especially the kinds of accounts that are described below:

- Children younger than 18 years old who have had an ADC

- Adults who had an ADC when they were under 18 years old

- Accounts of ADCs that occurred during prayer or meditation

- ADCs that include Jesus, Mary, angels, and other spiritual beings

- Accounts from the clergy: ministers, rabbis, priests, nuns, etc.

- Accounts of ADCs from people raised in other cultures or who practice different spiritual traditions and religious faiths

- ADCs that took place during a war, particularly in a combat zone

- Accounts of ADCs that include physical and/or spiritual healing

- ADCs that occurred during the transition of a loved one or patient: such as seeing deceased relatives or friends, spiritual figures, or colored lights who came to welcome and assist the one who was dying; sensing or seeing the soul of the person leaving his or her body; escorting the one who has died to the light; etc.

Everyone's anonymity will be protected at all times.

Judy & Bill Guggenheim
P.O. Box 916070
Longwood, Florida 32791, U.S.A.

Resources

*Those of us who have worked through our grief – and found
there is a future – are the ones who must meet others
in the valley of darkness and bring them to the light.*
—Rev. Simon E. Stephens
Founder of The Compassionate Friends

American Association of Suicidology
4201 Connecticut Avenue, N.W., Suite 310,
Washington, D.C. 20008; (202) 237-2280
Resources for suicide prevention and the survivors of suicide
(SOS); directory of local SOS chapters
Newsletter; referrals to local SOS chapters; conferences

American Suicide Foundation
120 Wall Street, 22nd Floor, New York, New York 10005;
(800) 531-4477
Resources for suicide prevention and the survivors of suicide
(SOS)
Newsletter; referrals to local SOS chapters; conferences

Association for Death Education and Counseling (ADEC)
638 Prospect Avenue, Hartford, Connecticut 06105;
(860) 586-7503
Professional association for death educators, caregivers, counselors, nurses, researchers, clergy, funeral directors, therapists,
and volunteers
Newsletter; local chapters; certification programs; conferences

Bereaved Parents of the U.S.A.
P.O. Box 95, Park Forest, Illinois 60466-0095;
(708) 748-7672
A self-help organization for parents, siblings, and grandparents
who have experienced the death of a child in their family
Newsletters; local chapters; conferences; books; tapes

Bereavement – A Magazine of Hope and Healing
Bereavement Publishing, 8133 Telegraph Drive, Colorado
Springs, Colorado 80920; (719) 282-1948; published six
times per year

Center for Attitudinal Healing
33 Buchanan Drive, Sausalito, California 94965;
(415) 331-6161
Support services for children and adults who have a life-
threatening illness and for bereaved families; workshops;
training sessions
Newsletter; referrals to over 100 independent centers worldwide

Centering Corporation
1531 N. Saddle Creek Road, Omaha, Nebraska 68104;
(402) 553-1200; Newsletter; catalog of books for the bereaved

The Compassionate Friends (TCF)
P.O. Box 3696, Oak Brook, Illinois 60522-3696;
(630) 990-0010
A worldwide organization offering friendship, understanding,
and support for bereaved parents, siblings, and grandparents
Newsletters; more than 600 local chapters in the United States;
national and regional conferences; books; tapes

The Compassionate Friends of Canada
685 William Avenue, Winnipeg, Manitoba, Canada R3E 0Z2;
(204) 787-4896; a worldwide organization offering friendship,
understanding, and support for bereaved parents, siblings, and
grandparents; newsletters; more than 100 local chapters and
telephone contacts; conferences; books; tapes

International Association for Near-Death Studies (IANDS)
P.O. Box 502, East Windsor Hill, Connecticut 06028-0502;
(860) 528-5144
For research and understanding of the near-death experience
(NDE)
Newsletter; professional journal; local support groups;
conferences

Mothers Against Drunk Driving (MADD)
511 E. John Carpenter Freeway, #700, Irving, Texas 75062;
(800) GET MADD
To stop drunk driving and to support victims of this violent
crime
Newsletter and magazine; about 500 local chapters; victim
support groups for the bereaved; training programs; conferences

The NAMES Project Foundation
310 Townsend Street, Suite 310, San Francisco, California
94107; (415) 882-5500
An AIDS support group that sponsors "The Quilt"; local
chapters and international affiliates; catalog; newsletter; sponsor of local and national memorial events

National Hospice Organization (NHO)
1901 North Moore Street, Suite 901, Arlington,
Virginia 22209; (800) 658-8898
Referrals to 2,600 hospices that offer programs, services,
support groups, and individual and family counseling for the
terminally ill and the bereaved; professional associations;
newsletters; conferences

Parents of Murdered Children (POMC)
100 East 8th Street, B-41, Cincinnati, Ohio 45202;
(513) 721-5683
The largest self-help organization in the world for parents,
families, friends, and other victims of homicide
Newsletters; more than 400 local chapters and contact persons
in the United States and abroad; conferences

Pen-Parents
P.O. Box 8738, Reno, Nevada 89507-8738; (702) 322-4773
An international support network for bereaved parents who
want to correspond with one another by mail
Newsletter

The Rainbow Connection
477 Hannah Branch Road, Burnsville, North Carolina 28714

(704) 675-5909;
Catalog of books and other materials for the bereaved

SHARE Pregnancy and Infant Loss Support
National SHARE Office, St. Joseph Health Center, 300 First
Capitol Drive, St. Charles, Missouri 63301; (800) 821-6819
For families bereaved by miscarriage, stillbirth, or neonatal
death
Newsletters; more than 100 local chapters; referrals; conferences

Sharing & Healing
Al & Linda Vigil, 11335-162 Affinity Court, San Diego,
California 92131; (619) 271-6889
Newsletter for the survivors of suicide

SIDS Alliance
1314 Bedford Avenue, Suite 210, Baltimore, Maryland 21208;
(800) 221-SIDS
Support for families who have suffered sudden infant death
syndrome
Newsletter; more than 50 local chapters; conferences

Suicide Information & Education Centre (SIEC)
Suite 201, 1615 – 10th Avenue S.W., Calgary, Alberta
T3C 0J7 Canada; (403) 245-3900
Resources for suicide prevention and the survivors of suicide
Newsletter; referrals to local suicide services; resource library

Widowed Persons Service (WPS)
AARP, 601 E Street, N.W., Washington, D.C. 20049;
(202) 434-2260
A program of the American Association of Retired Persons for
widows and widowers of all ages
Newsletter; more than 250 local programs; conferences

Many hospices, churches, hospitals, funeral homes, and
other independent organizations sponsor support groups for the
bereaved in your local community. Please call them for further
information, schedules, and referrals.

Sources of Quotations

The gull sees farthest who flies highest.
—*Richard Bach*

We acknowledge the following authors and publishers
for the material that we quoted throughout this book:

Bach, Richard. *Jonathan Livingston Seagull*. New York: Macmillan, 1970.

Bethards, Betty. *There Is No Death*, revised edition. Novato, California: Inner Light Foundation, 1985.

Cicero, Marcus Tullius. *On Divination*. Translated by Hubert M. Poteat. Chicago: University of Chicago Press, 1950.

Egan, Eileen, and Egan, Kathleen, O.S.B. *Blessed Are You – Mother Teresa and the Beatitudes*. Contains the quotes of Mother Teresa. Ann Arbor, Michigan: Servant Publications, 1992.

Elliott, William. *Tying Rocks to Clouds – Meetings and Conversations with Wise and Spiritual People*. Contains the quotes of Rabbi Harold Kushner and Swami Satchidananda. Wheaton, Illinois: Quest Books, 1995.

Gibran, Kahlil. *The Prophet*. New York: Alfred A. Knopf, 1923.

Graham, Billy. *Hope for the Troubled Heart*. Dallas: Word Publishing, 1991.

Greaves, Helen. *Testimony of Light*. Suffolk, Great Britain: Neville Spearman, 1969.

Jung, C. G. *Memories, Dreams, Reflections*, final revised edition. New York: Pantheon Books, 1973.

Kübler-Ross, Elisabeth. *On Life After Death*. Contains both of her quotes. Berkeley, California: Celestial Arts, 1991.
Life, Death, and Transition. An audiotape of a lecture she gave in California, containing the account of her experience with her deceased patient. July 1976.

Levine, Stephen. *Who Dies? An Investigation of Conscious Living and Conscious Dying*. New York: Anchor Books–Doubleday, 1982.

Marshall, Catherine. *The Helper*. Grand Rapids, Michigan: Fleming H. Revell, 1978.

Paulus, Trina. *Hope for the Flowers*. New York: Paulist Press, 1972.

Peale, Norman Vincent. "The Glorious Message of Easter." *Plus – The Magazine of Positive Thinking*. Pawling, New York: Peale Center for Christian Living. March 1994.

Puryear, Anne. *Stephen Lives! His Life, Suicide, and Afterlife*. Contains the quote of her son, Stephen Christopher. New York: Pocket Books, 1996.

Robinson, Jonathan. *Bridges to Heaven – How Well-Known Seekers Define and Deepen Their Connection with God*. Contains the quote of Dr. Wayne W. Dyer. Walpole, New Hampshire: Stillpoint Publishing, 1994.

Russell, Robert A. *Dry Those Tears*. Marina del Rey, California: DeVorss & Company, 1951.

Simpson, James B. *Simpson's Contemporary Quotations*. Contains the quote of Helen Keller. Boston: Houghton Mifflin, 1988.

Taylor, Susan L. *In the Spirit*. New York: Amistad Press, 1993.

Weatherhead, Leslie D. *Life Begins at Death*. Birmingham, Great Britain: National Christian Education Council, 1969.

White Eagle. *Morning Light – On the Spiritual Path*. Hampshire, England: The White Eagle Publishing Trust, 1957.

Woodson, Meg. *If I Die at Thirty*. Grand Rapids, Michigan: The Zondervan Corporation, 1975.

Yogananda, Paramahansa. *Where There Is Light – Insight and Inspiration for Meeting Life's Challenges*. Los Angeles: Self-Realization Fellowship, 1988.

Join Us on the Internet

The authors of *Hello From Heaven!* founded The ADC Project in 1988. It serves as a forum for sharing information and research on after-death communications and related spiritual subjects.

The ADC Project has a site on the the Internet. You are invited to visit its home page on the World Wide Web at:

http://www.after-death.com

Features include:

- Latest news about the field of after-death communication
- Lists of support groups and organizations for bereavement, personal growth, and spiritual development
- New, unpublished, firsthand accounts of ADCs and other kinds of spiritual experiences
- Interactive discussion groups and networking opportunities
- Articles on ADCs and similar topics
- Calendar of upcoming conferences, workshops, and lectures, including the authors' speaking engagements
- Suggested books, magazines, movies, TV shows, tapes, etc.
- Bibliography of factual and fictional ADCs
- Humor, quotes, and surveys
- And much more . . .

Other ways to contact The ADC Project are:

Fax: (407) 774-1260

Internet E-mail address:
adc-project@after-death.com

Mailing address:
The ADC Project
P.O. Box 916070
Longwood, Florida 32791, U.S.A

About the Authors

Bill Guggenheim and Judy Guggenheim have been conducting intensive after-death communication (ADC) research since 1988. Bill serves on the Board of Advisors of the International Association for Near-Death Studies. He is a member of the Association for Death Education and Counseling and several other organizations that minister to the needs of the terminally ill and the bereaved.

Judy Guggenheim is also a member of the Association for Death Education and Counseling. She and Bill have presented workshops and sharing sessions at national and regional conferences of The Compassionate Friends, Mothers Against Drunk Driving, the Association for Death Education and Counseling, In Loving Memory, the International Association for Near-Death Studies, Bereaved Parents of the USA, Parents of Murdered Children, other support groups for the bereaved, hospices, churches, and a wide variety of similar institutions that are devoted to personal and spiritual growth.

Judy and Bill and their ADC research have been featured on television and radio programs and in numerous newspaper and magazine articles throughout the United States and Canada. They have established a new field of research, and this is their first book.

Bill and Judy have three sons and were married for seventeen years before being divorced more than twelve years ago. They live separate personal lives in central Florida and continue to work together for The ADC Project.

Judy and Bill are available to present lectures and workshops about their ongoing research of after-death communication. For speaking engagements, please fax them at: (407) 774-1260.